Modelling Dual-Use Trade Control Systems

P.I.E. Peter Lang

Bruxelles · Bern · Berlin · Frankfurt am Main · New York · Oxford · Wien

Odette JANKOWITSCH-PREVOR, Quentin MICHEL,
Sylvain PAILE-CALVO (eds.)

Modelling Dual-Use Trade Control Systems

Security and Non-Proliferation
Vol. 10

This publication has been peer-reviewed.

Éditions scientifiques internationales
Brussels, 2014
1 avenue Maurice, B-1050 Brussels, Belgium
info@peterlang.com; www.peterlang.com

ISSN 1377-0608
ISBN 978-2-87574-203-2 (print)
ISBN 978-3-0352-6475-3 (eBook)
D/2014/5678/76

Printed in Germany

CIP available from the Library of Congress, USA, and the British Library.

Bibliographic information published by "Die Deutsche Nationalbibliothek".

"Die Deutsche Nationalbibliothek" lists this publication in the "Deutsche National-bibliografie"; detailed bibliographic data is available on the Internet at <http://dnb.d-nb.de>.

Disclaimer

The views and opinions expressed in this book do not represent those of the institutions the authors may be working for. The authors hereby present, discuss and express their views on the legislations and practices of States, international organisations and other entities only in their scientific capacities.

Acknowledgement

The directors would like to express their gratitude to the European Commission for its support in the funding and organisation of the seminar held in Chaudfontaine, together with the European Studies Unit of the Political Science Department of the University of Liège and ENCO.

Their gratitude goes also to Mr Wolfgang Lehofer, Mrs Marietje Schaake and her team, for their invaluable inputs in the debates of the "Chaudfontaine Group".

The directors would also like to thank the participants and authors of the following contributions, as well as Emily for her precious support.

May this raise new scientific interests and debates.

Contents

INTRODUCTION

Regional, Sub-Regional and National Trade Control Regimes Models: Choices for "Africa"?[1]

Dr. Odette JANKOWITSCH-PREVOR

Nuclear Lawyer – Consultant

Introduction

The growing importance attached to the "trade dimension"[2] of economic development and related industrial strategies in Africa may call for new approaches to national and possibly regional requirements for trade control regimes. This industrial evolution is essentially carried by trans- or multi-national corporations and characterised by international intra-industry transactions. Such developments are extremely relevant to States, though the individual State may not be the determinant actor in this worldwide development. Integration into the global market rather than within a regional market raises very different questions and concerns all actors: the individual State exporting industrial manufactured goods in addition to raw materials, the regional economic communities, and Africa as a whole. In the context of export control regimes this fast trend, if continued, might constitute a challenge for the individual State as well as for Africa's sub-regional economic communities of neighbouring or likeminded States.

1 Main sources consulted in addition to the chapters contributed to this publication by Algeria, the Democratic Republic of the Congo, Kenya Niger and Nigeria. Additional sources: seminar "Assessing Regional Integration in Africa V Towards an African Continental Free Trade Area" ECA; AU; African Development Bank, UNCA, Addis Ababa (Ethiopia), 2012. NTI, "Sub-Saharan Africa 1540 Reporting" 9 January 2014, CNS James Martin Centre for Non-proliferation Studies at the Monterey Institute of International Studies.

2 Seminar: "Building Trade Capacities for Africa's Transformation – A critical review of Aid for Trade". UN ECA, AU, ADB, Addis Ababa (Ethiopia), 2012.

At the same time, the individual State is called upon to adhere to increasingly specific, strict and binding international regimes directed at preventing all forms of proliferation of nuclear chemical or biological weapons,[3] sensitive trade and notably dual-use items; these amount to legal obligations that require the State to establish and implement *inter alia* "effective border controls, national export and trans-shipment controls and end-user controls".[4]

The question arises whether this is a fundamental, unsolvable dilemma or whether States will be able to find satisfactory solutions individually, within their regional economic communities and with the support by the African Union?

Intergovernmental organisations and trade control

Any attempt to analyse Africa in terms of its trade should first look at existing sub-regional economic communities, their composition, purpose, policies and activities, in order to discern their possible roles in assisting their respective Member States regarding implementation of trade control of dual-use and sensitive items.[5] This question requires some clarifications: what are the main concerns of these regional economic communities? How far are they comparable to the EU or to earlier cooperation and integration organisation in Europe, such as the European Free Trade Area? However, the contributions[6] to this volume covering individual African States clearly demonstrate the need to keep in focus the specific geographical, economic and political realities of each individual State.

Africa is a continent as is Latin America. It was and sometimes continues to be divided in terms of geographical rather than economic and policy denominated domains. This continues to apply e.g. to the regional approach to trade analysis of the UNECA, the Economic Commission for Africa,[7] considering the regions of North, East, West-Africa; Sub-Saharan Africa, the Sahel Zone. Another categorisation separates States

---

3 Document UNSC /Res/1540 (2004), Operative Paragraph 3.

4 UNSC Resolution 1540 (2004) Paragraph 3.(d).

5 This chapter uses the term "sensitive items", "dual-use items", or "related materials" as defined in UNSC.RES 1540 (2004) as "materials, equipment and technology covered by relevant multilateral treaties and arrangements or included on national control lists, which could be used for the design, development, production or use of nuclear, chemical and biological weapons and their means of delivery."

6 See chapters related to Algeria, the Democratic Republic of Congo, Kenya, Niger, Nigeria.

7 Seminar of the UNECA: "Building Trade Capacities for Africa's Transformation – African review of Aid for Trade", UNECA, WTO, OECD and AU, 2013.

according to (European) language groups which *per se* is not irrelevant as this reflects not only aspects of colonial history but what is more relevant today, common legal systems, national and societal rather than ethnic links and some durable trade patterns.

In the present context, attention is primarily on implementation of non-proliferation obligations – with reference to the NPT and more specifically to UNSC Resolution 1540 (2004) in the framework of the trade policies of States members of regional economic communities, as well as of the communities as a whole. Are States still acting mainly alone, or is there an existing or potential capacity of the Communities to establish elements of a common regulation and control of trade for their respective members? Is a regional trade – or sub-regional – control model possible, or is the more realistic policy of harmonising step-by-step national regulations preferable?

Considering the wider picture, there are domains where intergovernmental organisations cannot replace the obligations of the State: for example, legally binding obligations set forth by international treaties and conventions[8] rest exclusively upon the sovereign State. Such obligations seen in the present context require the State to enact national laws and appropriate regulations which apply to ensure strict border control of (sensitive or dual-use) exported goods as well as of those imported. Examples are demonstrated by the case studies on the export control regimes of selected African States contained in this volume. The basic question is how similar are national export control regimes at present to allow – without establishing a comprehensive "model" – for harmonisation of "basic provisions" to which States could conform within the scope of respective sub-regional economic communities.

At the continental level there are two well established intergovernmental organisations open to all sovereign States of the continent: the African Union (AU) with 53 States,[9] and the United Nations Economic Commission for Africa UNECA[10] 54 States. These 54 States constitute the Africa Regional Group in the UN General Assembly.

The African Union (AU) functions since its inception with a highly complex structure is somewhat similar to that of the UN, with an Assembly,

8 This applies also to obligations set forth by the UNSC, under Chapter VII of the UN Charter, see UNSC Resolution 1540/(2004) paragraph 3.(c).

9 The OAU was the first African intergovernmental organisation: http:// www.au.int: Note: Morocco left the AU on disagreement following the recognition by the AU of the "Spanish Sahara"/Western Sahara.

10 UNECA: UN Economic Commission for Africa. It has the same composition as the AU (plus Morocco) and seats in Addis Ababa (Ethiopia). See: http:// www.uneca.org.

a Parliament, an Executive Council, technical committees and commissions as well as a separate Economic and Social Council. It covers a huge diversity of political, economic, and legal subjects and acts through specific subordinate organs as well as through the Assembly of all its Member States.

Of particular interest in the present context is a new, different type of Treaty based continental organisation, the African Commission on Nuclear Energy (AFCONE),[11] a mechanism for Treaty compliance provided for by the Treaty of Pelindaba establishing the African Nuclear Weapon Free Zone. The Entry into force of the Treaty, 2009, and more recently the start of the work of its Commission (AFCONE), comes at a time when control of CBNR weapons by States is a permanent topical issue on the agenda of the UN, the IAEA and the EU. In light of its broad mandate this new institution might become relevant beyond its statutory mandate of nuclear non-proliferation[12] as a model for the implementation by States of other legal obligations notably those set forth by UNSC Resolution 1540 (2004) and thereby corroborating the basic concerns and to a large extent, the *raison d'être* of the Resolution.[13] Endowed with the necessary instrumentality for non-proliferation control, its powers as to verification of "peaceful uses"[14] (though of nuclear material only) may carry with it a parallel concern for the prohibition and control of biological and chemical weapons and acquire institutional knowledge as to the export /import control of dual-use items.

Treaties and conventions

As regards relevant international treaties and conventions on security and anti-terrorism, most African States have signed them (facilitated by the fact that these treaties were opened for signature at the UN or

---

11 Source: Treaty of Pelindaba adopted 11 April 1996 entered into force 15 July 2009: UNODA Treaties Data Base: Depositary African Union, (Article 12).

12 Treaty of Pelindaba: Article 7 obliges to dispose radioactive wastes and other radioactive materials in accordance with IAEA standards, Article 5: to conclude Safeguards agreements with the IAEA for full-scope safeguards; Article 10: establishment of a Control system to verify compliance with the obligations of the Treaty. Article 13: A State Party has the right to request the Executive. Committee to send a fact-finding mission to another State Party to clarify a situation which might give rise to doubts about treaty compliance.

13 See NTI "Sub-Saharan Africa 1540 Reporting". See "Conference Non-Paper to AU Commission: International Expert Workshop Establishing the Treaty of Pelindaba African Commission on Nuclear Energy". Institute for Security Studies and James Martin Centre for Non-proliferation Studies, March 2010, p. 19. Source: http://cns.miis.edu.

14 Treaty of Pelindaba, Article 9.

IAEA Headquarters or other IGO). However, the process of ratification and entry into force has taken a very long time and in many cases is still outstanding.[15] This needs not be considered as absence of political will by governments but can be well explained by the complex often technical nature of some conventions and the lack of their immediate relevance for the States e.g. the Convention on the Physical Protection of Nuclear Material (CPPNM) applies to the protection of "nuclear material in transport" which, except for uranium transported from a landlocked State[16] to the sea, is not commonly shipped from a State of origin to a State of destination within the African continent.[17] Moreover, the CPPNM and all UN "anti-terrorism instruments" adopted since 9/11 set forth detailed provisions defining criminal offenses, criminal procedure, international cooperation on criminal matters as e.g. extradition, which in any administration needs to be cleared or approved by several competent ministries and usually requires amendment of national laws and codes that are often difficult to transpose into national law due to different legal systems and concepts.

Moreover, after ratification of the instrument in accordance with the State's constitutional provisions, and transposition of its binding provisions into domestic law, a major obstacle to its implementation is often the weakness of the competent governmental authorities: any State control requires institutions equipped to supervise the implementation of the provisions of the law. Weakness of government bodies is a common problem not limited to African States, often due to lack of adequate funding and staffing or to overburdened staff facing a diversity of tasks and competences. In many smaller African States weak governmental institutions may constitute the single major difficulty in fulfilling trade control functions.

This is more relevant as the competence of the institutions at the national level is the first prerequisite for any form of coordination of import controls at a higher regional level: control of trade – notably exports and imports of sensitive items or dual-use goods – must take place at the country level before being coordinated at a supranational level. As well demonstrated in all of the five African case studies[18] the common comparable national competent authority is the national customs

---

15 The Amendment of the CPPNM adopted in 2005 is still not in force due to the large number of States required for its entry into force, requiring inter alia ratification by a number of African States.

16 See the chapter on Niger: export of uranium by land and sea via seaport of Benin.

17 Transport of yellow cake (uranium) from the mines of Niger to the Ocean but as in the case of e.g. uranium basically from the mine to the coast by States parties to the relevant Conventions.

18 Algeria, Democratic Republic of Congo, Kenya, Niger and Nigeria.

authority: this applies in terms of both its legal powers and its capacity for effective physical material border control. In this context the authors express general doubts as to the usefulness of defining a single model of an export control system that would be applicable to the hugely diverse economies and legal systems of the continent. Clear preference seems to be given to the elaboration of key common elements to be included in national trade control regimes as well as to national control practices.

Regional economic communities (REC)

The African Union recognises a number of intergovernmental "regional economic communities", some newly established, others succeeding earlier regional groups. Again there is great diversity in the purpose and activities of the REC. Some were established as monetary and administrative rather than as free trade zones, in particular those dating back to colonial administrations e.g. the AOF[19] and AEF and the East African Community. Today's broad based "new" economic communities appear to have more in common aiming e.g. accelerating integration of the respective economies and improving intra-African trade. The REC are however still facing major challenges – including inadequate financial and manpower resources to support their integration activities: In addition to a lack of compatibility of national economic policies,[20] one of the major problems seen by many as a real obstacle to "integration" is the overlapping membership in the different REC.

Overview of the regional economic communities[21]

A brief overview of the main AU recognised REC intends only to map out the complex structure of sub-regional integration of the continent and both the diversity and the common ground of these communities of States. Six recognised regional communities are considered here:[22] the main purpose common to all is to promote economic cooperation among

19 AOF and AEF (in French): Afrique Occidentale Francaise and Afrique Equatoriale Française.

20 See notably the case of Niger Chapter and the author's thoughts on these issues.

21 *Idem.*

22 *CEN-SAD: Community of Sahel-Saharan States* (28 States) works towards a free trade area among its Member countries with major development differences (e.g. by establishing technical studies to identify intra-community trade, including a specific scheme for least-developed members). "Assessing Regional Integration in Africa". *op. cit.*, p. 13.

COMESA: Common Market for Eastern and Southern Africa (26 States): established and implemented a customs union. Concluded tripartite arrangements of COMESA, EAC/SADC in 2008 in view of a common free trade area. Further works

them, to aim at establishing a common trade area, a customs union or beyond, to create an economic union. This applies notably to the Southern African Development Community (SADC).

Some conclusions

Trade control notably of sensitive or dual-use items remains predominantly a separate matter from trade studies and strictly within national competence: major comprehensive studies on African integration and trade do not include references to trade control, sensitive items or dual-use goods, to CBRN, to security-related treaties and relevant UN obligations regarding the control of potential WMD or weapons material. Issues of trade, of individual States or of regional communities of States are usually analysed exclusively in economic and developmental terms. Security, and non-proliferation, export of dual-use items belongs apparently to another book!

Questions of "importing" or copying a trade control model do not appear to be anywhere on the agenda.[23] A more detailed inside knowledge and, if published, case studies or other material issued by the regional economic communities as e.g. SADC may demonstrate how control regulations enacted in one or several of REC Member States could be harmonised with others to meet a common objective.

---

on harmonising financial and fiscal policies. Aims at a monetary union and single trade and investment space. "Assessing Regional Integration in Africa", *op. cit.*, p. 15.

ECOWAS: Economic Community of West African States (15 States): Aims at promoting cooperation and integration in economic, social etc. domains leading to a monetary union. Established a Bank for Investment and Development. Within ECOWAS 6 mostly Anglophone Members (Gambia, Ghana, Guinea, Liberia, Nigeria and Sierra Leone) are setting up a West African Monetary Zone (in view of future monetary union of the entire ECOWAS region). See: http:// www.ecowas.int.

EAC: East African Community (5 States) Mission: regional integration and development. Operational customs union, 2010. East African currency fully convertible. Jointly managed border points. See: http:// www.eac.int.

SADC: Southern Africa Development Community (15 States): customs union since 2012, accomplish a common market by 2015 and thereafter a monetary union and an economic union. *Inter alia*: promote intra-regional trade, productive investment and technological cooperation. Initiatives to harmonise customs procedures, instruments and a single customs administration document. Law on a customs model to facilitate harmonisation of national laws on customs. See: http://www.sadc.int.

UEMOA: West African Economic and Monetary Union (8 States): Commission; other political bodies includes: Court of Justice, Auditors, Inter parliamentary Committee. See: http://www.uemoa.int.

23 See chapters on Algeria and Niger in particular.

As defined above, obligations ensuing from international instruments on non-proliferation and related dual-use and sensitive trade control rest entirely with the individual State. However, the prime competence of the State in matters of trade control need not prevent States Members of a same sub-regional community, to mutually adjust and coordinate their trade control systems.

Another relevant issue is whether – with certain exceptions – the present composition of goods and the volume of exports of the majority of African States require an advanced, sophisticated export control regime. Without studying detailed economic reports and statistical data (as published by the ECA) nor, on the other hand, oversimplifying the reality of trade flows, it is a fact that outward trade consists predominantly of minerals, other raw materials i.e. metals such as copper and gold, oil and gas, tropical wood and of some crops, e.g. cocoa and coffee beans – at more or less processed levels – fruit and vegetables grown in export-oriented agriculture and… Flowers.

In fact, trade of industrial manufactured products out of Africa (south-south) or intra Africa is still an exception. There are indeed very few cases: South Africa[24] and increasingly, the sub-regional community which South Africa leads: (SADC); Nigeria and Algeria. It is worth mentioning that many African States need to export a very specific category of sensitive goods i.e. potentially dual-use or material for dirty bombs, that is the re-export of – imported and spent – radioactive sources[25] which are commonly used in mining, geology, medical facilities and in industry.[26]

Trade – both export and import appears to remain essentially carried out independently by individual States under agreements with a foreign importer. As noted above most exported items are not listed in any "sensitive trade list". As regards the issue of security, a regional overview of the "Sub Saharan Africa 1540 Reporting" notes that "[T]he major regional and sub-regional organisations on the continent "play almost no role in promoting Resolution 1540".[27]

24 The UN Register on annual imports and exports of major weapon systems, as submitted by national reports, lists as weapons exporters for the African continent only South Africa (and, to a lesser extent, Egypt). Source: http://www.un-register.org/HeavyWeapons/Index.aspx.

25 Code of Conduct on the Safety and Security of Radioactive Sources, adopted in 2003. IAEA Doc. 2004.

26 On this topic, see the chapter on Nigeria.

27 NTI, "Regional Overview. Reporting on UNSC Resolution 1540(2004)", Centre for Non-proliferation Studies, 9 January 2014. And J. du Preez, D. Dye, "Implementing Resolution 1540 in Africa, Balancing Competing Priorities", in L. Scheinman (ed.), "Implementing Resolution 1540", UNIDIR, 2008, p. 119.

None of the regional economic communities covers issues of trade control: as stressed by the African authors in this volume, it is difficult to conceive a trade control "model" that in view of the political and economic diversity of States would correspond to the needs – i.e. the economies and exports of the regional economic communities.

Part I

A Search for Harmonising Trade Controls…

Export Controls: Is a New Approach Needed?

Wolfgang LEHOFER

Directorate-General DEVCO (Development and Cooperation), European Commission

Introduction

We all have to live with the paradox that the threat of global nuclear war or other CBRN events has gone down, but the risk of violence in this area has gone up. International efforts to contain these dangers are centred on a global non-proliferation regime, but people and nations continually try to find new ways to break non-proliferation rules. However, we are far away reaching a "security of a world without nuclear weapon".[1]

Discussing export control issues seems pertinent following the concept to increase security aspects of international agreements such as the Chemical Weapons Convention (CWC), the Biological and Toxin Weapons Convention (BTWC) and the Nuclear Non-Proliferation Treaty (NPT), and of course multilateral export control regimes such as the Wassenaar Arrangement, the Nuclear Suppliers Group (NSG), the Australia Group, the Missile Technology Control Regime (MTCR) and certainly the UN Security Council Resolution 1540 (2004). The implementation of universal models for export controls is certainly continuing to be the clear objective, however the way to reaching these goals in export controls might need adjustments – a tailor-made approach – on country or regional level as the control list may not always reflect the economic realities every time.

The globalisation and the increasing levels of interdependence between nations have transformed the nature of power. It is much more difficult for individual nations – to dictate certain concepts in the security

1 Remarks by President Barack Obama, Hradcany Square Prague, Czech Republic, 5 April 2009.

field.[2] There is strong evidence for the need to look closer for finding a more systemic approach and to understand the clear nexus between (economic) development, trade and security as globalisation has facilitated the rise of transnational communities and other actors which may be de-legitimising nation-States.

EU non-proliferation efforts and export control

Since the end of the Cold War, the European Union is continually supporting countries to improve trade controls, engage scientists with weapons of mass destruction (WMD) skills so that they can put their expertise to use for peaceful purposes, secure biological laboratories that house deadly pathogens, and address the challenges posed by nuclear smuggling.

Proliferation of WMD cannot be prevented only by international treaties or export control regimes unless nations found wide political agreement, which allowed them to implement and enforce effectively. This lesson learned has clearly been demonstrated to non-proliferation community by the case of Abdul Qadeer Khan who played an important role in the Pakistan`s clandestine nuclear weapon programme and who was the organiser of a world wide smuggling operation. WMD proliferation is among the gravest threats to global security and regional stability. Proliferating States and terrorist networks continue to seek to acquire mankind's most deadly and destructive weapons. As technology changed and new risks emerged, the European Union has clearly understood the need to address and mitigate these risks in an evolving security landscape by supporting partner countries with outreach programmes to combat nuclear proliferation, including enforcing controls on the export of dual-use items.

Dual-use trade controls have been identified as one of the major area of activities in the EU Security Strategy 2003 (and updated in 2008) and current update of the New Lines for Actions (2013) against the proliferation of WMD as a key threat to European security. A key element was "the inclusion of a so-called non-proliferation clause in certain agreements between the EU and partner countries",[3] which introduced for both sides an obligation on existing commitments, a commitment to go further, and finally a commitment to establish an export control system. Consequently outreach activities on dual-use export controls with the aim to increase capacity building to ensure effective export control of dual-use goods by

2 Report, "Strategic Options for Europe's future", December 2013: www.newpactforeurope.eu.

3 B. Kienzle, "A European contribution to non-proliferation? The EU WMD Strategy at ten", in *International Affairs*, No. 89: 5 (2013), p. 1153.

providing export control and related border control assistance to third countries has been continually developed. Strategic trade controls' best practices include establishing a comprehensive strategic trade control system resting on several key principles. This includes the establishment of a transparent and comprehensive legal framework consistent with the guidelines and control lists of the four multilateral regimes and relevant Security Council resolutions. This framework identifies proliferation-sensitive dual-use and munitions items and enables regulation of their export, re-export, transit and transhipment.

The common EU export control system for dual-use items builds on the basic EU principle of the economic integration including a common market – the free movement of goods. Inside the EU a regime is in force binding all 28 Member States. Controlled items may not leave the EU customs' territory without an export authorisation. In the EU, roughly 1 to 2 per cent of exports out of the EU are licenced dual-use exports, obviously with notably differences per Member State.[4] The Commission is currently developing EU communication with a long-term vision for EU strategic export controls and may announce concrete policy initiatives.

Europe's role is central to the global "export control scene". The European export control framework has illustrated that a consensus on a regional basis to create standards which go beyond the classical control aspect and the need to establish "the right balance between security and competitiveness. There is a growing consensus as to where those balance lies: effective export controls must both prevent proliferation and be conducive to legitimate trade. Exporters would not benefit from lighter controls if these were to damage their reputations, or worse lead to financial or criminal sanctions".[5] Europe certainly has a crucial role in the sharing regional experience of export control framework measures and their variety of 28 different ways of implementing and enforcing the European Union's dual-use regulation. EU's regional concept already made the EU export control list as a global reference list for various countries in the world.

The nuclear threat

Energy remains the key factor for economic development. The example of "changing energy supply systems" around the world and, in

4 Commission Staff Working document, "Strategic export controls: ensuring security and competiveness in a changing world – A report on the public consultation launched under the Green Paper", COM (2011)393.

5 Interview of EU Trade Commissioner De Gucht on export controls with Commissioner De Gucht, in *Warder*, issue 25, Sept. 2013, pp. 7-9. See: http://trade.ec.europa.eu/doclib/docs/2014/february/tradoc_152182.pdf.

particular, in low and middle income countries has illustrated the nexus to national security, economic prosperity and the environment/climate. The Fukushima disaster has shown impact in Western countries but less impact on nuclear power expansion in emerging markets. As they endeavour to support economic modernisation, population growth, urbanisation and a growing middle-class choices have to be made on the energy mix, development paths and related security aspects. To meet rising electricity demand, while also lowering CO2 emissions, many countries see no alternative but to put nuclear energy on the table as a component of their economic development and energy security strategies. Particularly the "Middle East is showing the fastest progress in nuclear energy development among the newcomer countries. In a way, Middle Eastern States are now spearheading nuclear energy development in the newcomer countries on a global scale".[6]

This shows that nuclear security, in particular, is a key aspect to be considered when addressing effectively new energy demands. The establishment of new partnerships with relevant technical agencies and institutes to support governments outreach efforts to promote awareness of national export control requirements should strengthen three critical components of effective export control systems in partner countries: enterprise compliance, licencing analysis, and enforcement and interdict strategic commodities. In this session there should be an exchange on how to develop concepts to keep security aspects and economic development in a balance. New concepts urgently to be discussed on how instruments could be developed to follow up this matter further and how capacity building can be enhanced. Export control efforts play a key role to ensure economic development while respecting security obligations.

EU as global soft power

"There is a general agreement that the world is changing, but considerable disagreement about how it is changing".[7] Empowering Europa's future – in particularly to return on a growth path – also depends on the ability to find a census with partner countries around the world to ensure economic development while respecting security obligations including robust trade control systems consistent with international norms are an indispensable element to detect and prevent the illicit procurement of equipment, materials, and technological know-how by States and terrorist organisations

6 A. Khlopkov, "Prospects for nuclear power in the Middle East after Fukushima and the Arab Spring", in "UNIDIR ideas for peace and security", 2010, p. 2.

7 B. Buzan, G. Lawson, "Capitalism and the emergent world order", in *International Affairs*, No. 90, 2014, p. 71.

to avoid the proliferation of weapons of mass destruction (WMD) as economic exchange is based more and more on intangible technology transfer. Regarding the practical agenda for the future EU has the credibility – as it demonstrated the functioning of a regional export model – to support the global dialog process to develop a common approach to promote the adoption of advanced trade controls, such as catch-all, dual-use brokering controls on information technology and trans-shipment controls in partner countries avoiding harm to their economic development ability. "The transnational security governance approach" which also includes "relations between actors that are ideational"[8] remains a challenge in the set up of new export control systems.

[8] K. Zwolski, "How to explain the Transnational Security Governance of the European Union?", in *JCMS*, 2014, p. 6.

"Joined up Thinking"

The Pressing Need for Partnership in Compliance

Martin Palmer

Head of Export Controls – Transport Sector (Private)

Introduction

This chapter looks at the forgotten few in export controls and strategic exports; the "Middlemen" or more accurately the "service providers". For the purpose of this document the "service providers" are the carrier (air, sea, rail, road), transporter, freight forwarder, which contributes to the handling of the movement of goods from the seller, manufacturer, or supplier to the receiver, ship to address, end user, ultimate consignee, etc. In this chapter we will address some of the practical issues of the service providers, particularly the transport industry, the duplications and redundancies that exist, some of the costs of complying, and the desperate need for a true interdependency and partnership approach to export controls within the supply chain. Partnership including the manufacturers, the service providers, the law makers, and the law enforcers.

The ability to apply "joined up thinking" to assist in understanding all of the impacts within the international supply chain will allow smarter initiatives, more effective laws, and greater accountability and most importantly, a secured supply chain within an environment of global compliance.

Globalisation

The world has changed in ways that were impossible to foresee thirty years ago. Old World Globalisation goes back in time to nations exchanging of ideas, thoughts, and basic commodities. It often took weeks or months to transport even the simplest of message. Modern day Globalisation encompasses centuries of evolution, and new technology, products, ideas and multimodal transportation. The world is now indeed a very small place.

Trade barriers, treaties, quotas and tariffs have gradually been removed or simplified, whilst security demands have increased over time, particularly in the last twenty years and most notably in the last five years. In recent times, tragic events somewhere in the world have resulted in the introduction of a new security standard, tackling one particular problem rather than looking at the bigger picture. These "knee jerk reactions" create the impression that a security gap has been closed when often the root cause remains. Standards are developed and implemented both within government and industry, but independently.

Globalisation to a greater or lesser extent has effectively changed how all businesses work today. Countries once had control of their entire supply chain. Commodities would be designed on site, parts produced on site and assembled on site, all within their direct control and "in country". These protected and protective "in country" domains are now dispersed to all corners of the world and often different corners of the world for different elements of the same development, from conception to delivery.

The world has seen fast and furious development and improvement of the international supply chain infrastructure, using multimodal transport methods and transiting countries that were once closed to trade. This means that what would have taken weeks or more in the past to transport between the manufacturing country and the owner, in most cases is taking less than 36 hours door to door, across the extent of the globe, and across several jurisdictions.

Consumers' demand for cheaper products and access to international sourcing and shareholder hunger for increasing profits forces companies to look for more cost efficient ways of manufacture and distribution. Cheaper products and improved profitability is achieved in many ways. However, the first three options manufacturers often resort to are: i) produce the commodities in countries that have lower infrastructure costs (often subsidised) with lower labour costs, or ii) employ staff from countries that have lower labour costs to produce the commodities in their own domestic facilities, or iii) look for preferential trade treaties in countries which offer incentives and in which both i) & ii) may also apply. For compliance professionals, each of these scenarios presents major challenges when dealing with Export Controls and Strategic Exports. Why? – Several layers of regulatory regimes with overlay and conflict. Why is this a problem? – Because we live and operate in a globalised reality (we travel, we move, our supply chains are global), however, the rules of the game are not global. Regulators and enforcers (facing continuous budget restraints) in the countries struggle to keep up with the speed of change. The reality is that business can react faster and is more integrated than the regulatory world is.

Service Providers

Service providers are just that, they provide a service. They manufacture nothing, design nothing and seldom own anything other than the assets required to provide a service. The customers of the service providers are numbered in the hundreds, often thousands and sometimes millions. These millions of customers in turn between them serve many additional millions of customers, with tens of millions of commodities that they manufacture, manage and distribute.

The information supplied by the service provider's customer to the service provider is usually the only tangible data the service provider receives upon which to make any validation in relation to restricted parties, licence requirements, end use, *etc.* Service providers trust their customers to understand their own roles and responsibilities in relation to the regulatory requirements and that they have also provided the required documentation and have undertaken necessary screening requirements. Seldom does the service provider have access to details of all parties involved in the commercial transaction. Rarely are they aware of the technical nature of their customers' commodities. Nor does the service provider have the technical expertise to be able to identify a controlled commodity.

In the event of a compliance issue, service providers are often held jointly responsible / liable for a compliance failure with the legal consequences arising from that responsibility / liability. This is forcing service providers to undertake secondary screening of the millions of transactions processed, adding millions of Euros to the cost of transportation, unnecessary delays to delivery and negatively impacting international trade to protect the interest of the service providers' business. The extraterritorial approach of some authorities is adding to the complexity of the process and generating compliance screening paranoia.

Depending on where you are in the world, the regulatory authorities responsible for creating new or updating existing legalisation would traditionally engage representatives from the Aerospace and Defence sector in discussions, recognising these organisations as having a direct involvement and knowledge of managing commodities, controls and compliance standards. This level of engagement has been broadened over the years to include industries such as the high tech, bio chemical, petrochemical and communications sectors etc. The banking sector and sometimes the insurance industries have been engaged on a regular basis with the regulatory authorities. However the service provider is often excluded from the development of new regulations and only becomes actively involved once the regulation has come into law.

There are many other diverse service providers involved in an international transaction. These include, but are not limited to: collection company, domestic linehaul, customs broker, forwarder, airline, airline handling company, and transit warehouse, customs bond, delivery company and of course all the staff employed by these service providers. There are other parties that are often overlooked in an international transaction, including customs, security, secret service, *etc.* and these enforcers of law are usually left out of the law making.

Just to be clear *Service providers are often held jointly responsible / liable in law for a compliance failure* and today, with the extraterritoriality of some countries' export control regulations, transit controls and multiple jurisdictions involvement, this adds further complexity to an already complex and challenging environment.

More controls, weaker compliance?

In 2013, Accelus Thomas Reuters published the results of a survey of compliance professionals, entitled "Cost of Compliance",[1] there were two startling findings:

Over the next 12 months (2014), these compliance professionals expect:

81% of the respondents expect volumes of regulatory information to increase slightly or significantly this year.

80% of the respondents expect the focus on managing regulatory risk to increase slightly or significantly.

This is staggering and clearly puts the increasing burden and cost on industry to police compliance.

Such ever increasing demands and standards, sometimes duplicated, seldom mutual or interlinked, poorly communicated and with little support from the regulatory authorities, often lead to confusion and issues with implementation, and therefore impacts compliance.

Cost of compliance

Classification, licence application, restricted party screening, background checks, end use checks, customs clearance, etc., all cost time and money to the exporter of commodities. The regulatory authorities then require the various service providers to carry out similar validations and checks to those already completed by the manufacture / supplier / exporter.

1 Thomson Reuters Accelus "Cost of Compliance Survey 2013": http://accelus.thomsonreuters.com/special-report/cost-compliance-survey-2013 (retrieved on 30 January 2013).

Imagine if service providers were required to understand each industry's commodities and which regulations apply, effectively, the service provider would need to be an expert in every area of design, manufacture, production etc.

Whilst tools exist to help with this some of these process's, it is seldom that the initial process is the most complex part. The impact and risk is usually where manual intervention comes into play and that costs escalate markedly. For example, restricted parties screening. As a service provider, the many restricted party screening software tools available will help identify a potential restricted party within seconds. However, this is where the hard work starts.

Most restricted party screening software providers advise that the average "hit rate" for a potential restricted party match, is between 1 and 1.5%. Once you have identified a potential restricted party, you will need to carry out a secondary detailed validation using the same tool, but referring to the detail of a particular restricted / denial listing. This for a seasoned operator will take 15 minutes or more. So for a small service provider moving 100,000 consignments a week (many service providers transport millions of consignments each week), this would represent approximately 1,000 potential "hits". If you were then to take an average of 15 minutes per enquiry, this would cost 250 man hours per week for a compliance activity that should have (and in many cases has) already been completed by the exporter. All actors in the supply chain are expected to complete the same task. In addition to this task, the service provider will have the burden of contacting the relevant competent authority to agree what actions are to be taken. Often identifying the relevant authorities is a challenge, and they are occasionally unaware of what to do and who to contact, causing more details to be requested, resulting in additional man hours and further delays.

Where is the risk?

The majority of regulatory focus over the years has been given to the obvious targets, the major companies involved in the manufacture and exportation of nuclear, defence, aerospace, chemical commodities, etc. and towards the highest risk destinations. These industries are well aware of the commodities they produce or sell, and in many cases have been actively involved with the regulators in the creation of regulated and practical controls, licencing requirements and the like. Such companies are well aware of their Export Control obligations, the technical nature of their commodities and the possible dual-use implications that may exist.

These major industries have the luxury of substantial compliance, legal and training departments to help them develop, challenge, understand and implement these complex regulations. They often engage numerous suppliers to manufacture or supply certain parts to be contained within their own end products. Sometimes this activity is sub-contracted out to yet further parties. These sub-contractors often represent companies who count their turnover in tens or hundreds of thousands of Euros rather than the billions of their ultimate customers. They do not have the luxury of equivalent and substantial compliance, legal and training departments to keep them informed and protected.

Some concerns:

- How do these second or third level actors become aware of compliance requirements that are applicable to themselves?
- What outreach are regulators doing to educate and support the Small and Medium Enterprises (SME's)?
- What changes and updates are communicated to all relevant parties?
- What self-assessment tools exist?
- What training tools exist?

Joined up thinking

The terms "supply chain security' and "secured supply chain" are buzz words that have been over used in the last 15 years. We have seen the introduction of numerous secured supply chain programmes such as: Authorised Economic Operator (AEO), Custom and Trade Partnership Against Terrorism (C-TPAT), Partnership in Protection (PIP), Frontline, Golden List and many more introduced by the regulatory authorities globally. Industry have also introduced their own standards such as International Standards Organisation (ISO), Transported Asset Protection Association (TAPA), International Air Transport Association's (IATA) Known Shipper, etc. Advanced data screening initiatives such as Export Control System (ECS), Import Control System (ICS) within the EU and Air Cargo Advanced Screening (ACAS) in the USA have been implemented. All of these initiatives have over lapping and duplicated requirements and standards. Many organisations are accredited for *all* of these initiatives, as the regulatory authorities and customers now expect this.

What does this all mean?

What is the real value to compliance and trade?

Are we really more secure?

In their own right each of these initiatives, standards and programmes add value, but the sheer magnitude of the effort required by industry to obtain and maintain these various requirements, introduces complexity, human error, confusion and cost.

The lack of true mutual recognition between these initiatives is a compliance opportunity missed.

Conclusion

In reality, people and companies want to do the "right thing". Globalisation in a modern day market is fluid, dynamic and extensively growing with new technology, information and products. The need for controls for strategic commodities, both tangible and non-tangible, will remain and develop further to protect nations from non-proliferation and for national security purposes.

We need to foster a partnership to truly close the gaps within the supply chain and create a realistic and safe global environment, with all relevant parties involved in the overall supply chain.

Transnational Consortia For Dual-Use Goods and National Export Control Regimes

Facing Diversity

Harald HOHMANN

Attorney at law, Hohmann Rechtsanwälte

In spite of the existence of the EU dual-use Regulation (EC Regulation 428/2009, hereinafter "dual-use Regulation") which has harmonised all export trade with dual-use goods (all economic goods except weapons and defence items) in the EU Common Market, there remain important loopholes, so that national export control law of the EU Member States is still very decisive for the export law in action. This contribution wants to demonstrate some of the consequences of this diversity of different national export law of the EU Member States and what impact it can have on the export law in action.

Case 1: the organisational restructuring and its impacts on export law in action: former situation

Originally, the German company G was operating on its own and shipping its listed goods (especially listed electronic goods) directly to its clients overseas. G has a limited number of customers worldwide, most of them are research organisations which are supplied permanently.

Question: what must G do in order not to always apply for each export licences permanently?

New situation: G was bought by the US consortium A (now G is renamed: A-Germany); this leads to the following organisational restructuring: if a customer in India wants to order these goods from the Indian company A-India, a subsidiary of the US consortium A, A-India will send this order to the centralised ordering company A-UK, another subsidiary of the US consortium A. A-UK is not only collecting all world-wide orders but is also the responsible company for world-wide export controls of the US consortium A. A-UK sends this order to A-Germany, because only A-Germany is producing these goods. A-Germany will produce this good on behalf of A-UK and A-Germany will send this good on behalf of A-UK to the customer in India. The shipping documents including the bills are filled out by A-India (or if a national subsidiary of A is missing in this country: by A-UK).

Questions: which of these companies is now exporter? And what must this company do under which national law in order not to always apply for each export licence permanently? What are the main differences between former and new situation?

See the following picture:

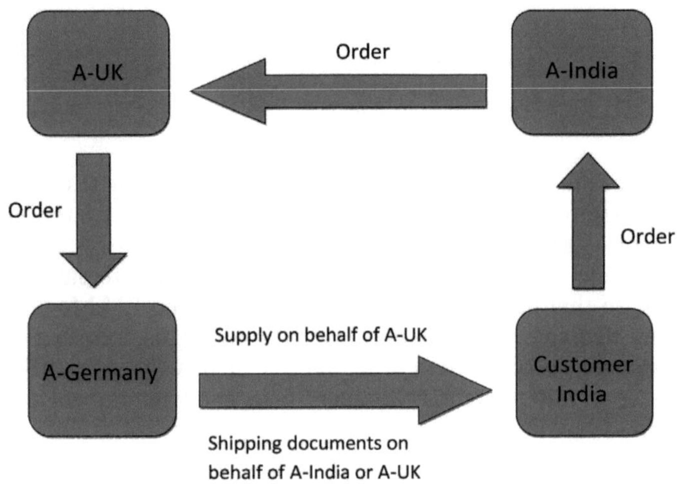

Case 1 in the former situation: bulk licences under national German export law

In the former situation, it was obvious that German national export law applied to the operating of G's exports: G was not a subsidiary of any international consortium, but was only acting in Germany.

Since the goods are listed, under Article 3 of the dual-use Regulation an export licence is required in each case of export to a third country (outside the EU). The question arises whether German national export law knows any trade facilitation in order to prevent that G has to apply for an export licence in each individual case. It must be checked whether any of the following two German bulk licences could be used by G, either the SAG (*Sammelausfuhrgenehmigung*) or the HBG (*Höchstbetragsgenehmigung*). The main difference between the SAG and the HBG in Germany consists in the fact that under the HBG G can export his goods only to one customer without applying for an individual export licence, while under the SAG he can do this to several reliable customers if he fulfils the high requirements of the SAG.

The differences between the two German bulk licences SAG and HBG are as follows:[1]

- The SAG can only be applied for in case that the German exporter is regarded as reliable by the German export agency BAFA and if he has received 50 export licences from BAFA within the last year, except that special circumstances can be demonstrated (e.g. that a dramatic increase of export numbers is to be expected). The German exporter must demonstrate that he has an ICP (internal compliance programme) for export controls, including formally nominating the Board's Export Director as responsible person (Ausfuhrverantwortlicher) to the BAFA. The SAG can be used for exports to several enumerated customers, under the two conditions that (1) these customers are regarded as reliable by BAFA and that (2) the German exporter checks whether the customers really comply with the use and end-use location indicated in their EUC (end-use certificate). The SAG is valid for 2 years (and can be extended once again).
- The HBG can only be applied for in case that the German exporter is regarded as reliable by BAFA; there is no need for him to demonstrate that he has received a specific number of export licences from BAFA, also an ICP is not necessarily required (although it is recommended). The HBG can be used for all successive shipments to only one customer. The German exporter must send the framework agreement for these successive shipments and an EUC of this one customer. The HBG is valid for 1 year (and can be extended once again).

Since the formal requirements for the SAG are very demanding, it is very likely that G will apply for the HBG for all customers he will ship to successively. In the case that he has 10 such customers, he will apply ten times for the HBG. Since the application procedure for this is only slightly longer than for individual export licences, it may take between 3 and 6 months to get this HBG from BAFA for these 10 customers.

---

1 Cf. German Runderlass Außenwirtschaft 10/2003 of 2 June 2003 (in BAFA (ed.), *HADDEX Handbuch der deutschen Exportkontrolle*, loose-leaf, Vol. 6, No. 730) concerning SAG, and comments by BAFA, in BAFA (ed.), *HADDEX*, Vol. 1, Part 7, No. 495 *et seq.* and No. 560 *et seq.* Cf. also Hohmann, *Angemessene Außenhandelsfreiheit im Vergleich*, Tübingen: Mohr 2002, pp. 243 *et seq.*

Case 1 in the new situation: bulk licences under national British export law

Here, the question which of the companies involved shall be regarded as "exporter" is decisive for the following reason: under Article 9 dual-use Regulation the place of establishment of an export company is decisive for the national export law to be applied for this export.[2] Therefore, it must be decided which of the companies involved shall be regarded as "exporter".

Under Article 2.3 (i) dual-use Regulation, it is decisive who is the "principal" of the export (so-called *procedural exporter*): this is the person "on whose behalf an export declaration is made", the person "who holds the contract with the consignee in the third country and has the power for determining the sending of the item out of the customs territory of the Community" and benefits most from this export. In this case, the export contract is concluded between A-UK and the customers, since the shipping papers regard A-India as supplier, while A-Germany and A-India are acting only as sub-suppliers of A-UK. And A-UK has the power of determining the sending of the item out of the customs territory of the Community. Very likely, A-UK will be regarded as procedural exporter.

Under national export law (Section 2 Paragraph 3 of the German Export Control Act), an additional exporter definition applies especially for purposes of criminal export law. The decisive factor here is which person is acting for the departure of goods from Germany to foreign countries (so-called *material exporter*).[3] It is very likely that A-Germany is regarded as "exporter" in this regard.

The question to decide here, namely what is the "place of establishment of an export company" in the sense of Article 9 dual-use Regulation, the EU definition of "exporter" under Article 2.3 (1) dual-use Regulation must be applied. Therefore, decisive is the place of establishment of A-UK, i.e. national British export law, and no longer national German export law.

British export law offers especially two kinds of bulk licences, namely OIEL (open individual export licence) and GPL (global project licence) – the latter is available only for military goods and defence items. If no bulk

---

2 For all other exports for which an authorisation is required under this Regulation, such authorisation shall be granted by the competent authorities of the Member State "where the exporter is established".

3 On the differentiation between procedural and material exporter, see Hohmann, John (eds.), *Kommentar zum Ausfuhrrecht*, Beck: Munich 2002, at pp. 289 *et seq.*, 363 *et seq.* and 1229-1231. See in particular: Hohmann, John, "Update Anhang 2 zur Dual-use-VO", note 15 *et seq.*; Just, "Paragraph 4 AWG", note 41 *et seq.*; Balzer, Hohmann, "Paragraph 8 AWV", notes 5 *et seq.*

licence is available, a SIEL (standard individual export licence) must be applied for. A-UK must now check, whether it wants to apply for SIEL or for the bulk licence OIEL. The differences are as follows:[4]

- The SIEL has similar functions as the German individual export licence, including some functions of the German HBG, since SIEL is often used for long-term contracts, projects and repeated business. SIEL is an export licence for controlled goods (especially for listed dual-use goods) specific to one exporter and only one consignee, and it is valid for 2 years. Thus SIEL is an individual export licence which can also be used if the British exporter wants to export these goods to only one customer in several successive shipments (based on a framework agreement) within 2 years.
- By contrast, the OIEL is a bulk licence having similar functions as the German SAG, since the OIEL can be used for the export of multiple shipments of specific controlled goods (especially of listed dual-use goods) to specific destinations, subject to meeting detailed terms and conditions. It may also name the consignees or end-users of the goods concerned – unlike the SIEL which always names these parties. To justify applying for an OIEL, the British exporter must have a record of at least 20 relevant SIEL applications in the previous year; where this is not possible (e.g. in case of new business), the British exporter should argue that there is an increasing number of export shipments. The British exporter should describe his ICP, he should add a list of very few countries to those the OIEL is applicable, and he should add the names and addresses of consignees and if possible of end-users (or at least a list of clients or end-users which could very likely be covered by his exports), and EUC undertakings from the consignees or end-users.

A-UK has now the choice whether it wants to apply for the SIEL; if he has 20 consignees to be delivered successively, he would need 20 SIEL. Or he could apply for the OIEL, in this case, this one bulk licence may be sufficient to undertake the exports to all consignees.

Case 1: main differences between former/current situations (German/British bulk licences)

While it is very cumbersome and time-consuming to apply for a SAG in Germany – already the requirement to have a record of at least 50 individual export licences in the previous year is a high barrier for most

4 Results of the author's phone calls with the BIS (July 2012).

companies, and the application procedure may take up to 1 year –, nearly the same functions can be received in the UK with the British OIEL, and the application procedure can be done within 60 working days (at least in 60-80% of cases). The conditions for applying the SAG are much higher than for the OIEL. The application procedure for the OIEL is quicker since the British export agency (in contrast to the German BAFA) will not check whether the exporter will fulfil with all requirements, instead BIS will undertake a compliance audit of the British exporter's business within three months after the first OIEL has been granted, and thereafter at intervals of between 3 and 36 months.[5]

The British OIEL is more flexible than the German SAG since not necessarily all end-users must be named during the application procedure, if at least a list of very typical end-users and those very likely to be named thereafter is submitted to BIS. It is no wonder that the number of granted OIELs is much higher than that of SAGs: in 2011, the BIS has issued OIELs to 406 exporting companies, while the number of German companies having a SAG is very limited, ca. 200 – 300 companies altogether, at least for the year 2001.[6]

Example 2: exports of a chemical company

CASE 2 A: The German chemicals company G sells a product to its subsidiary I in Italy. Later I sell this product outside the Community to S in South Africa. Who is the exporter: G or I? What practical steps should G and I take in order to simplify exports?

CASE 2 B: G wants to sell one of its products: a chemical mixture containing 15% aluminium powder, if possible from the stocks of its Italian subsidiary in Italy. This product is listed on position 1C111 lit. a under specific conditions. The interpretation of the German export agency is that it is only listed if at least 30% of this mixture contains aluminium powder. The interpretation of the Italian export agency is that it is already listed if the mixture contains only 10% aluminium powder. What should G do?

Concerning case 2 A

In Case 2 A it is very difficult to see which of the two parties is the procedural exporter, due to a triangle situation: the owner of the good (G) is not the contract partner of S, but G is supplying S, either directly

5 See: "Open Individual Export Licences OIEL", in: www.businesslink.gov.uk/exportcontrol.

6 See for these numbers: BIS, "UK Strategic Export Controls Annual Report 2011", at pp. 32 *et seq.*; Hohmann, "Bundestag Ausschuss-Drucksache 17(9) 1053 (neu)", at p. 8 *et seq.* and *Hohmann, op. cit.*, p. 244.

or via I, in both situations G is doing this under the instruction of I. It could be argued that G is procedural exporter, since I derives the power of control only from G, or that I is procedural exporter, since I is the principal. All depends on the contractual relationship and/or the division of labour between G and I.[7] The best recommendation for simplifying exports would be to have very clear contracts. Especially, if G wants to deliver the products directly to S, the best would be to have a contract between G and S. If only I has the contract and would deliver to S, then only I would be regarded as procedural exporter. In addition, the division of labour should be specified, that only the one doing the direct export to S should have control over the export, so that only he is regarded as procedural "exporter".

The question regarding which national export agency is competent also has two aspects: the German export agency BAFA has competence due to the *principle of residence* under Article 9 Paragraph 2 dual-use Regulation since the company's headquarter is in Germany. The other possibility is the *principle of the addressed agency:* that the Italian export agency is competent in case the export application is addressed to the Italian export agency under Article 11 Paragraph 1 dual-use Regulation and if the Italian and the other concerned national export agencies consult with one another. If the German export agency BAFA does not oppose to the Italian competence within 10 (or 30) working days, the Italian competence is accepted (Article 11 Paragraph 1 sentences 4 and 5 dual-use Regulation). In general, the end-use certificate of one country – regularly that of the final end-use (here South Africa) – is sufficient. If however the final end-use is not known at that time, than the EUC of the first destination could be accepted.

Concerning case 2 B

EU export law does not know any definition under which situations a mixture is listed, whether 10% or 30% would trigger this. At least one of the global non-proliferation regimes (MTCR) seems to accept a 30% rule for mixtures. Since there are no binding EU norms saying which mixture is decisive for triggering the match of the list position, EU Member States can decide which %-values is decisive for this. Therefore, there are no legal objections that the Italian export agency accepts a 10% level, while the German export agency accepts the 30% value.

In this case, G has the choice of a strategic selection which of the national export agencies is competent for this export application, depending on what G favours. Since G will prefer the situation not to be forced

[7] See BAFA, *op. cit.*, Vol. 1, Part 1, note 47 *et seq.*

to apply for an export licence, he will apply to the German export agency. Even if this good is already in the stocks of the Italian subsidiary I, this is possible due to the fact that the headquarters of G is in Germany. However in this case, G should consult with I whether a licence was already denied by Italy in the past. If denied, Germany may only decide on this application after having previously consulted with Italy (in order to meet the no-undercut notification requirement).

Results of case 2

Although the dual-use Regulation wanted to harmonise the conditions for exporting dual-use goods in the EU, it still offers some potential for "forum shopping". In order to apply at the national agency offering the lowest levels of export controls, transnational companies may sell their goods to a subsidiary in another EU Member State. This national export agency is then responsible, at least if it consults with the national export agency of the residence of the headquarters. This condition can be easily fulfilled by waiting 10 (or 30) working days whether the national export agency of the residence will object.

Results of both cases

The EU Common Market for dual-use goods is not yet a level-playing field in which all EU Members face same European conditions – instead the national export law of EU Member States still has a large influence on the export law in action.

- The question which national general licence is applicable or what kind of bulk licence could be used is largely dominated by national export law, in spite of all efforts of harmonisation by the EU. This can lead to results such as that an export licence is required under EU export law, while the national export law of one EU Member State renounces this requirement for all goods with a value below 5,000 EUR (German AG12). Or – as Case 1 shows – this can lead to results that a bulk licence like the British OIEL can be easily applied for within 2 months, while it would require more than 1 year to apply for the German SAG or half a year for the HBG, and in case of the SAG, it may even be too cumbersome or nearly impossible to comply with all conditions for it, while the corresponding British bulk licence gives nearly same advantages, although the bureaucratic burden is much less in case of Great Britain as compared with Germany.
- The question regarding which national interpretation standards will apply is also largely dominated by national export law. In case that EU export control law does not give binding results, all national export agencies can decide on their own which definition

and which standards should apply. As Case 2 shows, the standards in one EU Member can be much lower than in the other. This leads to competitive disadvantages between the EU Members.

- Some EU Member States still accept unilateral export controls which are applicable only in this State, but not in the other EU Members. Especially German export law knows several unilateral export controls which are not shared by the other EU Members.[8] Also in this case, the standards in one EU Member are much lower than in the other. This also leads to competitive disadvantages between the EU Members.
- This national diversity is a fact where especially transnational consortia can take advantage of it.
- They can sell their goods to the stocks of that EU Member having the lowest export control standards and then address the application to this national export agency.
- Or they can, if they want, also ask the national export agency of the headquarters to decide on this export matter. The question which national export agency has competence could be made dependent on the lowest export control standards.
- This can lead to a strategic "forum shopping" that always the national export agency with the lowest standards shall have competence.

Such a strategic "forum shopping" is not acceptable in the EU Common Market. Therefore, the Green Paper for the revision of the EU dual-use Regulation of 30 June 2011 (COM (2011) 393) has emphasised that differences in national approaches to dual-use export controls should be abolished as far as possible. The EU Commission has made clear that this task should cover administrative, substantive and operational measures:[9]

- Administrative: Member States should harmonise their approaches to such issues such as registration requirements and questions which kind of ICP is required for bulk licences.
- Substantive: Member States should harmonise their national authorisations available under the dual-use Regulation, in order to

8 See especially the licence requirements under Paragraph 9 of the German Export Control Order AWV (for non listed goods if there are "red flags" for a sensitive use in a nuclear installation in a nuclear sensitive country) and under Paragraph 11 Paragraph 2 AWV (for intra-Community transfers of nationally listed dual-use goods if there are Red Flags that these goods will be shipped to third countries); cf. the critical remarks by *Hohmann*, *op. cit.*, at pp. 323 *et seq.* and at pp. 511 *et seq.*

9 European Commission, "Green Paper", document COM (2011)393, p. 5.

prevent that broad national authorisations are applicable in one Member State which are not available for other EU Members.

- Operational: Member States should harmonise their different interpretations of control list entries and harmonise their use of the catch-all provisions for non-listed goods.

One of the main items of the Green Paper is the "level playing field for EU exporters" within all EU Member States. The EU principles of the economic freedoms (like the free movement of goods), the equality between the Member States, the Single Market with the EU Common Commercial Policy, they all urgently require that this "level playing field for EU exporters" is also created as soon as possible for the export policy in order to avoid facing diversity.

Dual-Use Trade Control

National and Sub-Regional Model for Africa

Yacine AMARA

Nuclear Lawyer

This chapter discusses first the UN Security Council Resolution 1540/(2004) with reference to its implementation in Africa. Second, it analyses the possibilities to examine export control models (regional or sub-regional) appropriate for the African continent and, finally, gives a brief description of the Algerian State practice in terms of its national export and import control system.

Briefly, the process of implementing the UNSC Resolution 1540 in Africa is often described as slow, primarily due to the fact that less than two thirds of African States have submitted their latest reports to the UN 1540 Committee. Most reports submitted so far contain very little detail about specific nuclear, chemical, and biological capabilities and safeguards, they simply list data on the status of disarmament and non-proliferation measures. Moreover, observers note that the legislations reported are often out-dated and insufficient to deal more effectively with recent WMD threats. As a response States in Africa have provided various reasons for the lack of detailed reporting which definitely should be understood in the context of the large number of competing priorities and challenges, rather than the low level of priority given to the WMD related commitments. The reasons that stand behind the reporting fatigue are the lack of human and financial resources and the politico-economic challenges. Deficient reporting does not necessarily mean that UNSC Resolution 1540 is not implemented on the continent, although submitting reports to the 1540 Committee is required by the resolution. However, most States would argue that it is better to submit a quality report, which takes more time and contains accurate information rather than submitting superficial and non-comprehensive reports.[1]

---

1 See the report of the 1540 Committee established under the reference S/2011/579.

The UNSC Resolution 1540 Committee acknowledges that States must determine how to implement the resolution domestically and suggests that States use the "1540 matrix" which constitutes a baseline for identifying priorities. However, only a few African States have a clear view on how the Resolution 1540 should be implemented and what ought to be done to make compliance easier and better. Possibly because some States in Africa present a danger of WMD proliferation, or consider any questioning on related materials subject to control as a way of exerting economic pressure for the continent. However, the most convincing argument that would strengthen the implementation of the 1540 resolution would be accelerated economic and social development of African States while maintaining control over WMD and related materials and technologies through a multilateral approach using existing regional or sub regional models.

The Resolution 1540 and the national export control system

As discussed above, the Resolution 1540 adopted in 2004 under Chapter VII of the UN establishes the obligation for all UN Member States to adopt and enforce controls over exports insofar as concerns materials and technologies related to nuclear, chemical, and biological weapons and theirs means of delivery.

Operational paragraph 6 encourages States to develop "effective national control lists" and in operational paragraph 8(d) calls upon States to "develop appropriate ways to work with and inform industry and the public regarding their obligations under such law".

Thus, under operational paragraphs 3, 6 and 8, the UN Security Council identified the key elements to effectively and safely control the trade in materials and technologies that could have legitimate commercial purposes, but also might be diverted by non-state actors to WMD related purposes.

African States have generally adopted one of two approaches to meet the UNSC Resolution 1540 requirement in terms of export and import control of WMD related items. The first is to include a list of WMD related items subject to export and import controls in their general foreign trade strategy. The second approach is to include export and import control provisions in a list of controlled items in a separate comprehensive export law. However, the first approach is deemed the best adapted.

As is the case with any UNSC resolution addressed to all UN members since the endorsement of the 1540 resolution, African governments are trying to implement it both at international and national levels. However, implementing the UNSC Resolution 1540 export requirements as an international binding instrument in the respective national legislations is not an easy task: there is a great diversity among States regarding the constitutional primary law as well as the legal system applying to government administration and to industrial organisation in the different countries.

The export control system in place in a country with a parliamentary political system and an open market economy is likely to be very different from such a system in place in a country with an authoritarian or one-party political system and a centrally planned economy. Therefore, it is very important to take into account the economic and political aspects while addressing national export and import regimes for Africa: each country being different, but in the final analysis, the UNSC Resolution 1540 is the main international commitment that all States have adopted and that they have to implement. National export and import regimes still constitute the utmost effective non-proliferation regime in place that is actually effective.

The primary export and import law should be easily ascertained to address the legal framework in order to make the essential non-proliferation objective transparent to both citizens and corporations, in essence to protect national security, to further foreign policy interests and to fulfil international commitment, notably those mentioned by the UNSC Resolution 1540. This statement demonstrates that the UNSC Resolution 1540 commitment requires all States to adopt legislation so as to meet the objective of non-proliferation rather than exercising export controls related to lists of items.

In general, some States have chosen to implement export and import regimes in accordance with procedures agreed upon by a group of States: expectations of global and strategic, commercial, and technological environments have led the EU Member States for example, to develop a comprehensive export control regime Regulation 428/2009, which includes tangible and intangible items. The EU Member States have taken a step forward beyond the UNSC Resolution 1540 requirements and toward a comprehensive dual-use control regime whereas most African States find themselves overwhelmed by the UNSC obligations, and are still looking to find a regional or sub regional approach in order to implement the Resolution 1540 as a promising way to overcome the implementation challenges.

Despite all available options, related *inter alia* to any global assistance that might be provided by the EU the US or the African Union to African States, any initiative in this context should not neglect or overlook the existing national comprehensive export and import regime of each African country. Any multilateral approach must necessarily assess the existing practice and eventually build upon either a specific model or a set of norms as an appropriate export and import regime consistent with the UNSC Resolution 1540 obligations and, at the same time, relevant to the African continent.

Appropriate national export and import model

As emphasised above, due to the great diversity of legal and administrative systems in the different African countries, no single model of an export control system can be defined which would apply to the entire African continent. Instead, there are some key legal elements to be considered for any model or norms at regional or sub regional level in order to be effective.

We acknowledge that the UNSC Resolution is making reference to WMD non-proliferation treaties, conventions and other related instruments. However, the status of ratification of these treaties shows that some African States remain outside WMD related international legal instruments. Nevertheless, this does not mean that the States that are neither signatories nor parties to WMD non-proliferation related treaties and conventions could take measures to defeat the object of the international instruments themselves.[2]

The option to put in place an export and import model or regime for African States could be undertaken among States notably that have the same international commitments relating to UNSC Resolution 1540, WMD, non-proliferation treaties and other relevant conventions. In any case whatever model – regional or sub regional – would be chosen by African States to implement the objective of non-proliferation of WMD, the following legal elements should be included or incorporated in such export and import models. The set of norms appropriate for the continent, legislations, thus have to be made in a way so as to translate the following key elements in norms and make them effective for national implementation and enforcement.

These key elements are:

- Jurisdiction over individuals and transactions;
- Implementation authority of the export control process;
- Penalties, investigation and prosecution;
- Responsibilities of the government;
- Responsibilities of the parties involved in the transaction supply chain.

---

2 See the Vienna Convention on the international treaties, Article 18.

It should be noted that these listed key elements do not constitute a menu from which national legislations or models have to choose or be inspired, but rather a set of elements found to be useful in the development of an effective legal framework in this area: there are a variety of ways to translate the aforementioned elements while drafting any model or setting up norms, assuming the perception that some of them are already included in existing countries legislation with effective export and import control law, as well as in countries with a comprehensive law on foreign trade to be implemented in conjunction with regular control of military items. In any case, no matter at which level these elements are already set forth, it is important that drafters of any effective export control legislation must take into account, these key elements when laying down the drafted model or norm.

Jurisdiction over territory, individuals, and transactions

The globalisation of production, distribution and financing of goods and services, as well as the development of technologies can constitute a threat to WMD proliferation. Governments thus should have the authority to control items moving into, through, or out of their physical territory including tangible and intangible technology. Unfortunately, domestic trade can also contribute to the proliferation of WMD or their means of delivery and undermine any export control regime in place by making it difficult to distinguish illicit from legitimate trade. To exercise control, States have relied on their national control lists that include both dual-use and restricted military items. However, we may wonder what would apply to items not listed in the respective national control list. An effective control regime should authorise government to control material and technology even if not listed in national control lists, especially when there is a potential diversion risk to an unauthorised end user related to WMD proliferation or for terrorist purposes.

Implementating authority of the export control process

A legal framework for export control should establish a clear assignment of responsibilities for the implementation of control, and designate the competent authorities in charge of the defined tasks with a clear view on the licencing process, allowing for decision making on specific licences as well as criteria (i.e. conditions for approval, and denial). In many African States, this task is normally not carried out by one authority or administrative body, rather to the contrary, there are different authorities in charge of issuing authorisations and licences related to nuclear, chemical, and biological items. Essentially, modern control systems should plan first and thereafter verify whether there are overlaps and interferences among authorities or agencies in charge of implementation. Therefore, it would be better to designate or assign an authority or agency and provide it with inputs from other authorities or agencies for processing the export criteria and licences. The licencing process should, where appropriate, include the required criteria, type of licences or authorisation that may be granted, procedures for submitting the said application, the timeline for reviewing and decision making on the application, the licence or authorisation validity period, etc.

Penalties, investigation and prosecution

An effective export legal framework should set forth a law enforcement system that applies specifically to implementation in order to monitor foreign trade and carry out investigations as to possible violations of relevant laws and regulations. In this context, it is very important to control the trade related foreign transactions in order to ensure consistency with the UNSC Resolution 1540, which requires control over financial asset of export transactions and funds. Many States subject such export and import transactions and operation to certain prerequisites, such as banking domiciliation, that do not necessarily imply restrictions. However, the export control system should be enforced in a way to allow verification of financial resources allocated to export and import operations or transactions.

In addition, an effective export model should set forth appropriate mechanisms to allow for the exercise of the right to enforcement including investigation and prosecution. In many countries, different authorities (customs, police, border, security and intelligence services) are involved in carrying out these tasks. In order to avoid overlaps and interferences between these authorities, it is very important for any model to clearly define the enforcement procedures including investigation and prosecution through clear specific administrative and judicial proceedings. First, the law should define the persons or authorities competent to settle export and import disputes, and second, the law should make clear the scope of jurisdiction under which such cases pertaining to export violation should fall.

In any case, no matter to which legal system a State may belong, the most important issue is – considering that all economic actors, notably exporters, are very sensitive about their trade reputation – that the laws regulating export and import should clearly state all administrative and judicial measures which might be taken as to the imposition in) of penalties and sanctions. The legal remedies against inappropriate measures or possible errors regarding prosecutions and accusation should be included.

Responsibilities of the Government (transparency, confidentiality, cooperation)

Transparency is an effective key element for any legal export framework that should address and set forth responsibilities of the government in terms of confidentiality and cooperation among governments. The legal framework should define the procedures or channels that governments will use to address the relevant industry (i.e. those involved in the export and import transaction chain).

The government for example should maintain accurate records related to the processing of licences, audit related issues, enforcement and implementation as well as outreach efforts. All related information is very important: most governments require this information be kept for many years as it might be needed to bring export dispute cases to completion in the courts. As such related licence information issues of controlled items can easily contribute to WMD proliferation, it is very important for any export and import model to regulate the time period required by the judicial systems to retain or keep related information. Governments should also identify the appropriate ways to maintain and publish up-to-date export control regulation and guidance. The relevant information should be made transparent, available and at the disposal of all economic actors, including changes brought to licencing criteria and procedures as well as to national control lists. The economic actors in African countries should support all those changes to ensure good compliance results. In some States, especially those with an open market economy system, operators can be involved at an early stage in the process of trade control system review (law, list of items, etc.), To the contrary, operators do not have this possibility in countries with a "command" economical system. In all cases, an effective export control model should facilitate the right of the economic actors to make comments and to be accordingly consulted for changes and updates brought to the control lists as well as to the regulations. The transparency principle also requires that the national licencing authorities make clear decisions on export licence applications in a prompt and transparent manner, and accordingly inform the applicant on decisions made.

Confidentiality is a further important responsibility of governments within the framework of any export and import control model, in order to build a common trust between government and industry and other economic actors; the business community (including industry) should have sufficient assurances regarding their business related information. In general to obtain a licence for controlled items, exporters should provide governments with information including as to the product, customers, and other data that if disclosed to a third party, to the general public or other companies could be used by competitors to gain a market advantage.

Companies should have assurances that the government will treat and keep such information confidential; If not there will be less compliance. This issue can possibly be also raised at the investigation level, where companies have to communicate sensitive information with more than one authority in charge of implementation and enforcement of the export law. Therefore, to enhance compliance it is very important that such information is kept confidential.

Cooperation is a core element for any effective export control model, as obviously no single authority or even country can alone successfully monitor WMD proliferation material or prevent sensitive exports dual-use items.

As emphasised above, most African countries are still facing difficulties to implement controls of WMD related material and technologies, even including those contained in national control lists. Therefore, to exercise real control over sensitive dual-use items, there must be a strong commitment to cooperation and coordination among countries. In any export control model, cooperation is needed to clarify the role of countries. First, on which basis is the cooperation conducted? Is it based on foreign policy interest of each country, or, only on violation against export laws that makes it necessary. As many African States are open to illicit trade given their low GDP and annual revenue, a matter that might incite and support illicit trade and make it very difficult to fight transnational illicit trade as well as organised crime. It is important to remind States of their international commitment. In this context support and help from developed countries is essential and can only be reached through cooperation.

Cooperation also needs investment in communication technology to facilitate regional and global participation in some regional and international initiatives such as the EU e-Customs and Export Control System. International cooperation means also preventing and detecting as well as investigating illicit export and import transactions, as without such cooperation it is very difficult to collect related information needed to proceed with prosecution and, thus, with the implementation of export control laws.

Adoption of many initiatives can be beneficial to maintain cooperation on a risk, sharing analysis and profiles as well as other information related to licence application for controlled items. Different export agencies or authorities can share related export information in one common accessible database. This will not only enhance the work of each unit, but also allow agencies to gather expertise in one unit and, thus, avoid duplication. The most important is to avoid all obstacles against cooperation between concerned governments within the framework of an export control model.

Responsibilities of the parties

As with the principle of transparency, the responsibility of the government towards all parties including exporters, re-exporters and other individuals and entities involved in transactions should be well clarified in any export control model; this would increase certainty and reliability for both industry and government. The responsibilities may include licence requirements, documentation, and compliance with the prevailing export laws and regulations: the law may also include restrictions for activities of intermediaries such as trade facilitators, brokers, carriers, and forwarders.

Algerian dual-use control items

The Algerian commitment to the implementation of the UNSC Resolution 1540 is more comprehensive than that of other countries in the Middle East and North African region, given its experience with cases of trafficking and terrorist activities on Algerian soil. However, in order to evaluate the implementation properly we need to consider state practice, which necessarily includes both the national and international legal and regulatory frameworks.

An overview of the Algerian treaties status as per the UNSC Resolution 1540 shows clearly that the State is a party to all major arms control and disarmament treaties. At the national level, we note that many laws and regulations have been recently enacted to regulate the export control regime in Algeria, but in general, the regulation put forth is not specific to dual-use items only. The Algerian export and import regime is subject to foreign exchange currency control.[3] In general, trade operations are conducted freely, only items are excluded that threaten security, public order and morality, as well as goods for which a licencing system or strict regulation may apply in accordance with the provisions of Ordinance 03-04[4] or, with international agreements to which Algeria is a party.

Different authorities are involved in the issuance of the import and export authorisations, and several Ministries must clear nuclear, biological and chemical products or items prior to entering the country. Dual-use items are considered but presently not specifically listed. Instead, issues regarding dual-use items are regulated through a Commission under the

---

3 Ordinance No. 03-11 of 26 August 2003 concerning the currency and credit. See Currency Regulations, Chapter 6, which subjects the export and import operations to certain prerequisites, such as banking domiciliation.

4 Ordinance No. 03-04 of July 19, 2003 concerning the general rules applicable to importing and exporting merchandise sets the general principle in this sector.

Ministry of Defence that has the authority to establish rules and regulations applicable to the export of sensitive material and dual-use items.[5]

These authorities involved in the licencing implementation process are not working alone, but in partnership with other authorities in charge of enforcement and implementation of the export and import control laws (such as the custom administration and security services), and, consequently also cooperating with relevant international bodies.

Cooperation in the chemical field is conducted through the African Commission and the Technical Secretariat of the Organization for the Prohibition of Chemical Weapons, for which Algeria has recently set up a ministerial Committee in charge of implementation and coordination with OPCW.[6] The Algerian effort regarding implementation of OPCW – specific obligations now also includes the provisions for sanctions against violations of the Convention.[7] The decision by the Head of Government that requires special authorisation for certain chemical products listed by the OPCW,[8] demonstrates the political will of Algeria to follow in a comprehensive and consistent manner the non-proliferation objectives of the Convention.

The nuclear field is fully regulated and international cooperation is well developed. As a result, all radioactive materials and sources, their users, permits, authorisations, inspections, etc., are shared with the IAEA. The country also participates in the IAEA Illicit Trafficking Database (ITDB). In addition, under the Comprehensive Safeguards Agreement (CSA) the IAEA, through it inspectors and together with the Algerian Atomic Energy Commission, are setting up the State Accounting System relating to all nuclear material within the Algerian facilities.

The customs administration plays an important role in terms of implementation of the export control law. It has, responsibility for collecting and safeguarding customs duties as well as controlling the flow of goods

---

5 Act of 8 December 2012, related to the Presidential Decree No. 2011-383 of 23 November 2011, which sets up the regulation applicable for export of sensitive material and dual-use items.

6 Ministerial Committee by virtue of Presidential Decree No. 97-125 of 26 April 1997.

7 Act No. 03-09, passed on 19 July 2003. It prohibits any natural or artificial person who is on the Algerian territory to take, under penalty of criminal and administrative sanctions, any action contrary to the relevant provisions of the Convention. The application of the Act extends to any activity prohibited for a State party to the Convention, undertaken in any place whatsoever, by a natural person having Algerian nationality.

8 Decision of the Head of Government of 24 March 2005 incorporating the chemicals in schedules 2 and 3 of the Annex on Chemicals of the Convention on the Prohibition of the Development, Production, Stockpiling and Use of Chemical Weapons and on their Destruction into the schedule of hazardous chemicals whose importation requires prior approval by the Ministry of Energy and Mines.

including animals, personal effects, and hazardous items in and out of the country. Its role is not limited to import and export processing declarations, collection of tax duties, classifications of and assessment of goods origin, but also includes the physical inspection, examination, the fight against smuggling and organised crime so as to ensure public security and health protection.

In this context, Algeria established at the national level a rigorous legislative and regulatory framework for border-control purposes further strengthened in the context of the war on terrorism. Consequently, all exported or imported hazardous items, in particular nuclear, chemical and biological substances are checked. The existing legislative and regulatory framework facilitates the internal cooperation among authorities in charge of export control implementation and enforcement. It is noted that a number of mixed customs/police working group posts were created along the national borders to back up customs officers in their fight against terrorist, fraud and cross-border criminal activities.

The border police works closely with the Algerian security services under the authority of the judiciary and cooperates well with the police on a bilateral level or through the International Criminal Police Organisation (Interpol).

The Algerian customs administration has taken the necessary steps to maintain international cooperation and signed agreements on mutual administrative assistance with several countries, including in the Mediterranean, Maghreb and Sahel regions. This trend has been confirmed with the effective application since September 2005 of the Association Agreement with the European Union (EU), and since 1st January 2009 with the Arab Free Trade Zone. Beside its membership and participation in the activities of the World Customs Organisation, the Algerian custom services are regularly updating the tariff heading code, which any exporters in Algeria must use in order to ascertain tariffs cost and to know whether any items subject to an export or import transaction is listed and requires prior authorisation.[9]

The level of awareness among the economic actors is rising too; the Algerian Government has made information available on the legal and regulatory framework relating to export control, as published in the official journal website.[10]

---

9 See: http://www.douane.gov.dz/applications/tarif/. Since 1995, Algerian Customs use the Automated Customs Management System (SIGAD) to codify merchandise and for the management of tax and fee collection systems. Goods can remain in bond in waiting for a special administrative authorisation.

10 See: www.joradp.dz. The web of the General Secretariat of the Algerian Government, where as all official laws, decrees, ordinance, Acts are published after theirs ratification either by the parliament or the president of the republic of Algeria.

Algerian law provides for sanctions and penalties in case of violations of the export regime. Offences are not all specific, but include offences committed in relation to dual-use CBRN items, matters related to non-compliance, to cases to combat fraud, and to detect illegal practices; Some sanctions fall under criminal law,[11] other cases pertaining to non-payment of duties and taxes or their refund, and opposition to seizures fall under the civil Code.

Overall export legislation in Algeria is comprehensive and it experienced significant developments; key gaps remain with respect to adopting export legislation related to dual-use end-use control, lists related to end-users and transhipment. This is a common deficit within the region, and, thus, should not detract from the comparatively good reporting and implementation behaviour exhibited by Algeria.

Conclusion

While almost all African countries still lag behind as to the dual-use control legislation, the only country with a developed legislation in this area is South Africa. As explained, most African States still voice concern about the real impact and effectiveness of the Resolution 1540, as well as with regard to the major flaw as to CBRN items to be regulated. Moreover, UNSC Resolution 1540 is usually seen as broadly drafted in terms that are vague and open to interpretation. Clarity is therefore essential for States to develop and enforce legislation based on their internal requirements and capabilities.

As much as possible the control lists should be more specific and inclusive regarding CBRN dual-use items. To overcome these challenges, it is certainly a good initiative to develop a model or a set of norms which could help African States in their national implementation of the UNSC Resolution 1540.

However, individual States, international, regional and sub-regional bodies such as the EU, the US, and the African Union can assist and support national implementation, especially by providing the necessary risk assessment tools in order to better identify transactions pertaining CBRN proliferation and terrorism.

---

[11] Article 87 bis 7 of the criminal law which prohibits import or export, use without authorisation of prohibited firearms or ammunitions. The Chapter 15 of the Customs Code deals with customs disputes under criminal jurisdiction, cases pertaining to payment of duties and taxes or their refund, and oppositions to seizures fall under the civil matters.

Export Controls of Dual-Use Goods and Technologies in the Democratic Republic of Congo?[1]

John Kabange MUKUBU

Customs Controller, Lawyer

Introduction

The Democratic Republic of Congo (DRC) is the second largest country in Africa after Algeria. The country stretches from the Atlantic Ocean to the eastern plateau of the continent covering the main part of the Congo River Basin.

The DRC shares nine borders with its neighbours that are Angola, South Sudan, Tanzania, Burundi, Zambia, Congo Brazzaville, Uganda and the Central African Republic. The need for intense customs activities is due to the length of national borders with its neighbours.

There is however, no export control regime applicable to dual-use goods that is strictly applied in the DRC, despite its strategic position and the economic potential of this "giant" located in the heart of Africa.

A number of law enforcement agencies are in charge of border control: namely the General Directorate of Customs and Taxes (DGDA),[2] the Border Police, the General Directorate of Migration (DGM) the Congolese Office of Controls (OCC), the Hygiene (health) control agency. Each agency applies its own regulations within the competencies attributed to it by the law.

Controls regarding transfers of dual-use goods and technologies are not carried out in systematic manner by the above referred offices and

1 Chapter submitted in French: "La Procédure d'export-contrôle des biens et technologies à double usage en République Démocratique du Congo". Translation by Dr. Odette Jankowitsch-Prevor.

2 Note of the translator: abbreviations are not translated into English but maintained in the original French.

agencies. Therefore, main emphasis is on the import and export controls carried out at the border crossings.

All exports of all types of goods regardless of their destination or further use – be it civilian or military – are regulated by national law.[3]

Further, the sanctions regime applicable to cases of violation of any given export provisions does not distinguish dual-use goods from any other merchandise that is not subject to any specific control.

Therefore, goods listed by customs for purpose of tariff and taxes – as well as non-listed goods – are subject to the same import and export controls regardless of their nature.[4]

The national defence policy introduced by the Government and applied by the Ministry of National Defence and Veterans does not attach any priority to the nuclear field. This is justifiable as the DRC does not develop or carry out any major nuclear activity and therefore security concerns are directed to other different domains.

This explains why national export policy and relevant security measures are implemented by specialised agencies (offices); notably the General Directorate of Customs and Taxes (DGDA), the Congolese Control Office (OCC), the General Commissariat for Atomic Energy (CGEA), and the National Committee for Protection Against Ionizing Radiation (CNPRI).

These Offices are under the authority of the following Ministries:

- Ministry of Finance;
- Ministry of Economy;
- Ministry of Higher Education and Scientific Research;
- Ministry of Mines;
- Ministry of Foreign Trade.

The lack of public awareness of the content of UN Security Council resolution 1540/ (2004) obviously does not facilitate implementation of its recommendations addressed directly to States. This international obligation is rather perceived as a constraint or a commitment.

Some African States argue that they are not in a position to blindly apply recommendations without having ever been associated to their adoption, although their delegates are represented in all Organs of the United Nations.

---

3 Articles 111 and 112 of the Code des douanes /ordonnance – Law No. 10/2010 (Customs Code).

4 Law No. 08/006 of 12 June 2008 modifying and completing Law No. 003/03 of 13 March 2003 setting forth a new customs tariff of dues and taxes.

However, it is a fact that Africa is involved in illicit trafficking of minerals, of light and small calibre arms, as well as in illegal activities aimed at destabilizing other States.

This situation – state of affairs – should not remain unnoticed by the international community considering that its main concern is the security of States and respect for their national sovereignty.

The main obstacles preventing the implementation of UNSC Resolution 1540 in Central Africa, a region to which the DRC belongs are however attributable to individual Governments.

Such obstacles are in particular:

- The lack of information on the very existence of Resolution 1540 provided to customs officers on duty at the borders;
- The lack of cooperation within the Region due to diverging interests;
- The specific situation of each individual State, notably concerns regarding the need to obtain income from the treasury through exports and interference by policy makers into customs controls;
- The uncontrollable national borders due essentially to the multiplicity of armed conflicts that prevail in the Region;
- The economic "dividend" accruing to certain States through such trade (i.e. minerals and arms);
- The society characterised by poverty of the population surviving by working in certain mining activities.

Laws and Regulations of the DRC applicable to the export of goods

The legal "weaponry" of the DRC does not specifically provide for norms regulating – as well as reprimanding violations of – exports of dual-use goods and technologies.

However, there are a number of laws that regulate the movement of goods at entry into and exit from the national territory.[5] These are as follows:

[5] See: Ordonnance-loi No. 10/002 du 20 août 2010 portant Code des Douanes; Ordonnance-loi No. 12/2012 du 21 septembre 2012 portant Tarif des droits et taxes à l'importation et à l'exportation; Code Pénal congolais livre II; loi No. 007/2002 du 11 juillet 2012 portant Code Minier; loi No. 73/003 du 05 janvier 1973 particulière sur le commerce en RDC; loi No. 017/2002 du 16 octobre 2002 portant dispositions relatives à la protection contre les dangers des rayonnements ionisants et à la protection physique des matières et des installations nucléaires ("loi nucléaire").

The Customs Code

The Customs Code provides that all imported or exported goods are subject to a declaration of goods under a specified customs regime (Article 112). The competency of Customs extends to the entire "customs territory" as specified by the law.

All goods entering or exiting the DRC must be controlled by a customs office and must follow *ex-ante* the conditions required or exit through the way authorised by the relevant law.

The fundamental law of the DRC regulates the movement of goods at the national border crossings. The law is further implemented by Ministerial Decree No. 016/CAB/MIN/FINANCES/2011 of 11 April 2011 setting forth the specific measures to be adopted as well as laws set forth by other authorities that the Customs Office has to impose.

The Legislator of the Customs Code has provided for certain measures enabling the customs office to carry out controls of sensitive goods as well as of dangerous goods.

Prohibited as well as restricted goods are specified by a Decree of the Minister of Foreign Trade. (Article 74 of the Customs Code.)

In regards to the export control of dual-use items, the Customs Code considers all goods as being prohibited that are not specifically authorised for import or export for any specified reason: such reasons include public order, public security, public morality, hygiene and public health, protection of the environment, protection of national cultural goods, intellectual property and consumer protection.

Moreover, subject to restrictions are all goods that are submitted to the application of special conditions or formalities other than customs controls and declaration (Article 73 Customs Code). It may be admitted, therefore, that the dual-use goods are ranked in the category of the restricted goods. Different from the prohibited goods, of which the entry and exit are forbidden, these goods may cross the border after the competent authorities have delivered licences.

In regards to customs procedures relating to export control, it is worth noting that as soon as the customs formalities are completed, the goods to be exported by sea, river, lake or airplane have to be immediately loaded on board of ships or planes (Article 140 OD Customs Code). Goods that are to be exported by land have to be taken immediately abroad by the most direct route. (Article 96 Customs Code.)

Goods for export by sea, river or lake may only be loaded at the harbour (docks) where customs offices are stationed. Goods to be exported by airfreight may only be loaded at customs airports.

The loading and unloading of goods is only *permitted upon request* of the transporter or shipper, or his representative holding a written authorisation by the customs office. Such transactions may take place during the customs office's working days and hours.

However, in case of specific requests by the shipper or his representative, for reasons considered valid by Customs, the Customs office may authorise loading of goods outside the working days or hours. In such cases, the shipper or the shipping representative must pay a fee. It is worth noting that activities implying export of goods concern seven items (products) subject to the export tariffs regarding duties and taxes in force notably: green coffee, minerals and their concentrates, mineral oils, electric energy, wood (logs) and polished wood, sweet water, and iron.[6]

This chapter focused specifically on minerals and its concentrates; potential dual-use of these goods appears to be evident. Indeed, the dual-use goods as it exists in other countries contain items which may be used for civilian or military purposes. Given the recommendations of the Resolution 1540 and in the context of the Democratic Republic of Congo, the mining products are more and more concerned. The Katanga province, located in the south of the country, as well as an important part of the eastern provinces have their economies based on this resource. The exports of the ores of cobalt, cobber, manganese and cassierite, and their use beyond the borders is yet left uncontrolled. Only the mining and export of uranium ore are effectively prohibited in the country, most probably with view to answer the objectives of the Resolution 1540.

Export of mineral products by the DRC

In addition to the lists of dual-use items established by the Ministry of National Defence, export controls are carried out by border offices on all goods regardless of their nature, except for items that could be "dangerous goods" as defined and prohibited by the Ministry of Trade.

Customs are the most relevant authority in the entire export procedure: Customs are expected to verify the application of the law by other government offices prior to any verification and release (*mainlevée*) of goods leaving the country.

The customs procedure is implemented in several steps, namely: taking the goods to customs, accepting the goods, verification, payment of exit fees and release of the goods.

6 Law No. 08/006 of 12 June 2008 amending and completing law No. 003/03 of 13 March 2003 sets up a new Customs Tariff.

Customs verifies the authenticity and conformity of the documents submitted by the exporter before agreeing to release the goods. The Congolese Control Office (OCC) verifies the quality of the product submitted to it for import-export by taking samples checked in specialised laboratories.

Submission of goods to customs

Submission of goods follows the steps mentioned under Title 4 of the Customs Code, (reference to articles 97 and 111 of the Code).

Upon arrival at the customs office, the driver of the vehicle transporting goods must present to customs the declaration of the load as well as annexed to it the commercial documents that usually accompany the goods – and, as appropriate, customs documents handed over by the customs office of the neighbouring State. Such documents include *inter alia* the name of the owner of the goods, the country of origin of the transporter, the country of destination, identification numbers, nature and quantity of transported goods, weight, etc.

Goods that arrive after closure of the customs office are kept at no fee in an adjacent office until the latter opens again. In this case, the documents mentioned above have to be handed over to the Customs office as soon as it opens.

At the borders it is prohibited to take any road or way that attempts to avoid the customs' offices. Goods to be exported can be placed in storage awaiting customs formalities.

Payment of export fees

Export fees are levied on all exports to foreign States. The amount of fees to be paid depends on the value of the goods exported as established by Decree of the Minister of Finance upon recommendation of the customs administration.

Public awareness

In the DRC, economic actors involved in import and export activities are not sufficiently aware about the nature of products designated as "dual-use" goods.

Such lack of relevant knowledge by economic actors, customs officials and other government staff explains the absence of control that should focus specifically on dual-use goods.

It is a fact that economic actors are not associated to the formulation and adoption of the relevant laws and thus do not play any role in influencing this process, as long as the Congolese legislator has not set forth any provisions regulating export control of dual-use items.[7]

Conclusions

The issue of the export control of dual-use goods and technologies is considered a new subject matter in the Democratic Republic of the Congo. However, this does not in any way imply the absence of controls at the national borders by customs and other government offices.

It has to be recognised that export-control as implemented in the European Union reflects the needs of its Member States regarding national security.

African States, notably the DRC, do not share the same concerns as to the protection of the population against chemical, biological radiological and nuclear risks (CBRN).

The African States have considerable resources, which may feed nuclear activities in many countries. However, the populations that mine

---

7 The Congolese Code of Penal Law book /livre II, the Customs Code, the Mining Code and the Nuclear Law set forth the penalties and sanctions.

"Article 386 alinéa 3 du code des douanes: Est passible de la confiscation des marchandises et d'une amende égale au double de la valeur de ces marchandises, toute fausse déclaration dans l'espèce tendant à éluder une prohibition ou à contourner une mesure de restriction.

Article 390 du code des douanes: Sont passibles d'une peine de servitude pénale maximum de 3 ans, de la confiscation des marchandises de fraude, de la confiscation des moyens de transport, de la confiscation des marchandises ayant servi à masquer la fraude et d'une amende dont la hauteur est comprise entre une et cinq fois la valeur des marchandises de fraude, tout fait de contrebande ainsi que tout fait d'importation ou d'exportation sans déclaration lorsqu'ils se rapportent à des marchandises prohibées ou soumises à des mesures de restriction.

Article 303 du code minier (détention illicite des substances minerales): Quiconque aura détenu illégalement des substances minérales sera puni d'une servitude pénale de deux mois au montant en francs congolais est l'équivalent de 2.000 $US à 20.000 $US ou d'une de ces peines seulement.

Article 304 du code minier (transport illicite des substances minerales): Celui qui sans autorisation aura transporté ou fait transporter des substances minérales est puni d'une amende dont le montant en francs congolais est l'équivalent de 200 à 20.000 $US ou d'une de ces peines seulement.

Article 305 du code minier (fraude): Toute exportation ou tentative d'exportation frauduleuse des substances minérales en contraventions du régime douanier et des accises prévu par le présent code est soumise aux pénalités et amendes prévues par la législation douanière et accisienne en la matière.

Article 306 du code minier: violations des règles d'hygiène et de sécurité: Est passible d'une servitude pénale d'un mois à un an et d'une amende dont le montant en francs congolais est l'équivalent de 5.000 dollars US à 10.000 dollars US".

and exploit these resources are accordingly and growingly exposed to the risks attached to radiation exposure.

A universal export control model might be a good solution in order to increase security in the DRC, and its neighbours as well as other States in the Region.

Implementation of an efficient control of dual-use goods has shown to be important for assuring States' commitments within the EU; in Africa however, States unite around strictly economic objectives thereby neglecting security targets.

Nonetheless, achievements made in the frame of regional organisations as COMESA where States have been cooperating for some time in setting up a common market which would be based on a customs union.

The effective realization of this project – launched at the 17th Summit meeting of COMESA,[8] held 26th to 28th of February at Kinshasa – will allow for States of the Region to integrate export control provisions regarding dual-use goods in their respective customs regulations and procedures.

However, regrettably, divergent interests of States concerned and difficulties in applying the principle of extraterritoriality are the main reasons that this aim has not yet been achieved.

8 COMESA: Common Market of East and South African States.

The Control of Export of Dual-Use Material from Kenya

Hamadi Iddi Boga

Professor of Microbiology, Taita Taveta University College

About Kenya[1]

Kenya lies in East Africa astride the equator. Kenya's neighbours include Uganda, Tanzania, Southern Sudan and the war torn Somalia. As a country that is located in a rather restless region beset by war in Somalia, Southern Sudan, parts of Ethiopia and also in the nearby Great Lakes Region, Kenya has been variously described as an Island of peace in a sea of turmoil. After many years as a single party republic, Kenya has always practiced a form democracy that is slightly more progressive than most of its neighbours. Currently, Kenya has a vibrant multiparty system, a robust civil society and a vibrant press.

Kenya thus attracts many people from within Africa and beyond, is a major transit point and retains an age-old reputation of being the place where sailors like Vasco Da Gama would rest en route to India. Because Kenya enjoys relative peace and is located strategically at the heart Africa it provides a home to many refugees from the region, and also is crucial transit point to Africa, Europe and Asia. The port of Mombasa is especially critical for imports and exports into and out of the region. Nairobi also is a major air transport hub for the region.

To quote Simon Limage, US Deputy Assistant Secretary for Nonproliferation Programs:

> Nowhere in the world is the nexus between security and development more complex than in East Africa. East African nations contend with a host of socio-economic and humanitarian problems, while simultaneously striving

[1] The author wishes to acknowledge Mr. Ali Gakweli of the Kenya Government Chemist Department, who gave insights into the CBRN issues in Kenya for this contribution.

to overcome a variety of challenges to governance, development, defence, and security.[2]

The East African Economic Community

Kenya is a partner in one of the oldest economic blocks i.e. the East African Community, which was formed in the sixties and involves Kenya, Tanzania, Uganda, Rwanda and Burundi. The five countries have signed a Customs Union and are flirting with a political federation and single currency. To facilitate the customs union the parties to the East African Community assented to the East African Community Customs Management Act of 2004,[3] which came into effect in January 2005. The Act is meant to "make provisions for the administrations and management of customs and for related matters". The Act also envisages "common border controls, joint customs controls, and also to ensure that goods which are imported or exported pass through competent customs authorities". Each Country has also in addition independent customs acts.

Kenya's commitment to international law

Apart from commitment to regional treaties, Kenya also aspires to be a global player and struggles to keep up with international laws and norms. The Constitution of Kenya 2010 Section 2 Article 5 asserts that "the general rules of international law shall form part of the Kenya Law" and in Article 6 that "any treaty or convention ratified by Kenya shall form part of the Kenyan law under this constitution".[4]

Among the Treaties ratified by Kenya are those aimed at curtailing the misuse of Nuclear and radioactive materials, chemical weapons, toxins and biological weapons.

Kenya signed the Chemical Weapons Convention (CWC) in 1993 and ratified it in 1997,[5] but there has been no domestic law enacted to implement the treaty. To its credit, Kenya has appointed the Government Chemist as its National Focal Point for the CWC and which coordinates the implementation of the convention and makes annual declarations to the Organisation for the Prohibition of Chemical Weapons (OPCW). The local chemical industry is periodically inspected by the OPCW inspectors accompanied by officers from the Government Chemist Division, which

---

2 S. Limage, "Trade Security in Kenya: Capitalizing Upon Opportunities", 2011. Available: http://www.state.gov/t/isn/rls/rm/172804.htm (accessed 24 February 2014).

3 2009 Edition.

4 The Constitution of Kenya, 2010.

5 Source: http://kenyalaw.org/treaties/.

has branches in Nairobi, Mombasa and Kisumu. A small number of personnel have been trained by OPCW in emergency preparedness, analytical skills and managing national authorities.[6]

Kenya also acceded to Biological Weapon and Toxin Convention in 1976.[7] Until recently, there was no agency charged with the implementation of provisions of the treaty. Currently the National Commission for Science, Technology and Innovation (NACOSTI) is the designated focal point. A draft policy and Bill to guide control over organisms that can be used for biological and toxin weapons is has been drafted and well received by the major stakeholders including the security agencies. The draft Bill and Policy were developed with the support of US agencies. Turf wars between government agencies over the BWTWC are delaying progress on this very critical point. Major challenges have been experienced with the National Biosafety Authority, which was tasked with the implementation of the Cartagena Protocol.

Kenya is also a signatory to the Treaty on the Non-Proliferation of Nuclear Weapons, which it signed in 1970.[8] For a number of years, the focal point for this treaty was the NACOSTI but in the last two years, Kenya formed "Nuclear Kenya" to be the focal point and to handle all matters to do with nuclear. As Kenya nurses ambitions of embracing nuclear energy, it has started training nuclear scientists to manage the sector. A lack of nuclear scientists will always hamper Kenya's ability to implement provisions of the Treaty and also to develop and manage its own nuclear power sources. The lack of a policy and legislation on the nuclear energy has seen the International Atomic Agency imploring Kenya to form a Nuclear Energy Agency.

Further, Kenya is also a signatory to the International Convention for the Suppression of Acts of Nuclear Terrorism, which it ratified in 2006.[9] Like all the other treaties this treaty has not been domesticated as well but the general rules of the treaty apply to Kenya also. The Radiation Protection Board is the designated focal point. The US have helped install radiation monitoring equipment at the port of Mombasa. There are also plans to construct a radiation waste facility and nuclear safety centre in Nairobi. The Radiation Protection Board has offices in Nairobi, Mombasa, Kisumu, Garissa and at the Jomo Kenyatta International Airport. It has the mandate of (i) Issuing Licenses for setting up Radiation facilities

---

6 *Idem.*

7 *Idem.*

8 *Idem.*

9 *Idem.*

(ii) Regulating registration of radiation workers and (iii) Inspection of radiation facilities.[10]

In general, Kenya has shown a readiness to embrace international treaties, without following through with the necessary legislation to domesticate these treaties. This could be due to lack of a capacity in the country to do so without much international input. Kenya like many other Countries in the African continent also lacks the technical expertise to handle some of the areas covered in these international conventions.

Kenya hosts the Eastern and Central Africa Regional Secretariat of the EU chemical, biological, radiological and nuclear (CBRN) Centres of Excellence. This is an initiative funded by the European Union and brings together six countries to jointly address CBRN risk mitigation in the region. CBRN-related issues are jointly handled by a CBRN Secretariat established in Nairobi with the aim of setting up a CBRN Centre of Excellence.[11] This brings together stakeholders in the East African region to exchange ideas and experiences on CBRN issues and also to build capacity. Workshops have been held under the auspices of the United Nations Interregional Crimes and Justice Research Institute (UNICRI) in collaboration with partners from the European Union.[12]

International collaboration

Potentially dual-use goods present a problem and danger for the entire international community. The fact that Kenya is a major transit route into and out of Africa makes it a critical country in the control of import and export of potentially dual-use goods. Limited capacity to manage the movement of dual-use goods in Kenya makes international collaboration absolutely essential. Collaboration within the East African Community Member States is managed under the general rules of the East African Community Customs Act 2004. Although dual-use goods are not listed under the restricted goods list, a firm foundation exists to expand the scope to include control of CBRN goods and this should be followed. Cooperation also exists with Sudan, Ethiopia, Djibouti and Somalia under the Inter Government Agency for Development (IGAD), although not to the same extent as the EAC. International agencies like the International Atomic Energy Agency (IAEA), the OPCW Secretariat, the EU and the US Government has collaborated with the Kenya in building capacity, raising awareness and even in installation of equipment. Some of the

10 Source: http://www.rpbkenya.org/.

11 Interview of Ali Gakweli, Coordinator of the CBRN activities at the Government Chemist in Nairobi, Kenya.

12 See, *CBRN COE Newsletter*, Vol. 2, January 2012.

focal nodes submit regular reports to the responsible international bodies and attend international meetings.

Role of customs in export control

As expected, the Kenya Customs and Excise Department play their traditional role of import and export verification. In doing so, they are guided by the East African Community Customs Act 2004 which mirrors very much the Kenya Customs and Excise Act of 2001.[13] Both these acts are however silent on CBRN goods in their lists of restricted goods.[14] The absence of any legislation domesticating the international conventions renders the Customs Department rather directionless in dealing with such issues. The Kenya Revenue Authority (KRA), under which the Customs Department lies, has a testing Laboratory, but its technical capacity and staffing is not clear. In their work, the Customs Department tends to work more closely with the Police and will tend to report any suspicious issues on CBRN to them. The focal points for the various CBRN issues are only brought into the picture by the police for identification and verification.[15] Thus the system is not well aligned and is poorly coordinated.

Sanctions for offenders

Kenya lacks legislation domesticating many of the international treaties that handle CBRN issues. Culprits are therefore mostly charged with offences like terrorism related offences. The Kenyan system has in the recent past arrested two Iranian nationals on suspicion of smuggling into the country RDX, a bomb-making chemical. Both suspects were sentenced to life imprisonment.[16] Kenya has also been successful in arresting drug, gold and ivory smugglers who pass through the Jomo Kenyatta International Airport as frequently reported in the media some of which have been jailed or fined heavily. There have been no reports made on arrest of persons with dual-use goods, although the danger is real.

Challenges facing export control regarding dual-use goods

Progress on the export control of dual-use goods remain a major challenge in Kenya and other African countries. The major challenge is the

---

13 Source: http://www.kra.go.ke/customs/pdf/CustomsAndExciseAct2001.pdf.

14 See: East African Community Customs Management Act, 2004 (2009 Edition) and http://www.kra.go.ke/customs/pdf/CustomsAndExciseAct2001.pdf.

15 Interview of Mr. Ali Gakeweli.

16 Source: http://www.longwarjournal.org/threat-matrix/archives/2013/05/kenyan_court_gives_life_senten.php#ixzz2mohdjhdq.

lack of capacity and expertise in the CBRN issues. Simply put, there are not enough qualified personnel in enough numbers and the few on the ground lack the necessary equipment to do the work. Corruption by immigration officials and the police at boarder points is a major challenge which allows illegal aliens to move in and out of Kenya freely with sometimes devastating consequences as was witnessed during Westgate attack in Nairobi in 2013 and also the bombing of the US Embassy in 1997. In both cases the suspects were able to acquire Kenya's identification documents through collusion with corrupt officials. Also clashing mandates between Government agencies lead to lack of progress as the agencies try to outrun each other. The domestication of the BTWC has basically stalled due to competition between NACOSTI and NBA over the mandate. At the border points in the East African Community, conflict between States is causing challenges. Uganda is wrestling with Kenya over Migingo Island. Uganda, Kenya and Rwanda appear to have formed a coalition of the willing as they appear to sideline Tanzania. Thus, cooperation in export control is made difficult at times because of the fights between the various States.

Raising awareness

Raising general awareness of the dangers posed by dual-use goods to the general public, custom officials, other enforcement agencies and policy makers is the key to formulating and implementing appropriate legislation and effective export control strategies. In general the level of awareness about dual-use goods in Kenya is low. In formulating any laws, the Kenya Constitution (2010) requires public and stakeholder participation. A robust debate on CBRN issues has not started in Kenya. Hence, the lead agencies need to start a campaign of information to sensitise the general public, implementing agencies and customs officials and policy makers on the importance of export control of dual-use goods. Kenya has a robust private sector spearheaded by the Kenya Association of Manufacturers, the Kenya Private Sector alliance and also a robust civil society, which would contribute positively to the process.

Conclusion

Kenya is located strategically with possibility for moving goods, people and services to other parts of Africa, Europe and Asia. It has a vibrant national carrier, the Kenya Airways, which is plying many routes in the world and has also the biggest port in the region, i.e. the port of Mombasa. These apparent advantages risk being misused by international terrorist networks and even state actors to smuggle CBRN materials. The lack of technical and equipment capacity will stifle any attempt by Kenya to exercise export control for CBRN issues, yet it has an obligation to uphold international best practices. The existing cooperation between members of the EAC and the collaboration with international partners like the UNICRI, EU and the US are therefore essential in building the capacity required to control movement and abuse of dual-use goods in the East African region. African countries should be encouraged and supported to domesticate the relevant international treaties. In addition, the lead agencies need to increasingly raise awareness in the general population, civil society among other technical persons and politicians to ensure the success of any programme that will be developed towards addressing CBRN issues.

Controlling Export of Nuclear Material and of Dual-Use Goods in Niger

Abdoul Rahimoune Massaoudou

Controller General, SOPAMIN-SA

Introduction

Niger is a landlocked country with a surface of 1,267.000 Km². The nearest access to the sea is the port of Cotonou, Benin, located at approximately 1,000 Km from Niamey, the Capital of Niger. Niger is the 4th world producer of uranium: uranium production requires massive imports of input materials for the production and, on the other end of the process, the export of unirradiated uranium from the mines located 2,200 km away from the port of Cotonou. The complete export process is carried out in three separate steps: the first step is the conveyance over land from the mines to the port of Cotonou, the second is the sea transport from Cotonou to Malvési in France and, the final step is the transport again over land from the seaport to the site of COMURHEX, to the conversion plant of AREVA. The overland segment carried out by Niger is the stretch ranging from the mining site to the port of Cotonou.

This chapter intends to provide a description of the export of specific materials as contained in the international list of goods defined as "dangerous" or as "radioactive goods" by the competent authorities, notably the Ministry of Transport and the Ministry of Mines. The aim is to present a factual account of this activity as carried out in Niger.

The legal framework

Niger is a member of several regional organisations as *inter alia* the UEOMA, (Economic and Monetary Union of West Africa), the CDEAO (Economic Community of West Africa) as well as the African Union. In the context of its membership in these regional associations, Niger is party to a number of treaties regulating the transport (import and export) of goods within the respective region. However, these community regulations are generally not concerned with the control of exports of radioactive, dual-use or dangerous goods: a good example is the "Uniform Act of the OHADA" (Organisation for the Harmonisation of Business Law in Africa), which applies to road transportation contracts only, more precisely, to the wording of such contract forms rather than to the nature of the goods transported. Niger is also a Member of the WTO, the IAEA, and Party to the NPT.

These organisations provide different definitions of dangerous, radioactive or dual-use materials and goods. The Ministry of Mines of Niger refers directly to the definitions established by the IAEA[1] for nuclear materials; the Ministry of Transport refers by specific decree to the IAEA definition of "dangerous goods" as applicable to transport. Dangerous goods are listed by decree[2] as follows:

- Ammunition and (pyrotechnic materials);
- Gas: compressed, liquid, dissolved, under pressure;
- Materials that release flammable gases when in contact with water;
- Pyrophoric materials;
- Flammable liquids;
- Flammable solids.
- Toxic materials;
- Materials that may be combustive to other materials;
- Radioactive materials;
- Corrosive materials;
- Infected materials;
- Organic peroxides.

Institutional framework

In the present context, the expression "institutional framework" designates all actors concerned with the export control process.

Ministry of Mines

The Ministry of Mines is the first governmental body to authorise the export of nuclear materials by a ministerial ordinance. Any mining company that wishes to export its products submits a request for an export

1 IAEA Safety Standards: Regulations for the Safe Transport of Radioactive Material. Safety Requirements No. TS-R-1 as updated.

2 Decree No. 2010//33/PCRD/MTT/A of 4 November 2010.

authorisation to the Ministry. The Ministry grants the authorisation to the company after the company has presented a document confirming or declaring "no objection" (i.e. to export) issued by the SOPAMIN-SA[3] i.e. the State owned company and shareholder in all mining companies.

It should be noted that the mining companies summit each month export control forms to the Ministry of Mines providing required information on the quantities (filled in the freight containers) the weight, the grade of uranium ore content and the chemical characteristics of the concentrate.

Ministry of Transport

This Ministry is responsible for all transports in Niger and establishes the specific conditions applicable to the transport of dangerous goods. Certain substances qualified as "dangerous" goods are in general imported for direct use in mining /extracting; in this case, the Ministry of Transport normally joins the Ministry of Mines in managing the transport operations of these particular products. An authorisation granted by the Ministry of Transport has to be obtained prior to any transport operation. There are however cases where a carrier (shippers) moves mining products without authorisation, either by sheer ignorance or in fraudulent manner to avoid paying the fees for obtaining a transport authorisation.

The mining companies

The mining companies are the main producers of radioactive materials and at the same time also the main consumers of imported "dangerous goods". At the beginning of the year, the companies, depending on their business plans, establish their import and export accounts covering both consumption and production. These "budget plans" are submitted to the Ministry of Mines as well as to all shareholders, allowing to establish approximately each company's needs for imports of dangerous goods as well as the foreseeable amounts of production for export.

As regards exports, the mining companies have to submit each month export control forms as described above. These forms allow to follow during the entire year both exports planned in the framework of the mining company's global annual budget and the requests for export authorisations (ordinances) required by them during the same year. These control forms are thereafter sent to the Customs Office to allow for the controls affected at arrival of the conveyance (vehicle) carrying the radioactive materials to the national borders. As concerns the technical

3 SOPAMIN-SA: Société de Patrimoine des Mines du Niger.

preparation of the materials for transport, the mining companies – under the supervision of AREVA, holder of the required expertise – fill the product into specific dedicated containment systems notably the freight containers. These containers are thereafter loaded onto vehicles of the National Transport Company for Strategic Products (CNTPS-SA). This company has been set up specifically for transport of strategic goods, including dangerous goods.

Ministry of National Defence

The Ministry is responsible for the physical protection of the convoys carrying dangerous goods within the territory of Niger. National Defence and Security Forces escort the convoy from the border of Benin to the mining sites as well as from the mines in Niger to the Benin border. Physical protection (security) is thereafter provided by the defence forces of Benin.

Customs

The responsibility of Customs in the export process of radioactive material is to control the convoys carrying these goods when crossing the national border. The Customs Offices will have received in advance a copy of the export ordinance specifying the quantities and properties as well as the final destination of the material. At the border, Customs officials verify the transport documents and check these documents against the papers submitted earlier so as to ensure their concurrence.

AREVA

AREVA is shareholder of the mining companies and, moreover, contributes through one of its subsidiaries, TNI (*Transport Nucléaire International*), its specific expertise in matters of transport security of dangerous and radioactive products. TNI acts as the commission agent for the mining companies concerning these particular products both for import and export. TNI is responsible for transport security of the products from the site (mines) to the port and return.

The "Patrimonial"[4] (national endowment Mining Company of Niger (SOPAMIN-SA)

SOPAMIN-SA is a State company in charge of managing the State'shares (participation) in the Mining Companies. In this capacity,

[4] Note by the translater: the term "patrimonial" in the French language may corresponds to "national", the country's endowment in natural resources.

SOPAMIN is a shareholder in all mining companies of Niger and, at the same time, a client of the part of the company's production that corresponds to its participation in the overall capital of each mining company. Exports of these companies accrue to the shareholders. In its capacity as shareholder SOPAMIN holds all statistical information as well as the projections of the mining companies as to consumption of (imported) dangerous goods as well as production of uranium concentrates. SOPAMIN is also a recipient of the export control forms established by the mining companies.

A prior written agreement or a "no-objection" statement by SOPAMIN has to be obtained by the mining company before submitting a request for an export ordinance authorising the export of uranium concentrates. The Ministry will not grant an export authorisation without the agreement by SOPAMIN. As SOPAMIN is a shareholder, it will thereafter no longer be able to verify specifically the production plan and the calendar of material to be bought, and to check this information against the export forms. In addition to its role as shareholder of the mining companies, SOPAMIN established a company devoted exclusively to the transport of strategic goods.

National Transport Company of Strategic Goods (CNPTS-SA)

This company was established specifically for the purpose of transporting dangerous goods – notably including uranium concentrates. The company cooperates with the TNI as well as with the National Defence and Security Forces to assure that transport of these goods is carried out securely in conformity with international security norms.

This company also facilitates the control/supervision of material accounting of the imported and exported goods and contributes to limit cases of fraud committed by non-authorised shippers.

For each shipment, the documents pertaining to the transported products as well as the relevant authorisations are transmitted to the heads of the convoys allowing them to submit these documents to Customs officials at the border crossing. After the border crossing, the level of security is usually lowered as the perception of risk is lower. This tends to increase risks and decrease application of security norms.

Export control of nuclear materials: risks and difficulties

This section addresses import and export in view of the fact that transport is the most important issue in our context.

As concerns exports, there have never been any problems within the territory of Niger, as each stakeholder knows his role in this process. However, the security and defence forces of Niger stop at the national border and are relayed by those of Benin; this creates security risks for the convoys due essentially to different perceptions of the risks to man and the environment emanating from uranium. In Niger the entire population is well aware of the dangers specific to uranium whereas on the other side of the border the population is not at all familiar with this particular danger; the vehicles loaded with uranium are perceived as being just like any kind of transport of goods. In fact, all road accidents that occurred involving uranium transports took place outside the territory of Niger. It is notably the transport of the imported dangerous goods that creates the main problems. It must be noted, that the sheer quantity of goods transported is huge and represents an economic activity which is supposed to have a major impact on some economic sectors in the country where the port is located. The regulations of Niger applicable to transport of dangerous goods require that the driver of vehicles transporting such goods is a citizen of Niger and that the vehicle is registered in Niger. This raises an issue of extraterritoriality as transport is an economic activity of the port that – in the present case – should generate employment in the neighbouring country that struggles with poverty and unemployment as does any other African State. It is very difficult to respect this principle and it even leads occasionally to negative practices when loading the vehicles in the port.

Contributing thoughts to a harmonised practice of export control in Africa's sub-regional associations

With a view to setting up a harmonised practice in Africa as a whole or within sub-regional groups of States, competent institutions should, in our view, take into account the following considerations:

Extraterritoriality

In Africa the regional associations (States assembled in a given space) are not very strong: this is not only due to their history (i.e. colonisation by different States), but also because of border disputes which prevail in many parts of Africa. This situation hampers the implementation of regulations set by one State in another, even in cases where official working groups have been established to minimise irritations at the different border crossings. The positive approach to be followed consists in settling these problems in a regional rather than bilateral manner, within the same institutions of which the States are Members.

The Economy

Reflecting on export controls, it is evident that for African countries, the entry and exit of goods is first of all an economic issue. The concept of "security" is generally connected with the trade of products usually understood as being "illicit" (narcotics, weapons etc.).

Poverty and unemployment are still the daily concerns of these countries that are caught in a real competition for the survival of their national economies. Each country tries thus to obtain maximum benefits for an economic activity that crosses its national borders, be it financial or job-creating for the local economy. It would be very difficult indeed to ask a country that struggles to pay the salaries of its officials to spend part of its human and financial resources in order to control the shipment of uranium or of explosives which do not bring them much income. In fact, spending the same amount of resources for the control of second hand cars arriving at the port, the country would make the equivalent of three monthly salaries of an official for each second hand car. In order to make countries understand and join in a common endeavour, it will be necessary to show these countries the economic value of this type of control. But, national interests are sometimes far too divergent. For instance, the interest of Niger as regards a uranium convoy for export – is its secure arrival at the port; for Benin on the other hand, its main concern is the income received for the crossing of its territory by that same convoy. These are the sorts of antagonisms which impede the control of exports of dangerous substances. The search for a balance of interests must be sought by the regional organisations to which the States belong in order to avoid difficult and partisan bilateral discussions.

Communication: raising awareness and training

Communication is a very important component of export control of dangerous goods considering that the concept of security for a given product varies from one country to another; it is indeed relative rather than absolute except for the universally known terminology discussed above. Stakeholders must however have exactly the same perception of security required for exporting a given product within a given space. This task is entrusted to the international organisations in charge of developing a harmonised practice of export controls. In addition to the institutional actors in the countries, who would be regularly trained, awareness programmes need to be carried out further so that the general public would adopt the concept of security for products that have to be controlled for export. This aspect is of determinant value for the success of a common approach to controls; both training and awareness raising need to be provided by organisations such as the IAEA or the European Union. The global objective of these communications should be beyond demonstrating to the local actors that security is a matter for all and guaranties the well functioning of economic activities, but also training the stakeholders for implementing the export control measures.

Conclusion

In conclusion, we believe that a good dose of realism is required in looking for a harmonised practice of export control of radioactive or dual-use products in Africa; this is needed in the light of the analysis made of the African reality rather than of specific countries named above. Organisations entrusted with conceiving, promoting and following these control "models" need to keep in mind that the European model cannot be directly transposed for implementation in Africa. It will need to be adapted to the local realities.

Implementation of the United Nations Security Council Resolution 1540 in Nigeria

Shamsideen B. ELEGBA

Professor – Department of Physics, University of Abuja

Introduction

In April 2004, the United Nations (UN) Security Council unanimously passed Resolution 1540, which is intended to reduce the threat of terrorist groups gaining access to weapons of mass destruction (WMD). The resolution mandates that all States adopt and enforce "appropriate effective laws which prohibit any non-State actor to manufacture, acquire, possess, develop, transport, transfer or use nuclear, chemical or biological weapons and their means of delivery", as well as attempts to engage in such activities, assist, or finance them. The resolution requires States to establish export controls for such weapons and the means of their delivery, and "related materials". It also requires States to implement effective export controls and physical protection measures, in order to prevent the diversion of sensitive materials and technologies.[1] The scope of the resolution, encompassing not only weapons of mass destruction but also the means of their delivery and related materials, makes it one of the broadest legal instruments in the non-proliferation field. It is also legally binding on all UN Member States, owing to its passage under Chapter VII of the UN charter. Since its adoption, Resolution 1540 has been widely recognised as a useful multilateral tool to help prevent the acquisition of weapons of mass destruction by non-State actors, and to facilitate the exchange of information and assistance among States.[2]

1 "Security Council Decides All States Shall Act to Prevent Proliferation of Mass Destruction Weapons", United Nations, 28 April 2004: www.un.org.

2 "Perceptions, Resources Challenge Implementation of UN Security Council Resolution 1540 Ahead of April Renewal", Stanley Foundation, 1 March 2011, see: www.stanley-foundation.org.

It is important to note here that there is no unique definition of the term WMD[3] as many African States consider WMD as weapons of mass destabilization. This interpretation was strongly and eloquently affirmed by the Nigerian President Goodluck Jonathan in his statement at the maiden edition of the Nuclear Security Summit in 2010 in Washington DC (USA).[4] According to President Jonathan, there was "the need to pay adequate attention to an equally debilitating weapons of mass destabilization (WMD): the small and light weapons which are widely proliferated in Africa but produced by the industrialized countries". Similarly, Nigeria like most African States does not "manufacture, acquire, possess, develop, transport, transfer or use nuclear, chemical or biological weapons and their means of delivery".[5] But radioactive sources are widely used in all African countries and they are all imported except in the case of South Africa, which has facilities for the production radioactive sources on a commercial scale. Radioactive sources have however been implicated in the improvisation of the so called "dirty bomb" or radiological dispersal devices (RDD). It was in response to the growing global concern over nuclear weapons and RDD, that the US President Barack Obama[6] in April 2004 elaborated a three-step strategy to address international nuclear threats and in particular the increase in the risk of nuclear material diversion and illicit trafficking by:

- Proposing measures to reduce and eventually eliminate existing nuclear weapon arsenals;
- Strengthening the Non-Proliferation Treaty (NPT); and
- Preventing "terrorists" from acquiring nuclear weapons or materials.

Despite the differences between RDD and WMD, on one hand and the interpretation of "WMD" on the other, all these materials from the viewpoint of Nigeria, nay many African countries are imported. There is therefore the need for symmetry in the formulation and application of export and import control on the two "types" of WMD.

---

3 "Security Council Decides All States Shall Act to Prevent Proliferation of Mass Destruction Weapons", United Nations, 28 April 2004, see: www.un.org. See Operative Paragraph 4.

4 Q. Michel, S. Paile, M. Tsukanova, A. Viski, *Controlling the Trade of Dual-Use Goods: A handbook*, Brussels, PIE Peter Lang, 2013.

5 "Statement by HE Goodluck Jonathan, the Acting President, Federal Republic of Nigeria to the Nuclear Security Summit, Washington, DC, USA", 12-13 April 2010.

6 "Address by US President Barack Obama, US Embassy, (Prague)", 5 April 2009.

Safety and security of nuclear and radioactive materials

Nigeria is highly committed to the peaceful uses of nuclear energy as can be demonstrated by the fact that as far back as 1968 Nigeria became the second country to sign the NPT,[7] after joining the International Atomic Energy Agency (IAEA). It has also demonstrated its commitment to the full implementation of the NPT by voting in 1995 for its indefinite extension. In 1988 Nigeria also signed the *Comprehensive Safeguards Agreement*[8] with the Agency and ratified the *Convention on Early Notification of a Nuclear Accident*[9] and in 1990, the *Convention on Assistance in the Case of Nuclear Accident or Radiological Emergency.*[10] Also in 2001, Nigeria signed the *Model Additional Protocol to the NPT.*[11] Furthermore, Nigeria in 2007 acceded to the *Convention on Physical Protection of Nuclear Materials*[12] and its *Amendment*[13] which has yet to go into force. Nigeria also supports other legally non-binding instruments of the IAEA such as the IAEA *Code of Conduct on the Safety and Security of Radioactive Source*[14] and its associated *Guidance on the Import and Export of Radioactive Sources.*[15] In addition to her robust engagement with the IAEA, Nigeria is also an active member of the Comprehensive Test Ban Treaty Organisation, World Customs Organisation, Organisation for the Prohibition of Chemical Weapons and party to their several conventions and agreements, such as the Chemical Weapons Convention and the Biological and Toxin Weapons Convention. In the Africa region, Nigeria is equally committed to the international safeguards regime and continues to pursue the goal of general disarmament. This has been amply demonstrated by her early ratification of the *Africa Nuclear Weapons-Free Zone Treaty*[16] otherwise referred to as the "Pelindaba Treaty", which entered into force on 15 July 2009 and resulted in the establishment of the African Commission for Nuclear Energy (AFCONE).

---

7 Nuclear Non-Proliferation Treaty (NPT).

8 Comprehensive Safeguards Agreement, 1988.

9 Convention on Early Notification of a Nuclear Accident 1990.

10 Convention on Assistance in the Case of Nuclear Accident or Radiological Emergency 1990.

11 Model Additional Protocol to the NPT 2001.

12 Convention on Physical Protection of Nuclear Materials 2007.

13 Amendment to the Convention on Physical Protection of Nuclear Materials 2007.

14 Code of Conduct on the Safety and Security of Radioactive Sources, IAEA, Vienna, Austria (2004).

15 Guidance on the Import and Export of Radioactive Sources, IAEA, Vienna, Austria (2005).

16 Africa Nuclear Weapons-Free Zone Treaty, otherwise referred to as the "Pelindaba Treaty".

Nigeria has a nascent nuclear power programme with a small nuclear research reactor. Nigeria is however a major user of radioactive sources, all of which are *imported*. Radioactive sources are used in several sectors of the Nigerian economy. The petroleum industry is the largest importer and user of radioactive sources in the country and the Niger Delta is the hub of the petroleum industry in the Gulf Guinea and the entire West Africa sub-region. The security of radioactive sources is therefore of great national importance. Furthermore, Nigeria does not have a radioactive waste disposal facility, therefore disused radioactive sources and spent nuclear fuel (when the time comes) all have to be exported to countries of manufacture. Therefore import and export control of nuclear and radioactive materials is of great economic and security importance to the country.[17]

Prior to May 2001, radioactive sources were imported and exported without any form of authorisation, although the *Nuclear Safety and Radiation Protection Act*[18] was promulgated in 1995. The Act provides for the establishment of the Nigerian Nuclear Regulatory Authority (NNRA), which was established in May 2001. The NNRA has the overall responsibility for nuclear safety and radiological protection regulation in the country. Consequently, radiation protection, safety and security of radiation sources, safeguard of nuclear materials and physical protection of nuclear installations constitutes the five major regulatory functions of the NNRA. The safety and security of sources is guaranteed through an effective regulatory control programme. This regulatory control must necessarily include the ports of entry, hence the close working relationship between the NNRA, the Nigerian Custom Service and other law enforcement agencies such as the Nigerian Police, the Nigeria Immigration Service and the State Security Service. This coordinated approach to the safety and security of radioactive sources from the port of entry through use, to the port of exit has lead to the establishment of the inter-ministerial Committee on Nuclear Security. The effectiveness of the regulatory programme for the import of radioactive sources has been attested to by the *London Times*[19] publication of 6 October 2002. This network has also been tested and failed once in May 2003, when sources were exported as scrap metal. The second incident was in December 2004, when a duly authorised export of a spent radioactive source was re-packaged and mis-declared as "mould".

17 2006 Annual Report, Nigerian Nuclear Regulatory Authority (unpublished).

18 The Nuclear Safety and Radiation Protection Decree 19, 1995, Official Gazette of the Federal republic of Nigeria, Vol. 82, A547-A569, (1995).

19 J. Sparks, P. Conradi, "Revealed: radioactive material for dirty bomb is just a phone call away", *The Sunday Times*, London, 6 October 2002, p. 14.

These lapses were attributed to inadequate radiation detection capability at the ports and inadequate training of the officials at the ports and airports. These challenges have been overcome with the support of the IAEA, European Union Commission and the US Department of Energy through provision of training for frontline officers and equipment for NNRA. The regulatory control of import and export nuclear and radioactive materials in Nigeria has been shown to be very effective and efficacious.

Legislative and regulatory infrastructure

Whereas the *Nuclear Safety and Radiation Protection Act* empowers the Nigerian Nuclear Regulatory Authority (NNRA), to amongst others control the *import* and *export* of any radioactive material, nuclear material, radioactive waste, prescribed substance and any apparatus emitting ionising radiation; *Customs & Excise Management Act* (CEMA)[20] vests legal authority in the Nigeria Customs Service to act on behalf of the Federal Government of Nigeria in all customs matters.

Accordingly, the Nigerian Nuclear Regulatory Authority has responsibilities for, amongst others: the regulation of the possession and application of radioactive substances and devices emitting ionising radiation; ensuring protection of life, health, property and the environment from the harmful effects of ionising radiation, while allowing beneficial practices involving exposure to ionising radiation; performing all necessary functions to enable Nigeria meet its national and international safeguards and safety obligations in the application of nuclear energy and ionising radiation. Correspondingly, the NNRA is empowered to, amongst others, to: categorise and licence all activities involving exposure to ionising radiation, in particular, the possession, production, processing, manufacture, purchase, sale, *import*, *export*, handling, use, transformation, transfer, trading, assignment, transport, storage and disposal of any radioactive material, nuclear material, radioactive waste, prescribed substance and any apparatus emitting ionising radiation; liaise with and foster co-operation with international and other organisations or bodies concerned having similar objectives.

Furthermore, the control of radiation sources and premises where they can be used or stored are strengthened by section 15 of the Act. In fact no person can carry out any activity under the Act and at the end of the activity abandon, de-commission or rehabilitate installations thereof without a licence issued by the NNRA. This essentially is a codified demonstration of the "from cradle to grave" principle of the IAEA. In this regard, the NNRA has from its inception taken steps to put in place the

[20] Customs & Excise Management Act (CEMA), Cap 45, Law of the Federation of Nigeria, 2004.

proper regulatory framework, within the context of its enabling Act, to effectively register, licence, inspect practices involving ionising radiation and to enforce nuclear safety and radiological protection nationwide. It has also taken necessary measures to have in place the basic administrative and technical capability to support its activities. These have been achieved through a very rigorous regulatory control program.

The regulatory control of radioactive sources in Nigeria is derived from Section 4(1) of the Nuclear Safety and Radiation Protection Act. The main elements of the regulatory control programme are:

- Regulations and guidance;
- Authorisation;
- Oversight functions (inspections and enforcement);
- Emergency planning and response;
- Ancillary functions.

In accordance with sections 47(1 and 2) and sections 6(d and e), the NNRA developed and promulgated in 2003 the *Nigeria Basic Ionizing Radiation Regulations* (NIBIRR),[21] which cover all uses of radiation sources in the country, including *import* and *export*. According to Regulation 79 of the NIBIRR, any employer who intends to import a sealed source containing any radioactive material for any practice shall:

(a) Require the supplier, as a condition of any contract for the purchase or transfer, to receive the source back;

(b) Submit to the NNRA a copy of relevant parts of the purchase or transfer document and obtain its authorisation prior to entering the contract in force or accepting the source; and

(c) Return the source to the supplier within six months after its useful lifetime.

Furthermore, the NNRA has adopted and domesticated the IAEA *Code of Conduct for the Safety and Security of Radioactive Sources* And the associated *Guidance on the Import and Export of Radioactive Sources* by promulgating the:

- *Nigerian Safety and Security of Radioactive Sources Regulations, 2006;*[22]
- *Nigerian Transportation of Radioactive Sources Regulations 2006.*[23]

---

21 Nigeria Basic Ionizing Radiation Regulations, Official Gazette of the Federal Republic of Nigeria, Vol. 90, B165-B247, (2003).

22 Nigerian Safety and Security of Radioactive Sources Regulations, 2006.

23 Nigerian Transportation of Radioactive Sources Regulations, 2006.

In addition, Section 6(1) of the Act empowers the NNRA to issue authorisation for all activities involving exposure to ionising radiation. Thus the *import* and *export* of radioactive sources require authorisation in the form of licence. The authorisation presently can be in the form of notification, registration or licence. Copies of import/export licences issued are always sent to Nigerian Customs Service, the Nigerian Police Force and the Department of State Security. Furthermore, Section 19 of the Act requires that no source or practice shall be authorised except through a system of application, notification, registration or licencing as established by the NNRA. This is very important for the safety and security of nuclear and radioactive materials in the country.

Institutional framework

With its mandate and the scope of its responsibilities, the NNRA established linkages and Memorandum of Understanding with several national agencies such as: The Nigeriac Customs Service, The Nigeriac Police Force, Federal Ministry of Health and the Federal Ministry of Justice. This was further strengthened with the establishment of the Nuclear Security Committee. The NSC had been very useful in carrying out investigative inspections and enforcement actions, which sometimes required arrest and prosecution.

Furthermore, the NSC provides a platform for the training of all stakeholders using both national expertise and international experts supported by international counterparts such as the IAEA, the US Department of Energy (DoE) and the EU Commission. This institutional framework has been very consistent with the Communiqué of the Second Nuclear Security Summit held in Seoul on 26-27 March 2012. The Communiqué recognised "that investment in human capacity building is fundamental to promoting and sustaining a strong nuclear security culture" and therefore encourages "States to share best practices and build national capabilities, including through bilateral and international cooperation". The Summit also encourages at the national level, "all stakeholders, including the government, regulatory bodies, industry, academia, non-governmental organisations, and the media, to fully commit to enhancing security culture and maintain robust communication and coordination of activities (...) and to promote human resource development through education and training".

It is in this spirit of training, sharing and networking that the NNRA in collaboration with the Nigerian Ministry of Foreign Affairs and the ECOWAS Secretariat organised a one-day workshop on nuclear security for the Economic Community of West African States (ECOWAS) and States in the Gulf of Guinea in Abuja (Nigeria), on 13 April 2011. The workshop was attended by diplomatic missions from ECOWAS countries in Abuja and countries from the Gulf of Guinea. The workshop identified the common challenges and threats to the security of radioactive sources during transportation in the Gulf Guinea and in the entire West Africa sub-region.

Lessons and experience

The import/export control of radioactive sources suffered several setbacks both within the country and from abroad. The challenges were both real and concocted. Three examples of the teething problems will suffice. It is noteworthy that all the three incidents described below involved trans-national shipment (virtual and real) between Nigeria and Europe and even with North America.

The 6 October 2002 edition of the *London Sunday Times* carried a centre page article with a screaming title, "Revealed: Radioactive Material for Dirty Bomb is Just a Phone Call Away" by Justin Sparks and Peter Conradi. According to the article, highly radioactive material that could be used by terrorists to make a "dirty bomb" can be bought on the open market in Europe and shipped across inter-national borders, a *Sunday Times* investigation has revealed "undercover reporters, posing as representatives of a bogus British company identified only as CMI, reached an agreement with a Czech manufacturer to buy a cancer radiotherapy machine containing 70 grams of radioactive cobalt 60. Packed into a 500 kg bomb, the material could contaminate up to a square mile of any city, experts say".

The reporters said they wanted to send the machine to Nigeria under an aid project. They were assured both by *Skoda-UJP*, its manufacturer, and by Czech nuclear authorities that they would face no problems in obtaining export clearance. As part of the covert operation, the service of a transnational shipping company, *PANALPINA*, was sought to contact NNRA for the procedure for such importation and use of radioactive sources. In response, NNRA sent its ten-item requirement list, which included detailed drawings of the facility where the sources will be stored and used and that the site must be *inspected* before a licence can be issued for construction. Furthermore, names and qualification of the experts must be submitted to the NNRA for security clearance before the facility could be licenced for radiotherapy practice; and it is only after all these requirements have been satisfied that the NNRA would consider issuing an import licence for radioactive sources into the country. All these exchanges took place in June 2002 and NNRA received no other communication from *PANALPINA* or her sponsors before the *London Sunday Times* article. On the other hand, the perpetrators of the operation did not relent but rather contacted another arm of the Nigerian Government, the

Federal Ministry of Health, the purported beneficiary of an additional radiotherapy (cancer treatment) centre in the country.

According to the publication, a single fax from CMI was sent to a senior civil servant in the Nigerian health ministry for his help. He promised to help with the "acquisition of documents" necessary to import the machine into the country because "the Nigerian nuclear authorities are bureaucratic and difficult". The sting operation was foiled by the Nigerian Nuclear Regulatory Authority and marked the first lesson or success story of the NNRA in the combat of illegal and illicit importation of radioactive sources to Nigeria.

While the first lesson was a virtual violation of the import control of radioactive sources into Nigeria, it involved two continents: Africa and Europe. The second lesson was real and involved not only Africa and Europe but also North America (USA).

In December 2002, a multi-national nuclear well-logging company, *Halliburton Energy Services Nigeria Limited* (HESNL), reported the loss/theft two high-risk neutron (Americium-Beryllium) sources with activities 19.5 Curie and 0.5 Curie in the Niger Delta in December 2002. The organisation was not under regulatory control and therefore had no import licence in the first place and had not applied for one to retroactively cover all the legacy sources in its custody. The stolen/lost sources were sold as scrap metals because radioactive sources are usually shielded in very heavy steel containers which turn out to be very attractive and lucrative for scavengers of scrap metal. Furthermore, it was legal to export scrap metal out of the country prior to the ban in September 2003, so the stolen sources were exported "legitimately" out of the country to Germany by sea as scrap metal. This was made easy by the fact that neither the seaports nor the airports are equipped with portal radiation monitors (PRM) to detect radioactive sources and nuclear materials. Similarly, men of the Nigerian Customs Service, the Nigerian Police and the Security Services were neither trained nor equipped to identify and detect radiation sources at entry points.

The Nigerian company, *Cabomet International Metal Trade*, deals in scrap metals, which it used to export before the ban (September 2003) on the export of scrap metals from the country. The radioactive sources, labelled as "stainless steel" were shipped in containers with other scrap metals to a German company, *Eldelstahl Recycling GMBH Germany* via Antwerp in Belgium. With the PRM installed at the gates of *Eldelstahl Recycling GMBH Germany*, the stolen sources were detected, but were unfortunately sent to the US instead of to Nigeria. HESNL was suspended by NNRA from using radioactive sources for about 18 months. After several diplomatic efforts and meetings between the governments of Nigeria, Germany, the US and the IAEA. The two radioactive sources improperly imported into and taken out of Nigeria, and subsequently exported to Germany and finally to the US, were returned to the country in October 2004. Although the multinational company was not prosecuted, the suspension resulted in huge losses in the form of cancelled contracts. This action by the NNRA sent very strong signals to all users, foreign and indigenous, of radioactive materials in the country as it took the intervention of the governments of Nigeria, Germany and the US for its resolution.

The third and final case took place in December 2004, when a multinational industrial radiography company which was duly authorised to export two spent radioactive sources (Iridium 192 and Selenium 75) from a designated airport chose to use a different airport without authorisation. In the process, the licencee transferred the already inspected and properly labelled consignment to an unauthorised Nigerian freight forwarding company, which in turn illegally transported the radioactive package by road over a distance of about 500 kilometres to a different airport. The freight forwarder or his agent shipped the consignment of radioactive material without declaring it to be such, another gross violation of the Act. Its external surface was not marked or labelled as dangerous goods and no shipper's declaration of dangerous goods (DDG) accompanied the consignment, which upon inspection at the destination in the UK was discovered to be a correctly marked and labelled wooden crate, which had been over wrapped with a fibreboard box that was unmarked. The consignment escaped the attention of the Nigerian Customs because of the wrong labelling and because there was no portal radiation monitor at this airport. The two companies were prosecuted and convicted. All these cases went to strengthen the need for international cooperation between the various regulatory bodies concerned with safety and security of radioactive sources.

International cooperation

With these incidents, Nigeria became very active in the various activities related to the implementation of the ENAC (early notification and assistance conventions), to which it is party. In fact it was under the instrumentality of the *Convention on Early Notification of a Nuclear Accident* that Nigeria reported the loss of the two neutron sources in 2002 to the IAEA; sought and obtained assistance from the IAEA under the *Convention on Assistance in the Case of Nuclear Accident or Radiological Emergency;* while Germany reported the interdiction of the same neutron sources to the IAEA *Illicit Trafficking Data Base*. In addition to the multilateral arrangements with the IAEA, NNRA in collaboration with other regulatory bodies in 2008 established the Forum of Nuclear Regulatory Bodies in Africa (FNRBA), the objectives of which are to:

- Provide a platform for fostering regional cooperation;
- Provide for the exchange of expertise, information and experience;
- Provide opportunity for mutual support and coordination of regional initiatives; and
- Leverage the development and optimization of resource utilisation.

The FNRBA carries out its activities through ten thematic groups, one of which deals with security of radioactive sources (including experiences in import/export control). Thus, with the support of its member regulatory bodies, their governments, the African Union Commission, the IAEA and indeed the international community, the FNRBA strives to improve and enhance radiation protection and nuclear safety and security in the Region. In fact, the FNRBA has received support for its activities from the United States Nuclear Regulatory Commission (US NRC), the European Union Commission (EUC) and the Korean Institute of Nuclear Safety (KINS) through the IAEA Nuclear Security Fund.

Furthermore, the coming into force of the *Africa Nuclear Weapons-Free Zone Treaty* otherwise referred to as the "Pelindaba Treaty" and the consequent establishment of the African Commission for Nuclear Energy (AFCONE) provides a veritable platform for a region-wide monitoring and control of movement (including import and export) of radioactive and nuclear materials in the region. This in turn will bolster the confidence of the international community and prevent Africa from being a victim of a "universal trade control regime". In that regard, it should be appreciated that Africa is the only region with a Nuclear Weapon Free Zone Treaty (NWFZT) that is truly free of nuclear weapons and never embarked on a nuclear weapon race; and where a nuclear device was tested and nuclear power programme was voluntarily de-weaponized. Furthermore, Africa is a region where uranium is produced but rarely utilised; yet the Treaty, through its protocols, provides for the involvement of the P5 States and Spain, and the IAEA through the IAEA Safeguards. Against this backdrop however, the region as a whole generally has weak regulatory infrastructure for radiation safety, nuclear safety, security and safeguards, but the situation is changing with the establishment of AFCONE. AFCONE initiates changes by developing appropriate regional legislation and regulatory infrastructure; and working with national regulatory bodies for the domestication and enforcement of such legislation. Africa is therefore justifiably very sensitive to a "universal trade control regime" that does not take cognizance of its peculiar economic interests.

Conclusion and recommendations

Nigeria has diligently been implementing the United Nation Security Council Resolution 1540 in the area of nuclear and radioactive materials. The NNRA took steps to prevent accidental or undeclared import and export of radioactive sources by designating only some airports and seaports for the import and export of radioactive and nuclear materials. This was further strengthened when the European Union Commission, through the IAEA, donated the first radiation portal monitor (RPM), which was installed at an airport designated for the export of radioactive sources. The efficacy of the RPM convinced the Nigerian Government through the NNRA to install similar devices at other import/export terminals. Leveraging her collaboration with the IAEA and her participation in the Global Threat Reduction Initiative (GTRI) of the US Government, several national training courses were organised for the front line officers in the customs, immigration, Police, Army and other Security Agencies. There is thus a significant improvement in the import/export control of radioactive courses in Nigeria. This can also be said of several countries in the region.

All the 33 Member States of the IAEA (nay all the 53 countries) in the region use radioactive sources, with only one Member State actively involved in their commercial production and sale throughout the world. The need for radioactive sources for cancer treatment (radiotherapy) clinics and for industry in the region is rapidly on the increase. Yet there are reported cases of shipment denial, some which the IAEA resolved successfully. It may be indicative of the degree of the implementation of the UNSC resolution 1540 can be deduced from the voluntary compliance of several African Member States to the non-legally binding IAEA Code *of Conduct on the Safety and Security of Radioactive Source* and its associated *Guidance on the Import and Export of Radioactive Sources*· It is noteworthy that in 2013, there are 32 African countries which have expressed support for the Code of Conduct while 24 have expressed support for the Guidance and are therefore implementing the recommendations on import/export control of radioactive sources.

There is still a lot of room for improvement. The EU Commission may want to consider direct engagement with States in the ECOWAS and with States in the Gulf of Guinea. This can build on the outcome of the seminar organised by the NNRA for the ECOWAS missions in Abuja (Nigeria) in April 2011. Furthermore, this can be replicated in the other sub-regions of Africa. Most importantly, the EU Commission may want to use this platform to engage the African Union Commission or the AFCONE on forging a common platform for the effective implementation and monitoring of import/export control in the entire region.

The approach adopted at the end of the recently concluded International Conference on the Safety and Security of Radioactive Sources, 27-31 October 2013 in Abu Dhabi (UAE)[24] is instructive. The Conference, according to the final address by the Conference President, recommended amongst others that the "IAEA should convene a working group to assess the merits of developing a Convention on the safety and security of radioactive sources, and to make recommendations". This would enable an informed decision to be made with regard either to continue with the extant "Code of Conduct" or to seek Member State support for the development of a legally binding "Convention". The Conference however noted that since the approval of the Code of Conduct in 2003 "National regulatory infrastructures have been strengthened and, in many cases where they previously did not exist, they have now been developed". A regional export/import control pattern seems to be emerging and therefore any model with this type of geography may achieve quicker and more enduring satisfactory results. Nigeria is a good example of this where there has been no incidence of unauthorised import or export of radioactive or nuclear materials since 2004. A regional export control model may therefore be preferred.

24 Proceedings of the "International Conference on the Safety and Security of Radioactive Sources", 27-31 October 2013, Abu Dhabi (UAE).

United Nations Security Council Resolution 1540

A Universal Model?

Dr. Andrea VISKI

Scientific Officer – Joint Research Centre, European Commission

Introduction

Unlike many other domains, the field of dual-use export controls lacks a single institution, or international treaty, soley responsible for delineating measures and ensuring compliance of those measures to ensure harmonisation and implementation.[1] This is due to the crosscutting nature of export controls, as they relate to measures to manage the trade of dual-use chemical, biological, and nuclear materials, technology, and equipment. The adoption of United Nations Security Council Resolution 1540 in 2004 appears to provide a solution to this issue due to the language of Operating Paragraph III, calling on States to take and enforce appropriate and effective measures for export controls and related measures such as trans-shipment control and financing. However, ten years since the Resolution, universal implementation of export controls remains a challenge, due in part to a lack of universal agreement over what is, in essence, necessary for an "appropriate and effective" export control system.

This chapter discusses the extent to which Resolution 1540 can realistically serve as a model for dual-use export controls. It will first give a brief introduction to the Resolution and discuss the link between it and the trajectory of international law in order to demonstrate the far-reaching effect that it presumably has on States. The chapter will then discuss the elements of the Resolution that could be drawn upon as a basis for an international model, including an analysis of efforts by the

---

1 For example, in the nuclear field the International Atomic Energy Agency (IAEA) is dedicated to nuclear safeguards, security, and safety issues, as well as ensuring compliance of international law related to the nuclear field. For the control of chemical weapons, the Organisation for the Prohibition of Chemical Weapons (OPCW) serves a similar role.

1540 Committee to identify specific measures necessary for compliance with the Resolution. Finally, the chapter will identify obstacles to using the Resolution as a model, particularly based on observations of implementation efforts by countries. The overall discussion will conclude that while Resolution 1540 is a useful tool to encourage States and mobilise resources and give attention to export control issues, it cannot serve as a definitive model for the implementation of dual-use export controls.

Towards an export control model: an objective worth consideration?

Before moving onto concrete implementation issues, it is helpful to take a step back and observe the link and potential role of international law *vis-à-vis* export controls. In order to do so, it is helpful to consider why a model is needed in the first place for export controls, and indeed, why universality is a goal worth moving towards in this regard.

What has become clear over the past decades, and especially in the post Cold War context, is that problems stemming from within States can take on international dimensions. In addition, due to a globalised world as well as rapidly evolving technology, countries are more interlinked than ever. In terms of export controls, it is not enough for merely the main suppliers of trigger list items to implement export control measures. The threat of transnational trafficking networks, with the potential involvement of terrorist organisations, can form in any State, including, and often targeted, to States without any export control measures in place. In sum, due to globalisation, any country can serve as a trans-shipment point, supplier of fake documentation, financing, or a variety of other roles that facilitate the proliferation of weapons of mass destruction (WMD). On the flip side, every country can also be effective and play a potential role in stemming the threat of proliferation, thereby establishing a use for a universal export control model.

UNSC Resolution is an example of how international law has adapted to the internationalisation of national shortcomings in the general area of the threat of WMD acquisition or use by terrorist actors. In particular, the Resolution was passed as a response to IAEA investigations revealing "an extensive gray market of nuclear and nuclear-related goods and technologies", particularly following the discovery of the AQ Khan network, the terrorist attacks of 11 September 2001 and the threat made by terrorist organisations to try to acquire and use a WMD.

As a consequence, the Resolution obliges all States to implement a large number of measures within their States that can affect domestic politics, a step not exemplified in international legal tradition. The Westphalian origin of international law was to solve interstate issues without interfering in national policy-that is, to tackle issues between States, not stemming from within them. As aptly put by the legal scholars Anne-Marie Slaughter and William Burke-White, "by ensuring that governments actually function in pursuit of collective aims, international law is starting to play a far more active role in shaping these national political choices".[2]

Nevertheless, while Resolution 1540 takes a significant step in universalising certain measures related to WMD proliferation in international law, consideration of the Resolution as a specific model for dual-use export controls is a far trickier proposition. The following section discusses the Resolution in more detail.

UNSC Resolution 1540: searching for a dual-use export control model

Resolution 1540 was adopted under Chapter VII of the United Nations Charter, meaning that it is legally binding for all Member States of the UN. The Resolution obliges States to refrain from supporting by any means non-State actors from developing, acquiring, manufacturing, possessing, transporting, transferring, or using nuclear weapons and their delivery systems. The Resolution further commits States to establish domestic legislation in order to preclude nuclear proliferation by creating controls over related materials and encourages international cooperation and adherence to prior legal non-proliferation instruments. Through Operative Paragraph 3, the Resolution creates an obligation for States to establish and maintain effective national export and transhipment controls over items that could be used in a terrorist WMD attack. The paragraph obliges States to:[3]

> Take and enforce effective measures to establish domestic controls to prevent the proliferation of nuclear, chemical, or biological weapons and their means of delivery, including by establishing appropriate controls over related materials and to this end shall:
>
> (a) Develop and maintain appropriate effective measures to account for and secure such items in production, use, storage or transport;
>
> (b) Develop and maintain appropriate effective physical protection measures;

---

2 A.-M. Slaughter; W. Burke-White, "The future of international law is domestic", Harvard International Law Journal, 1 June 2006.

3 Note that the text of Resolution 1540 does not explicitly refer to dual-use export controls. The term "related material" can be interpreted as relating to this function, however.

(c) Develop and maintain appropriate effective border controls and law enforcement efforts to detect, deter, prevent and combat, including through international cooperation when necessary, the illicit trafficking and brokering in such items in accordance with their national legal authorities and legislation and consistent with international law;

(d) Establish, develop, review and maintain appropriate effective national export and trans-shipment controls over such items, including appropriate laws and regulations to control export, transit, trans-shipment and re-export and controls on providing funds and services related to such export and trans-shipment such as financing, and transporting that would contribute to proliferation, as well as establishing end-user controls; and establishing and enforcing appropriate criminal or civil penalties for violations of such export control laws and regulations.

If Resolution 1540 is considered a model for dual-use export controls, Operative Paragraph 3 is certainly the guiding section. In order to facilitate and monitor the implementation of the Resolution, Operative Paragraph 4 provides for the establishment of a Committee of the Security Council – originally for two years and later extended, the "1540 Committee". The Committee reports to the Security Council and gathers national reports that each country is required to submit regarding steps taken or intended to take to implement the Resolution.

Based on these reports, the 1540 Committee developed a tool to identify which specific measures a State would have to implement in order to comply with Operative Paragraph 3. The tool organises the vast influx of information by using national reports as well as supplemental information supplied by governments and inter-governmental organisations. The matrix tool shows how utterly complex it is to implement the Resolution as there are dozens of measures to be taken by States in order to comply with Operative Paragraph 3. The Committee states that the matrices are not a tool for implementation or measuring compliance with the Resolution but rather "a reference tool for facilitating technical assistance" and "(enhancing) dialogue with States." Nevertheless, the specificity designated in the matrices is the closest model for export controls that exists at the international level.

Before discussing the measures, it is worth remarking that the 1540 Committee matrices shed light on the vague wording of the Resolution, especially in areas where words such as "appropriate" and "effective" are used. The matrices offer insight into what the Committee means by its language as they list the components necessary to comply with the separate parts of the Resolution. They are therefore a useful tool for understanding and organising the varying measures necessary for the implementation of the Resolution, and or establishing a basic rubric for the domestic implementation of export controls in particular.

While it is beyond the scope of this chapter to analyse in detail each measure identified by the committee as necessary for compliance with Operative Paragraph 3, the 26 measures are listed here:[4]

- Border control;
- Technical support of border control measures;
- Control of brokering, trading in, negotiating, otherwise assisting in sale of goods and technology;
- Enforcement agencies/authorities;
- Export control legislation in place;
- Licencing Provisions;
- Individual licencing;
- General licencing;
- Exceptions from licencing;
- Licencing of deemed export/visa;
- National licencing authority;
- Interagency review for licences;
- Control lists;
- Updating of lists;
- Inclusion of technologies;
- Inclusion of means of delivery;
- End-user controls;
- Catch-all clause;
- Intangible Transfers;
- Transit control;
- Trans-shipment control;
- Re-export control;
- Control of providing funds;
- Control of providing transport services;
- Control of importation;
- Extraterritorial applicability.

4 The 1540 Matrix template is available at the following address: http://www.un.org/en/sc/1540/national-implementation/1540-matrix/matrix-template.shtml.

Different countries may interpret these measures differently, not to mention with regard to practical implementation concerns.[5] Nevertheless, the measures listed above are one possible example of a dual-use export control model that could be accepted by the international community. This is the model created by the 1540 Committee and in fact the matrix has been recently updated with all of these specific measures remaining intact, but this does not exclude that other models could fit just as well under Operative Paragraph 3 language.

While the 1540 Committee is an official Committee charged with monitoring the implementation of the Resolution, the matrix is not an official legally-binding document, leaving Operative Paragraph 3 nevertheless open to broad interpretation. In order to assess whether such is the case, it is necessary to observe the level of implementation of the specific measures noted by the Committee, as well as to consider all other relevant factors, as discussed in the next section.

UNSC Resolution 1540: a working model?

Resolution 1540 has been a significant achievement in terms of mobilising countries around the implementation of measures to combat the threat of nuclear WMD terrorism. The measures specified in the Resolution have also had effects beyond that specific goal, as they pertain essentially also to States, not just non-State actors. Barring these achievements, whether the Resolution serves as a model for dual-use export controls is a more complicated matter. This section identifies four general obstacles to Operative Paragraph 3 as a model:

- The broad scope of the resolution;
- The vague wording of Operative Paragraph 3;
- Controversy over the power of the Security Council to adopt a universally-binding resolution;
- The issue of a “one-size-fits-all” approach;
- The broad scope of the resolution.

Although Operative Paragraph 3 pertains also to export controls, the Resolution taken as a whole is extremely broad. First, the Resolution refers to chemical and biological, as well as nuclear, weapons. The usage of the umbrella term WMD achieves the goal of bringing greater attention to the terrorist threat of using such weapons against the international

5 A. Viski, “The national implementation of export controls: Developing a best practices model”, European Safeguards and Research Development Association (ESARDA) Bulletin, Vol. 46, (2012).

community, yet the practical consequence of using the term likewise multiplies the difficulty in implementing national laws that protect against all three types of threats. The risk presented by the diversion of nuclear materials and equipment is different from that of chemical or biological substances, and logically different international treaties and conventions should apply to each type of threat. This differentiation, however, is never enunciated in the Resolution, and therefore leaves the question of how to deal with the three in legislation and enforcement – separately or together – up to States. As a result, States vary widely in terms of implementation on this issue.

The Resolution is broad also in terms of what it expects from States. The broader the command, the more difficult it is to implement in practical terms, and the more room there is for fudging on the part of States if they wish to do so. Furthermore, the Resolution does not address the consequences of non-compliance, such as possible enforcement actions or sanctions, giving States leeway in terms of the extent to which they implement the resolution. In cases of non-compliance, the Security Council would be hard-pressed to impose sanctions or other punishment, even if such a response would be legally possible, due to the inevitable controversy such actions would create.

The vague wording of Operative Paragraph 3

While the language of Operative Paragraph 3 lays down broad and far-reaching obligations for States, the specific measures necessary to comply with the text are not specified in the Resolution itself. As a result, many States find the wording, especially the use of the terms "appropriate and effective", too vague.[6] In terms of the implementation of the Resolution, one difficulty countries have faced lies in understanding what exactly is specified by the language used. As Peter Crail notes, "what is considered to be an appropriate and effective legal mechanism varies between States, thereby complicating any such assessment and leaving room for political considerations to come into play as States assert that they are in compliance".[7]

The vague wording also pertains to the measures identified by the matrix. While some measures are extremely clear, such as having a law in place, others are less so, not just in terms of interpretation, but also in terms of whether they are accepted as standard export control measures. Some examples are measures concerning extraterritorial applicability,

6 J. Bergenas, "A piece of the global puzzle", Stimson Center Report, 9 December 2010.

7 P. Crail, "Implementing UN Security Council Resolution 1540: A risk-based approach", Non-proliferation Review, (13:2), 2006, pp. 355-399.

deemed exports, import controls, and intangible transfers, without being exhaustive.

Controversy over the power of the Security Council to pass a universally-binding resolution

Some States, especially following the initial passage of Resolution 1540, expressed reservations at the broad powers of the Security Council to enact such a powerful international law. These reservations tie the evolution of international law into, sometimes, the domestic policies of States. While the need for such scope has been established previously in this chapter, many States are nevertheless uncomfortable with the growing power of international law and institutions.

In the context of Resolution 1540, a few States felt that the Security Council had usurped the powers of the General Assembly and other organisations, especially as the Resolution was passed under Chapter VII, making it obligatory under international law. This further meant that most countries were excluded from the Resolution negotiations, fuelling the viewpoint of a North-South divide and underscoring resentment voiced by Members of the non-aligned Movement.[8] The weaker the legitimacy of the Resolution, the weaker the motivation on the part of States to implement it effectively. Nevertheless, this issue appears to have relented in the past few years, as evidenced by the large number of submitted national reports to the 1540 Committee.

The issue of a "one-size-fits-all" approach

Of those countries that have submitted reports, almost none have implemented all of the measures identified by the 1540 Committee matrices.[9] It is therefore an initial starting point to mention that submitting a report to the 1540 Committee is not equivalent to fully complying with the Resolution. Even for a supplier country of WMD materials and equipment, the task of complying with the broad language of Resolution 1540 can be a challenge. Because most States significantly lack the institutional mechanisms required by the Resolution, the task of implementation can become costly and complex.

Moreover, different country profiles, resources, geography, and national priorities can make the implementation of a very broad Resolution practically impossible on a universal, harmonised level. A more adequate dual-use export control model would focus rather on implementing key

8 J. Bergenas, *op. cit.*

9 A. Viski, *op. cit.*

measures identified as basic for all States, with supplemental and voluntary measures for States where such measures would be appropriate.

Conclusion

This chapter has examined the extent to which UNSC Resolution 1540 can be considered a model for dual-use export controls. An attempt was made at justifying the need for such a model, have it been in the Resolution on another document, in the first place, and tying this need to the trajectory of international law from a historical context. The Resolution was then presented, followed by a discussion of the specific measures identified by the 1540 Committee, in their matrix tool, pursuant to Operative Paragraph 3. The last section outlined broad reasons limiting the usefulness of the Resolution as a model, underscored by the weak overall implementation of the 26 measures outlined by the Committee per its own reports to the Security Council.

While using the Resolution and supplemental guidance in the form of the matrix measures may not be an ideal model for dual-use export controls from an analytical perspective, it nevertheless remains the closest possible universal model currently available to the international community. No other models exist that have international legitimacy. On the other hand, many States and regions have developed their own model, often in non-conformity with the 1540 matrix measures. These alternative models are furthermore often "exported" in the form of capacity-building projects, with the result that many competing models for dual-use export controls have been adopted worldwide. It is for the future to tell whether a new model is necessary that aims to truly universalise and harmonise supply-side non-proliferation measures, or whether the status quo can provide the necessary security to keep the world free from the threat or use of WMD.

Arms Export Controls

Setting Common International Standards

Rosa Rosanelli

International Trade Compliance Specialist

As essentially political instruments in the context of the Cold War, conventional arms controls have later evolved in to a much broader need, aimed at regulating exports towards critical destinations, protecting strategic technologies and reducing the role played by small arms.[1]

Consistent with Article 51 of the United Nations (UN) Charter, is the sovereign right of each State to manufacture, import, export, transfer and possess conventional arms for their legitimate self-defence and security needs and for the maintenance of order.

However, to avoid adverse effects on regional stability and international security, this right corresponds to the responsibility to take steps to prevent the diversion to illegal channels and to combat illicit trade.

In a domain that is very closely linked to national sovereignty, reaching a shared international understanding of the risks and a common identification of international standards represents a key-challenge to set up an effective global system of control.

The aim of this chapter is to analyse arms export controls at several levels and to critically evaluate, notably in the light of the recent Arms Trade Treaty (ATT), the challenges and opportunities to establish universal legal standards.

Peculiarities of arms export controls

During the Cold war, arms export controls were a powerful political tool. Conventional weapons transfers had little restraint within the two blocs and were strictly blocked across the borders of their spheres of influence.

---

1 See also Advisory Council on International Affairs (Netherlands), "Conventional Arms Control: Urgent Need, Limited Opportunities", No. 2, April 1998, p. 50.

Today, the global threat scenario has changed significantly, and focus has shifted to the need to prevent acquisition of weapons by "unsafe" governments but also international criminal and terrorist organisations. Yet, conventional armaments remain closely linked to issues of national sovereignty and military capacity.

A State will generally list and regulate as "conventional arms" the items involved in the process of "preparing for war". Within conventional weapons we can discriminate between major weapons systems and small and light weapons (SALW).[2] Small arms are particularly critical because of their relative ease of availability; however major weapons systems have the potential to influence regional balances of power.[3]

For this reason, the measures adopted to control exports of weapons and sophisticated military technology will generally reflect national sovereignty priorities, specific national risk analysis and political relations.

On the other hand, conventional weapons represent an important element in the equation of international security and regional stability. Their availability can improve national military capabilities, but also raise the level of tension, allow the use of weapons in internal repression and make them potentially available for diversion to undesirable recipients.

States have been making collective efforts to effectively control arms exports, for instance in furtherance of strategic embargos under decisions of the United Nations (UN) Security Council. But while there is a widespread consensus that the proliferation of weapons of mass destruction (including chemical, biological, radiological and nuclear) and their delivery systems should be controlled, the exports of conventional weapons are still considered as a national prerogative.

States have traditionally been reluctant to give up any element of national control in this area, which is very closely linked to their right to sovereign self-defence, as stated in Article 51 of the UN Charter.

For these reasons, *de facto* arms export controls mostly rely on national regulations.

2 This Chapter will not focus specifically on the issue of SALW, which represent an exception in virtue of their easier availability in the illegal traffic of armaments. For this reason they have been object of a specific concern since the late 1990s, both at EU and UN level, in order to avoid their proliferation.

3 R. Smith, B. Udis, "New Challenges to Arms Export Control: Whither Wassenaar?", The Non-proliferation Review, Vol. 8, No. 2, 2001, p. 82.

Harmonisation of arms export controls in Europe

EU regulations are considered among the most stringent for dual-use goods and technology. However, the initiatives that have been carried out to achieve a progressive harmonisation in the field of arms export controls still remain in the realm of the "politically binding".

In the European Union, efforts to harmonise national policies on arms export controls have been carried out since the 1990s as a prerequisite of further integration for both foreign policy and trade and competition. Legal harmonisation was in this sense a preliminary step to promote multilevel governance, enforce common "ethical" foreign policies, and enhance defence industrial cooperation.

A political will to establish harmonised rules on the control of exports of military items and technology to third countries started to appear during the European Council meeting in Luxembourg in June 1991, when the "Declaration on Non-Proliferation and the Export of Weapons" was adopted.[4]

In a time when pressure of the public opinion was high, after arms transfer-related scandals like the continued sale of arms to Saddam Hussein in the period preceding the invasion of Kuwait in 1990, seven common criteria to govern arms exports were agreed by the Heads of State. The following Council meeting in Lisbon later added the eighth "economic" criteria. However, opinions continued to diverge on interpretation, the principles were not mandatory and it was never made clear how they should be applied.

A step forward was made in December 1992, when the European Council of Edinburgh designated arms exports as a joint action area.[5] Under impulsion of the German presidency in 1994, the Council tried to reach a common interpretation, nevertheless aware that "exports of conventional arms touch upon important and legitimate national interests".

A series of cases showed the need of a common policy on arms exports: in 1994 Germany refused to agree to a warship contract with Taiwan, France supplied Mirage fighters and fregates for 6,1 billion dollars; when Portugal imposed a unilateral arms embargo on Indonesia

---

4 For the text of the declaration, see "EC Council Decisions on Non-proliferation and Arms Exports", http://archives.sipri.org/contents/expcon/eu_criteria.html.

5 The report published by an ad hoc working group referred to "economic aspects of security", including "the adoption [...] of common arms export criteria" and "common licence revocation procedures and review of existing UN and European arms embargoes". See C. E. Golumbic and R. S. Ruff III, "Who Do I Call for an EU Sanctions Exemption?: Why the EU Economic Sanctions Regime Should Centralise Licencing", Georgetown Journal of International Law, Vol. 44, Issue 3, Spring 2013, p. 1018.

after the invasion of East Timor, Germany and the UK continued to supply warships and aircraft.[6]

A long political process led to a "Code of Conduct on Arms Exports" in 1998, that restated the eight criteria, established a notification and consultation mechanism for denials and introduced the publication of annual reports.[7] Still, it remained a declaration which enforced political commitments and was not legally binding.[8]

Its successor, the Common Position 2008/944/CFSP of 8 December 2008, would extend controls to brokering, transit transactions and intangible transfers of technology but also change the status of the Code. As a common position, it imposed on States an obligation (although not a legal requirement) to ensure that national laws are in compliance.[9]

Besides the political objective, the economic need was a fundamental driver. During the 1990s, the European defence industry went through a process of important consolidation and internationalisation.

In its submission to the Intergovernmental Conference in 1997, the European Defence Industries Group (EDIG) denounced the disparities between national export control policies as an obstacle for European cooperative programmes and called for a harmonisation that would strengthen the European commercial position.[10]

---

6 I. Davis, *The Regulation of Arms and Dual-Use Exports: Germany, Sweden and the UK*, Sipri, Oxford University Press, 2002, p. 98.

7 See also NATO Industrial Advisory Group, High Level Advice Study No. 154, "Developments in Europe to reform Export Control and Defence Procurement Processes: Implications and Opportunities Resulting, Particularly with Regard to Multinational Programs Supporting NATO Capabilities and Interoperability", Annex 2 to TADIC Paper Panel 1, p. 7.

8 It played nevertheless an important role, as part of a EU agenda intended to promote more responsible licencing of exports. In this sense went also the Joint Actions on Small Arms and Light Weapons of December 1998 and July 2002, and the Council Common Position on arms brokering of June 2003. See also M. Bromley, M. Brzoska, "Towards a Common, Restrictive EU Arms Export Policy? The Impact of the EU Code of Conduct on Major Conventional Arms Exports", in European Foreign Affairs Review No. 13; 333-356, 2008.

9 A. Hudson, "Case Study: EU Code of Conduct on Arms Exports", Overseas Development institute, available online: http://www.odi.org.uk/sites/odi.org.uk/files/odi-assets/publications-opinion-files/3677.pdf.

10 "It would be difficult, if not impossible, for a major company to contemplate collaboration with another company unless that company exists in a country where the Government has accepted common principles of exporting policy. An absence of national Government agreement could therefore mean that its national industry would find itself effectively debarred from participation in collaborative projects". European Defence Industries Group, "The European defence industry: an agenda item for the 1996 Inter-governmental Conference, Memorandum by EDIG", 30 May 1995, p. 11.

The European Commission recognised that unharmonised national export control policies created market distortions. The gradual elimination of the differences was a matter of competition policy, rather than a politico-strategic necessity. However, fearing the effects on the transatlantic relationship, its proposals remained limited to measures to achieve greater transparency.

But if the Communication "Challenges for the European defence industry: a contribution to action at a European level" was published in 1996,[11] it was only in December 2007 that a "Defence Package" was designed to improve the competitiveness of the European Defence sector. One of the two related directives that followed in 2009 was Directive 2009/43/EC *simplifying terms and conditions of transfers of defence-related products within the community*.

The Directive essentially attempts to extend the common market to the trade in defence-related products, by reducing individual licencing within the EU. Member States are invited to replace them with general licences in a number of cases in which risk of re-export is limited, for instance in the case of purchases by armed forces or "certified" companies.

Directive 2009/43 was certainly a step further towards a more fluid internal defence market. However, its implementation did not succeed into achieving simplification: Member States were expected to transpose the Directive by 30 June 2011 and to implement it by 30 June 2012, but there was a significant time shift for some of them. National implementations were also highly unharmonised, and this ultimately generated perplexity in many European companies *vis-à-vis* the utility and effectiveness of becoming "certified".

Multilateral efforts for arms export controls' harmonisation and the path to a treaty on conventional armaments

Collective efforts to regulate international arms transfers at the global level have been on the international agenda since the early 20th century.[12] However, unlike chemical, biological and nuclear weapons, conventional arms have been, until recently, the only type of arms not covered by global multilateral treaties.

[11] Communication of the European Commission "Challenges for the European defence industry: a contribution to action at a European level" COM (96) 10, 24 January 1996.

[12] 1919 St Germain Convention for the Control of the Trade in Arms and Ammunitions and the 1925 Convention of the League of Nations for the Supervision of the International Trade in Arms and Ammunition and in Implements of War were, in this sense, two missed opportunities.

As the UN Secretary General Ban Ki-moon argued, "there are common standards for the global trade in armchairs but not the global trade in arms".[13]

The Wassenaar Agreement, formally established in 1996, covers export controls for conventional arms and dual-use goods and technologies.[14] Yet, designed as a forum of exchange of information, it does not have a legally binding nature or a universal membership.

Within the United Nations, a first important initiative was the establishment of a register in 1991, in order to increase transparency in imports and exports of seven categories of arms, which are deemed the most lethal.[15] In its Resolution 46/36H of 6 December 1991, the UN General Assembly (UNGA) urged Member States to exercise "effective control over their arms imports and exports and to ensure that they have in place an adequate body of laws, regulations and strict enforcement measures". It also invited States to cooperate effectively for the harmonisation of relevant laws, regulations, administrative procedures and enforcement measures with the goal of eradicating illicit arms trafficking.[16]

In 2002, the General Assembly adopted Resolution 57/66 "National Legislation on Transfer of Arms, Military Equipment and Dual-Use Goods and Technology". A non-legally binding document, it recommends to enact or improve national legislation, regulations and procedures to exercise effective control over transfers of arms, military and dual-use goods and technology and to cooperate on a voluntary basis.

In the late 1990s a campaign for a universal and legally binding Arms Trade Treaty was initiated by non-governmental organisations and later supported by a group of Nobel Peace Prize laureates. It persuaded a large number of States to promote the initiative, which was successfully brought to the UN.

The result was UNGA Resolution 61/89 *towards an arms trade treaty: establishing common international standards for the import, export and*

---

13 Ban Ki-moon, "Secretary General's remarks to Final UN Conference on the Arms Trade Treaty", New York, 18 March 2013.

14 R. Smith, B. Udis, "New Challenges to Arms Export Control: Whither Wassenaar?", *op. cit.*, p. 81.

15 It has to be noted that Article 3 of Resolution 46/36 L of 9 December 1991 establishing the UN Register of Conventional Arms reaffirmed the right to self-defence, "which implies that States also have the right to acquire arms with which to defend themselves". See http://www.un.org/disarmament/convarms/Register/. See also I. Davis, "The Regulation of Arms and Dual-Use Exports: Germany, Sweden and the UK", *op. cit.*, p. 23.

16 UNGA Resolution 46/36H of 6 December 1991, "International Arms Transfers", A/RES/46/36, available online http://www.un.org/documents/ga/res/46/a46r036.htm.

transfer of conventional arms of 6 December 2006, that requested the Secretary General to "seek the views of Member States on the feasibility, scope and draft parameters for a comprehensive, legally binding instrument".

In December 2009 an overwhelming majority of UN Member States voted to consider the issue in an *ad hoc* Conference convened in 2012 "to elaborate a legally binding instrument on the highest possible common international standards for the transfer of conventional arms".

The Arms Trade Treaty: a missed opportunity?

It was only in 2013 that an international Arms Trade Treaty (ATT) put an end to the lack of international agreements for the prohibition or restriction of transfers of conventional weapons. However its wording and membership did not succeed in shifting national patterns of arms exports and making it a milestone in international law.

The Treaty was adopted and open for signature on June 3, 2013. 50 ratifications are needed for it to enter into force, but to date it has been signed by 116 States, and only ratified by 9.

While uncertainty remains as to when and how the Arms Trade Treaty will enter into force, the Conference has been a historical opportunity to establish "the highest possible common international standards" for the import, export and transfer of conventional arms. But was it a missed opportunity?

The ATT was a unique occasion to strengthen State responsibility for the control of transfers of conventional armaments, including by non-State actors as it was meant to cover both "licit" and "illicit" arms transfers.

However, its final construction is such that it only sets a list of elements to be included in the national control systems, like national control lists, regulation on imports, transits and brokering, enforcement measures to prevent diversion, and record keeping practices.

Otherwise, it reaffirms the sovereign right of each State to regulate and control armaments exported nationally. Uniform guidelines will have to be taken into account when assessing transfers, but the Treaty will be implemented primarily at the national level, and the implementation will remain at national discretion.[17]

---

[17] D. Fiott, K. Prizeman, "The Arms Trade Treaty and the Control of Dual-Use of Goods and Technologies: What can the European Union's Export Control Regime Offer?", IES Working Paper 1/2013, p. 21.

The effective enforcement and implementation inevitably will rest on strong political will and its effectiveness will very likely depend on pre-existing robust export control mechanisms in each arms exporting country.

Yet, the ATT initiative remains the most relevant development in conventional arms controls in decades. It reaffirmed that all States have a primary responsibility to effectively establish and implement their respective national control systems. It also has the merit of having helped reach a common understanding of armaments export controls as an area that needs to be regulated through legally binding rules, but also cooperation, transparency and responsible action.

Which common international standards?

Whether the ATT could have done more to harmonise and coordinate the domestic regulation of conventional armaments control is certainly debatable. However, as shown by ATT discussions, national prerogatives are not the only issue.

It is also very difficult to identify common paradigms, assess the degree of subjectivity of assessments and build on core shared interests.

The draft text of the treaty has been subject to controversies around objectivity, notably on issues such as human rights violations, and all the attempts to achieve harmonisation based on political and ethical principles and humanitarian objectives have been repeatedly frustrated.

However, as we can draw from the European experience, export controls would probably achieve a more effective harmonisation if arms trade was considered primarily as a "trade" issue.

A well-regulated system cannot only guarantee international peace and security. It is also one where legitimate trade in military material, equipment and technology and international commercial cooperations are protected. In this sense, an international legally binding instrument could achieve more effectiveness if it focuses on the economic drive more than the political and social rationale.

The ATT can be an "opportunity structure" to develop further. While there is no appetite among governments for authorisation decisions to be taken by a supranational body, the establishment of common paradigms has proven to be a useful step to achieve coordinated export controls and also a ground where it is possible to reach a global agreement.

However, the elements identified in the ATT represent necessary but not sufficient requirements for domestic change to occur. They need to be enriched with clear and pragmatic elements that focus on the commercial aspects and the operational effectiveness of control mechanisms.

National arms export control laws and regulations usually involve:
- Lists of items that are subject to authorisation procedures,
- Lists of transfers that are to be controlled,
- Lists of countries to which exports are restricted and criteria to employ to assess ambiguous cases,
- Custom procedures to halt unauthorised exports and
- Enforcement measures to guarantee consistency in the declared end-use of the items, and prohibit re-exports.

Yet, to achieve successful harmonisation, a common language and common definitions could make the several national lists of items "compatible".

A step further would be the definition of common products and destinations' lists. To date, there is no common international understanding of which goods and services should be controlled and subject to authorisation and which should be traded freely, nor a commonly agreed identification of "unsafe" destinations. A common global standardised marking and tracing procedure for manufacturers and exporters could also be beneficial to international tracking efforts.

Common standards should allow lower administrative costs in presence of collaborative projects or fairs and expositions, harmonise laws and regulations at least in their language and structure, and thus federate efforts to restrict access to conventional armaments in the most "unsafe" circumstances.

Finally, an international instrument should impose international cooperation between competent national authorities and mutual assistance, an element that is indispensable to guarantee effective enforcement, tracking and end-user verification.

Lessons Learnt from Strategic Trade Control Enforcement Capacity-Building in Western Africa

Renaud CHATELUS

Senior Scientist Grant Holder,
European Commission – Joint Research Centre

Can export control systems be shaped according to universal or regional models? Recent experiences of strategic trade control enforcement training in Western Africa[1] was the occasion to get hints about the answer to this question, at least for the enforcement aspects of it. Enforcement is one of the most challenging aspects of export control, even in so-called developed countries. It is legitimate to seek models which can be exported to help building capacity in countries where they don't exist yet, but it requires three conditions at least: good models must exist, they must be suitable to the local context and they must be transferable (i.e. the elements of the model can be built or provided via assistance programmes). We will see that these conditions are difficult to fulfil when it comes to export control enforcement in a context like Western Africa. However, talking about export control enforcement models may be looking at it from the wrong angle. As often, taking a broader perspective and thinking out of the export control and non-proliferation box may help. Export control enforcement is not only about export control, it is also about enforcement. Models from other enforcement subjects than export control may exist, be suitable and be transferable.

---

1 One of these experiences was the Advanced Interdiction Training of the Container Control Program is a joint UNODC-WCO programme aiming at establishing container risk profiling teams in major container ports of participating countries. These teams are a mix of several services (customs, police, intelligence and other services operating at the border) and originally focus on narcotics, but may look at other types of cross-border trafficking. In 2011, the program expanded its focus to cover strategic trade controls. Thematic workshops were organised for profiling units in Western Africa. See: http://www.unodc.org/documents/toc/CCP_Year_End_Report_2011.pdf.

Is there a good model for export control enforcement?

The first question to raise regards the existence of good models. When it comes to enforcement, it is not obvious. Export control enforcement is a challenge in every country. Of course, some are more advanced than others, thanks to accumulated experience, effective legal framework, good organisation or simply strong political will. Assessing the performance of national export control enforcement is however difficult. Indicators are problematic and when they exist, the "performance" measured can be the result of many factors, beyond the efficacy of the system. For example, an apparent absence of seizures may mean either very dissuasive enforcement, or very ineffective enforcement, or an absence of operations to which export control would apply, or an absence of publicity about seizures.

What we can observe is that enforcing export control is a struggle everywhere. Certain enforcement challenges are very difficult to overcome even for the most advanced countries. There are many reasons to explain this and in particular, to explain why customs may have difficulties with this subject. At the national level, border services face the same big issues, and found only imperfect ways to tackle them. Lack of technical expertise, competing priorities, large volumes of control, pressure to facilitate trade, or compatibility with customs processes are amongst them. For customs, there is in addition the question of compatibility between export control requirements and the international trade legal framework: World Trade Organisation rules, international maritime laws, the Revised Kyoto Convention,[2] international transit agreements,[3] recommendations of the World Customs Organisation, regional trade agreements, etc. These are often seen as more binding legally and politically.

The two dominant "models" from which international capacity building programmes originate, have themselves short comings.

The US has a very broad and far reaching export control system with, in particular, heavy penalties in the form of fines and imprisonment, but also withdrawal of export privileges, black listing and other kinds of economic punishments. Because of the central position of the US and its currency in the world economy, the extraterritorial reach of US regulation and US enforcement means, these tough provisions have deterrent

2 "The International Convention on the Simplification And Harmonization of Customs Procedures", Customs Cooperation Council (now World Customs Organisation), June 1999.

3 For example, the United Nation Convention on Transit Trade of Land-locked States (1967) or the Convention Relating To Inter-States Road Transit Of Goods A/P.4/5/82, ECOWAS (1982). Many other legal instruments relating to transit and right of passage could be quoted here.

effects far beyond US borders. But the system has its limitations. It is still a complex authorisation regime. International companies have difficulties coping with re-export and deemed export provisions, and the rather confrontational relation between companies and enforcement services does not always facilitate proactive and voluntary participation of the industry to the system.

In Europe, the regulation and its integrated control lists are models for many countries in the world. But enforcement as well as licencing, is a Member State's responsibility. Both remain unevenly implemented amongst Member States. Enforcement services also have to cope with coordination and communication between licencing and customs authorities in different Member States, with different enforcement regulations, different interpretations of EU laws and different licencing policies. All this applies to a common market where most dual-use goods move freely and are only controlled when leaving the EU territory.

Many other potential models exist, but there is no model that would perfectly combine the different dimensions of export control to which enforcement contributes: compliance (is the law respected?), trade facilitation (is the system not hindering legitimate trade?), border control and investigations (do violators have a good chance to be caught?), prosecutions and penalties (are prospects of sanctions against violators dissuasive?) and non-proliferation (is proliferation made more difficult?). Implementers of international outreach programmes sometimes find themselves in a slightly uncomfortable position when they have to explain best practices in implementing the most challenging export control provisions like transit or intangible transfers.

Possible models are not necessarily adapted and transferable to a context like Western Africa

Even if good models exist, the next question is whether they would be adapted to countries where capacity needs to be built.

In the case of Western Africa, questions on the means and resources are certainly central. In absolute terms, border services often don't have the means to conduct general border controls that more developed or even intermediate countries process. Potential export control enforcement models may rely on means of communication, technical analysis capacity, IT systems (including databases), means of transportations, if not capacity to conduct undercover operations which may just not be there. At some border points, the first operational need may well be to have a telephone line working, electricity to power it or a motorbike to move inspectors in the port from their office to the clearance sites.

But we must examine the question of resources in relative terms too. The limited resources for enforcement are focused on priorities relating to the protection of the national territory from criminal activities, the protection of national economic interests against unfair competition and the collection of revenue for the government. Objectives relating to international responsibility and global security like export control necessarily belong to a secondary set of priorities. Dedicating resources to it may be seen as a luxury that rich countries can afford. It requires important investments in terms of staff allocation, training, establishing procedures, IT systems, communication, etc. for few trade operations concerned, little chances to find a violation at and likely lack of understanding by operators and higher management. It is often argued that doing good export control brings economic benefits by facilitating trade and allowing customs facilitations in partner countries. But whether the argument is sufficient will depend on the country's trade profile and on how much it will be affected by import facilitations in Europe or the US.

From a human resources perspective, export control belongs to a category of controls which do not generate revenue for the government. But in many countries part of the officers' revenue is calculated from the number of cleared imports. Working on non-revenue related export controls may mean loosing this part of the salary.[4]

On a different level, corruption and the fight against it cannot be overlooked. Corruption is not an exclusivity of customs services or Western Africa, but it has dimensions which maybe absent from potential models. Export control combines an authorisation regime, controls at the border, no national security issue at stake and commercial activities involved: a risk configuration from a corruption point of view. Hence, capacity building and assistance programmes should always evaluate the potential effect on corruption of proposed models, for example when recommending how to organise licencing. Potential for corruption should be a parameter in the choice of how licences are requested and delivered, who issues them and whether they should be centralised within one agency or split between ministries. For example, it may be sensible to avoid creating a new and independent set of export control permits for commodities already subject to authorisations.[5] Anti-corruption specialists' input would certainly be useful in this regard.

---

4 To take the example of the container control programme, mixed profiling teams in western Africa may have difficulty attracting customs participation because customs officers may loose the revenue associated with the clearance process when they join teams.

5 In one Western African country, violations found following a CCP training related absence of one of the four permits required for a given chemical. This was still without a licencing requirement for proliferation related export control.

For Customs, measures to prevent corruption have very concrete consequences. Western African countries are signatories of the revised Arusha declaration[6] and the Maputo declaration.[7] The WCO made recommendations in connection with these commitments. They include for example, centralised and automated risk management systems associated with random selection of officers for inspections. When implemented, such parameters are certainly to consider in determining where enforcement trainings should be directed.

Additionally, beyond border operations, two key components of export control enforcement are likely to be lacking in Western Africa: technical reach back and intelligence. Most of the functioning models available in the world would in fact make heavy use of both capacities.

One last particularity of Western Africa is the existence of many landlocked countries. Mali, Niger, Burkina Faso and Tchad have no maritime façade and depend on transit trade through countries at their southern and western borders. This makes control on transit on the Atlantic façade politically sensitive, if not subject to legal limitations set by international, regional and bilateral conventions.

As we see, whatever model is chosen, it will have to be extensively adapted to the local context. But the next question is how much of these models can be transferred, i.e. how much of the export control elements can be supplied or transferred through international assistance.

Some elements of potential export control models are not transferable

Advanced technical expertise and specialised intelligence capacity are essential in many potential models, as we have seen above. But they are not likely to be transferred in the short run, if at all, and especially not through international export control capacity building programmes. Models built around these elements are therefore not always relevant. Other elements difficult to transfer are large integrated IT systems. In Europe, in the US but also in a number of intermediate countries in South East Asia or Latin America, enforcement officers can count on databases handling customs declarations, recording past violations, ensuring the monitoring of transit, recording export permits, etc. These elements are not always present in Western Africa, and definitely not at every border

6 The Revised Arusha Declaration Concerning Good Governance And Integrity In Customs, Declaration of the Customs Co-Operation Council, June 2003.

7 The "Maputo Declaration: A Commitment to Integrity in Customs", WCO and the Government of Mozambique, March 2002, adopted by African Heads of Customs.

crossing point. Some may be built with international support, but not in the framework of export control.

When it comes to field detection and analysis equipment like scanners, densi meters, chemical field analysers or metal analysers, supply through assistance programmes is possible, but in relatively poor countries, they bear challenges of their own. One is maintenance over years, which is not always ensured by support programmes. But the simple fact of supplying portable equipment worth several customs agents' annual salaries is a problem. The history of international development programmes is full of stories of donated equipments disappearing shortly after their arrival. International export control capacity building is no exception.[8]

At this point of our demonstration, it appears difficult to conclude that export control enforcement "models" can be applied in Western Africa, at least not without a thorough adaptation to the local context. But we may want to examine the question from another perspective, focusing on where to find elements of models already present in these countries, in other fields than export control. These elements may be legal provisions or enforcement practices that capacity building programmes can build on.

Looking at mechanisms and practices outside export control

We can here review a number of export control enforcement challenges as well as existing expertise and experience to address them.

To start with, border services already enforce many kinds of import-export permit regimes, sometime in application of international conventions. Examples include the control on trade in medicines, dangerous chemicals, radioactive material, waste and small arms and light weapons.[9] Some of them even apply to exports like for endangered species[10] or national cultural treasures. Even if these are imperfectly applied, their existence means that similar procedures exist, that challenges have been identified and that enforcement staff already know some export control principles. Even when it comes to detecting smuggling, there may be some experience of checking exports and transit for narcotics.[11] In other

8 For example, it has been reported that batteries of portable equipment have been stolen by officers in some countries to supply electricity to their home.

9 Convention on Small Arms and Light Weapons, Their Ammunition and Other Related Materials, ECOWAS, June 2006.

10 The Convention on International Trade in Endangered Species of Wild Fauna and Flora (CITES), also known as the "Washington Convention", 1973.

11 Western Africa has become a major transit platform for cocaine from South America to Europe.

words, there are elements of a model already in place for export control, in a literal sense.

We could also mention customs audit procedures for authorised economic operators (AEO)[12] and other audits associated with customs procedures or safety/security related authorisations. All these processes and experiences are relevant for audits in the framework of export control.

Another area where experience may be present is the implementation of controls requiring technical and legal reachback provided by another organisation. It is not always a comfortable situation for enforcement services which must take the risk and bear the cost of a control not knowing whether the operation will be assessed as illegal (or not) by the relevant technical body. Customs services already have to face such situations for medicines, endangered species and counterfeit commodities (when a regulation is in place for these).

Other relevant know how include the knowledge of legitimate trade[13] which is so important to identify areas of trade concerned by export control or detect abnormal risk profiles of shipments. We may also recall that services already deal with strategic security issues when they work on arms trade or explosives precursors[14] and that the verification of the destination and consignee of shipments which is a part of export control enforcement, is also conducted to profile other high risk shipments.

As a conclusion, export control enforcement models that would work for Western Africa may be difficult to find or even adapt. A tailored approach is certainly needed. But observing things on the ground beyond the export control horizon gives us interesting leads on where to find foundations to build it upon. The Western African context is not just a source of limitation, it is also a source of opportunities to tackle this challenging subject in this challenging context.

---

12 The authorised economic operator (AEO) certificate is an internationally recognised quality mark indicating the companies' role in the international supply chain is secure, and that its internal customs controls and procedures are efficient and compliant. It derives from WCO Framework of Standards guidelines and entitles operators to get customs benefits and trade facilitations along the international supply chain.

13 Through the clearance process, Customs officers are in a unique position to intimately know the trade going through their border crossing point.

14 Explosives precursors may be controlled in the framework of the WCO/Interpol/ UNODC Global Shield Program, which aims to thwart the smuggling of precursor chemicals that could be used to build improvised explosive devices (IED).

Part II

… Without Standardising

From Global Straggler to Regional Exemplar

Japan's Export Control System 1990-present

Crystal D. PRYOR

PhD Candidate – University of Washington

In this chapter, I offer a brief update on the progress of US export control reform and an in-depth description of the contemporary Japanese export control system. I suggest that other countries have much to learn from Japan's failures and successes in the field of export controls.

US export control system

The United States used its export control system to prevent the Soviet Union and its allies from gaining a military advantage during the Cold War. The Export Administration Act of 1979 formed the basis of this system. The export control system grew less effective and more cumbersome in the post-Cold War period, causing businesspeople, bureaucrats, and politicians to press for reform. In 2009, the Obama Administration finally launched a comprehensive review of the system. People assigned to this task included representatives from the Departments of State, Defence, Commerce, Energy, Treasury, Justice, Homeland Security, and the Office of the Director of National Intelligence.[1]

In April 2010, then-Defence Secretary Robert M. Gates proposed a new system based on what the government has called the "four singularities, which signifies 1) a single export control list, 2) a single licencing agency for munitions and dual-use items and technologies, 3) a single enforcement coordination agency, and 4) a single integrated information technology (IT) infrastructure". As of March 2014, the government is now in phase two of three of export control reform.

1 US Department of State, "Export Control Reform Update", 24 July 2013. See: http://www.state.gov/t/pm/rls/rm/2013/212545.htm (accessed 7 March 2014).

Update on export control reform progress

Prior to reform, multiple departments responsible for processing licences on sensitive technologies and too many dual-use items on the US Munitions List (USML) strained the export control system to the breaking point. The Department of State controls the export of defence articles and services on the USML while the Department of Commerce licences items on the Commerce Control List (CCL), which primarily covers dual-use items and some military items of lesser sensitivity. (The Department of Defence is deeply involved in the export control process but does not issue licences). The Export Control Reform (ECR) initiative is implementing the creation of a single export control list in three phases. In phase two, the government has been rationalising the USML and CCL lists such that they use common terminologies and structures in preparation for merging them. The first changes in the control lists took place in October 2013, on aircraft and gas turbine engines. According to the government, "these two control categories account for the largest volume of US export licences and represent the highest percentage of licenced exports from 43 countries, with licenced shipments of almost 21 billion Dollars a year. These two categories also account for the largest amount (75%) of USML export licences approved solely for parts and components".[2] Ultimately, the government plans on updating every category of defence articles to better meet current national security and economic challenges. Many of the items moved to the CCL are now eligible for export without specific licences as long as their intended end-use is by governments of 36 US allies and partners, while items remaining on the USML are still subject to the most stringent controls. The government has been careful to note that that all of the controlled items on either list remain subject to the same US arms embargoes as before.[3] Indeed, in February 2014, the ECR tightened existing arms embargoes, especially against human rights violators.

In March 2012, the government opened the Export Enforcement Coordination Centre (EECC) within the Department of Homeland Security as part of the effort to create a single export enforcement coordination centre. The Department of Defence has used the export licencing database and software platform "USXPORTS" to track licence applications referred to it. In July 2013, the Department of State transferred over to USXPORTS. The Department of Commerce is slated to begin using

2 The White House Office of the Press Secretary, "Fact Sheet: Announcing the Revised U.S. Export Control System", 15 October 2013. http://www.whitehouse.gov/the-press-office/2013/10/15/fact-sheet-announcing-revised-us-export-control-system (accessed 7 March 2014).

3 "Fact Sheet: Announcing the Revised US Export Control System".

USXPORTS in early 2014, although as of this writing it has not yet transitioned. The end goal is for these three largest departments involved in export licencing to move to a single IT system for better coordination among them.

The Obama Administration has not yet offered a proposal concerning the creation of a single licencing agency, "although elements of a future single system such as the consolidated screening list and harmonisation of certain licencing policies have been achieved". The government has reportedly prepared legislation for the final stage of export control reform, but as of March 2014, has not yet introduced it to Congress.[4] In phase three, the administration is to work with Congress on legislation to conclude the reform initiative by creating a single export control agency and consolidating some of the enforcement units.

More than 30 years after its original implementation and in a move many felt was long overdue, the United States is currently overhauling its export control system. How long it will take to complete phase two and conclude with phase three depends on how easily legislation passes through Congress – a new administration may be in power by the time export control reform finally finishes. Nevertheless, the government has already enacted many important changes that are having a major impact on bureaucracy and business.

Japanese export control system

Japan has a well-developed export control system. It was an original member of the Coordinating Committee for Export Controls (COCOM) (and the subsequent Wassenaar Arrangement), the Nuclear Suppliers Group, the Missile Technology Control Regime, and the Australia Group. Japan bases its national control list on the lists of each of these international regimes plus the EU Dual-Use Control Regime list. And while Japan was slow to implement them, it also now practices catch-all controls.

Two elements distinguish Japan's contemporary export control system from peer countries. The first is its ban on the export of arms. Japan has a long history of controlling exports of weapons and sensitive military technology. In 1967, the Prime Minister introduced a Japanese government policy of "Three Principles" for restricting arms exports, and these principles still are in effect today. These guidelines state that Japan shall not export weapons to 1) communist countries, 2) countries subject to an arms embargo authorised by the UN Security Council, or 3) countries

[4] I. Fergusson, P. Kerr, "The U.S. Export Control System and the President's Reform Initiative", Congressional Research Service (13 January 2014).

engaged in, or likely to be engaged in, international conflict. The second element unique to the Japanese system is a third-party organisation that interfaces between the government and corporations on export controls. I believe that other countries could benefit from a greater understanding of how this organisation works.

Although it has received less attention than the American and European systems, a review of Japan's historical and current experience with export controls may provide relevant "best-practices" for African States currently developing their own export control systems in line with UN Security Council Resolution 1540 (2004). In the remainder of this chapter, I offer an overall picture of how the Japanese export control system works, then focus on the aspects that could serve as a model for other countries. I close with the challenges in export controls that Japan continues to face.

Major events

At least two international events are of great importance to understanding the trajectory of the Japanese export control system. In the Toshiba Machinery Incident of 1987 (also known as the Toshiba-Kongsberg Scandal), the United States discovered that the Toshiba Machinery company had been exporting machine tools to the Soviet Union. The Soviet Union used these machine tools to improve its submarine propeller production capabilities, making them harder to detect. The export was domestically illegal because Toshiba Machinery and Kongsberg Trade (a Norwegian company to which Toshiba contracted) submitted false end certificates to obtain export licences. This export also went against COCOM rules. The discovery of these illegal exports caused an international uproar, and especially drew the United States' ire as it saw Japan as aiding the Soviet enemy with these technologies.

Japan's response to its lax oversight of its exports was the establishment of internal compliance programmes, or ICP, a system through which Japanese civilian companies that produce and/or export high-tech products regulate themselves. It also led to the creation of the Centre for Information on Strategic Trade Control, or CISTEC, the third-party research organisation for security export controls I discuss in detail later in this chapter. As in many other countries across the globe, the events of 11 September 2001, also strengthened Japan's focus on terrorism and the threat of WMD proliferation.

Other major reforms

In recent years, Japan has made three major reforms to its export control system. First, the Japanese government passed legislation for its first brokering and transshipment controls in 2006, implementing them in 2007. This legislation was in direct response to UNSC Resolution 1540. Second, the government issued an amendment of the Foreign Exchange and Foreign Trade Act in April of 2009, enacting it in November 2009. The main points of amendment were reviewing export controls on technology transfers, strengthening penalties, and establishing standards for the Internal Compliance Programme. Third, in December 2011, the ruling party, the Democratic Party of Japan (DPJ), decided to begin relaxing the ban on arms exports – the "Three Principles" described earlier. The current party in power, the Liberal Democrat Party (LDP), is moving forward with this policy. Under the new arms exports laws, arms exports are now permissible for two reasons: 1) peace contribution and international cooperation; and 2) international joint development and production under strict control. The reasons behind this reform in arms exports are twofold. First, they allow Japanese manufacturers to participate more readily in joint development projects with allied nations. Second, allowing exports brings down development costs, a concern for most developed countries with defence industries.

Since the initial relaxing of the arms export ban in 2011, Japan announced that it would cooperate with the United Kingdom to jointly research and develop "arms" like chemical protective suits. In March 2013, Japan's Cabinet announced plans to participate in an F-35 joint strike fighter production and parts procurement programme. Importantly, arms export licence applications are still under a de facto "policy of denial" unless governments are involved in the export process. As such, Japanese defence contractors do not seek to become global arms suppliers. Therefore, it is unlikely that Japan will become a major exporter of arms in the near future, but this policy shift is perhaps some indication that Japan is becoming a more military-oriented power in the region. Japan also continues to be one of the world's largest producers of dual-use technologies.

Legal basis: law and acts

A general trade law, the Foreign Exchange and Foreign Trade Act (Law No. 228; "Gaitame-ho" or the "Trade Law"), enacted in December 1949, forms the legal basis for Japan's export controls. Article 25 covers technologies, while Article 48 covers goods. Legislation supporting the act includes (1) Cabinet Orders, (2) Ministerial Orders, and (3) notifications and guidance. The most important statutes under the Act are two Cabinet Orders: the Export Trade Control Order (ETCO, or "Yushutsu-rei") and the Foreign Exchange Order (FEO, or "Gaitame-rei"). The ETCO refers to controlled *goods* (Article 25 of the Trade Law) while FEO specifies controlled *technologies* (Article 48 of the Trade Law). Ministerial

Orders provide details like the specification and interpretation of listed items. Finally, notifications and guidance/notices (interpretations) sit below Ministerial Orders in Japan's legal structure. CISTEC notes that Japan's multi-layer legal structure, although pervasive in the Japanese legal system, makes any regulatory change in export controls difficult to implement.[5] CISTEC therefore proposed in 2010 to shift legal delegation for issues such as amending the control list from Cabinet Orders to the lower levels of Ministerial Ordinances and Notifications.[6] Although the Japanese legal structure differs from the United States, its actual practices resemble the US Department of Commerce's administration of the Export Administration Regulations (EAR; the licencing policy implementing the Export Administration Act).[7]

Administrative structure

The administration of Japan's export control system is more streamlined than that of the United States, where the Commerce, State, and Defence departments and many other agencies have a major say in the export control process. Japan issues about the same number of licences as the United Kingdom or France, a figure drastically smaller than that of the United States.[8] In Japan, the Ministry of Economy, Trade and Industry (METI) is the main player in export controls, although the Ministry of Foreign Affairs (MOFA) has some input and represents Japan at the multilateral export control regimes, while the Ministry of Defence deals with export controls on arms specifically.[9] Although METI is the main ministry handling the majority of Japan's export control licencing, it has a relatively small number of bureaucrats working on export controls. About one hundred officers work on export controls, including those in regional offices.[10]

---

5 CISTEC, "Overview of Japan's Export Controls (Third Edition)", (October 2012) p. 5.

6 CISTEC, "Request for a Comprehensive Review of Japan's Security Export Control Legal System", (17 October 2010), p. 4.

7 Pillsbury, Winthrop, Shaw, Pittman, "Nuclear Export Controls" (October 2012), http://www.nei.org/corporatesite/media/filefolder/ExportControlsComparativeAnalysis.pdf (accessed 7 March 2014).

8 US Governmental Accountability Office, "Export Controls: Observations on Selected Countries' Systems and Proposed Treaties", 2010. According to a 2014 Congressional Research Service (CRS) report, in FY2012, BIS processed 23,229 export licence applications worth about 204.1 billion Dollars, 113.6 billion Dollars of which were licences for crude oil exports.

9 Currently, the Ministry of Defence only has experience with processing the "export" of US military items from Japan to the United States for repair, overhauls, etc. Not surprisingly, no organisation can currently support MOD on export control matters.

10 "Overview of Japan's Export Controls", p. 3.

There are three units within METI, all under the Trade Control Department, involved in export control administration: (1) the Security Export Control Policy Division, responsible for export control policy setting, legislation and overall administration; (2) the Security Export Licencing Division, responsible for issuing licences; and (3) the Security Export Inspection Office, responsible for enforcement, inspections and educational activity to prevent illegal exports.

Types of controls

Like many other countries, Japan has a control list based on the multilateral export control regimes. Exporters must obtain a licence if they want to export any item on the control list. Japan's control list has 16 total categories: 1 category for military items, 14 categories for dual-use technologies (4 WMD-related and 11 conventional-arms related), plus a catch-all control which includes items not in these 15 categories.

Commodity Watch List

The government first published the Commodity Watch List in 2003. Besides the 15 categories of sensitive items on Japan's standard control list, an additional 40 are on the Commodity Watch List. These are items with high risk of diversion for the development of WMD or their delivery, including items like tributyl phosphate (TBP), carbon fibre, titanium alloys, filament winding machines, and gyroscopes. In 2013, Japan also added 12 items of specific concern (such as certain chemicals) for export to Syria. Exporters are required to check and verify the end-use and end-user carefully when exporting any of the 40 items or transferring any related technologies. Exporters are not required to apply for a licence for technologies on the Commodity Watch List, but are responsible for ensuring their appropriate end-use before export.

Furthermore, when exporting any items on the Commodity Watch List to any organisation listed on Japan's End User List, a licence is required if WMD use agrees between the watch list and the end user. For example, the exporter must obtain a licence when exporting a missile-related item on the Commodity Watch List to a missile-related entity on the End User List.

End-User Lists and Categories of Export Destinations

Japan has two ways of categorising end-users, by destination country ("white countries", "non-sensitive countries", UN arms embargo countries, and "countries of concern") and by a foreign end-user list that enumerates specific entities. These categories are as follows:

White Countries (countries with strict export control practices – 27 total)

Argentina, Australia, Austria, Belgium, Bulgaria (*most recent addition*), Canada, Czech Republic, Denmark, Finland, France, Germany, Greece, Hungary, Ireland, Italy, Republic of Korea, Luxembourg, Netherlands, New Zealand, Norway, Poland, Portugal, Spain, Sweden, Switzerland, United Kingdom, the United States.

UN Arms Embargo Countries

Afghanistan, DR Congo, Cote D'Ivoire, Eritrea, Iraq, Lebanon, Liberia, Sierra Leone, Syria, N. Korea, Somalia, Sudan.

"Countries of Concern"

Iran, Iraq, North Korea.

Non-Sensitive Countries

Countries not under UN embargo or Iran, Iraq, North Korea.

Foreign end-user list

Not an embargo list, but as of late 2013, lists 452 entities for which there is concern about WMD.

Catch-all controls

While late to the game, Japan has also developed catch-all controls. Japan originally had a "know" system, which held that a company that suspects its goods may be used for military purposes is required to consult with the government and apply for an export licence. The government first introduced a form of catch-all controls in 1996 as "Complementary Controls", in which 87 specific items were listed as those subject to control. In that sense, this system was like an extension of the List Control, or what CISTEC has called a "Catch-Some Control."

The government introduced the present style of WMD Catch-All Controls in 2002, replacing the "Complementary Controls", and further introduced the Military Catch-All Controls in 2008.[11] Exporters must obtain a licence 1) when aware item could contribute to WMD, or 2) when informed by METI to do so. The catch-all controls apply to: 1) all non-white countries and entities on the foreign end-user list; and 2) the "Commodity Watch List."

With the current catch-all controls, exporters have to obtain a licence if requested (or "informed") by METI to do so with respect to a specific export transaction. When METI believes there is a considerable risk that the item in question will be used for the development, manufacture, use, or storage of WMD, this constitutes the "informed" condition. Meanwhile, a

[11] "Overview of Japan's Export Controls".

"know/objective" condition generally corresponds to the "know" condition adopted by Western countries. Exporters must apply for a licence if:

1) Exporters have come to know that the items will be used for the development, manufacture, use, storage, etc. of WMD.
2) Exporters have come to know that the end user is/was involved in a WMD-related programme through relevant documents such as Foreign End User List, except for when the item in question will clearly be used for a purpose other than WMD-related activities.

Brokering and transshipment

In June 2007, METI enacted regulations to control WMD-related brokering and transshipment services. METI introduced these new regulations to meet the requirements of the UNSC Resolution 1540. The brokering control was further enhanced in April 2009.[12] Any transshipment or brokering of arms-related technology now requires a licence.

Licencing

Exporters submit licence applications to METI's security export licencing divisions; the officers review the application and check the end-use and end-user of the technology, and then will issue a licence if the export does not contribute to the design, development, or production of WMD.

In 2012, Japan made a major revision to its licencing rules. Before 1st April 2012, as a condition to grant an Individual Export Licence for certain sensitive products, METI required an applicant to submit two end-use assurances – one from the end-user and the other from the applicant. In this scheme, besides the WMD-related end-use assurance, end-users had to declare that they would never re-export, re-sell or re-locate the products without prior consent of the exporter. Exporters also had to assure METI that if they received a request for prior consent from the end-user, they would inform METI and prohibit the end-user from re-transferring without approval from the authorities.

After the 2012 revision, only the end-user has to make an assurance, and for this METI provides a prescribed end-use certificate (EUC) form, which the end-user needs only to fill in and sign. The end-use must also provide a statement, "Notice relating to the End-Use Certificate". The practical significance of this change is that because the end-user's assurance is now given directly to MET instead of through the exporter, in principle the government no longer holds the exporter responsible for any breach of the assurance by the end-user.

---

12 *Idem.*

Licence types

Like many countries, Japan has two major licence types. The individual licence is transaction-based while the bulk licence is valid for multiple transactions for 3 years. The exporter is supposed to practice controls on bulk licence exports. According to CISTEC statistics (2010), 12,000 individual licences are applied for each year.[13] To obtain a bulk export licence, exporters must:

1. Establish an appropriate internal control system based on internal compliance programme (ICP) and submit it to METI,
2. Implement controls complying strictly with the ICP, and
3. Participate in seminars held by METI.

The type of licence (such as individual, white country bulk, special general bulk, and special bulk licences) METI will issue to the exporter depends on the item's control list category and the destination country (whether it is a white country, a non-sensitive country, etc.).[14]

Penalties

As mentioned above, the Japanese government strengthened penalties for violating export control laws in the April 2009 amendment to the Trade Act. The minimum imprisonment term is now 10 years, and the fine at least 7 million JPY (approximately 70,000 US Dollars) for export control violations. If the export control violation WMD-related, the minimum imprisonment term is 10 years while the minimum fine is 10 million JPY (approximately 100,000 US Dollars) or five times the value of the export. Companies face a ban on exporting or transferring technology for at least three years, and the government makes a public statement about the violation, thus potentially damaging the company's reputation.

Institutions supporting METI

The existence of internal compliance programmes and CISTEC make Japan's rationalised bureaucratic structure possible and are therefore are advantageous elements of an efficient export control system.[15] Here I provide details on these institutions.

---

13 METI outreach presentation, "Overview of Japanese Export Control Legal Framework" (2013).

14 For more details, see: "Changes to Japan's export licencing system", *WorldECR*, No. 15 (September 2012), p. 17.

15 As a close associate of METI, CISTEC has provided services for exporters, but its focus has been on dual-use items. This may change in the future as arms exports grow.

Internal compliance programmes (ICP)

CISTEC inaugurated a compliance programme model in 1996. Since 2003, companies that create and maintain their own compliance programmes and register with METI can have their names published on the METI website. This is designed as an incentive for companies to develop their own compliance programmes. Until 2009, exporters only had to have an ICP if they wanted to obtain a bulk licence, but after the 2009 Trade Act amendment, all exporters must observe ICP standards. While most countries with developed export control systems incorporate government-industry outreach and internal compliance programmes, Japan's ICP system is somewhat unique in that all major technology exporters are expected to have an internal export control system with the following nine elements put forth by METI:

1. Standard company principles for export control;
2. Control and responsibility systems in the company organisation;
3. Company procedures for determining export propriety;
4. A shipping control system;
5. An internal inspection system;
6. An education and training system for employees;
7. A document control system;
8. A guiding system for subsidiary companies and associated companies;
9. Penalties for breaches of company regulations.

The ICP exist so companies 1) strictly comply with the export control act and regulations when exporting goods or transferring technologies; and 2) establish their own internal programmemes for export control, which cover management policy, export control organisation, procedure, shipment confirmation, internal audit, training, record keeping, etc. METI also annually issues an Export Control Compliance Self-Check List to companies. As of 2012, approximately 1,600 ICP had registered, and METI's website published 570 names as "compliant companies".

METI says the ICP are beneficial for the government because they reduce violations, allowing it to concentrate on more sensitive cases; and beneficial for the companies because they get public recognition as "good exporters" and can minimize the risk of mistakes and streamline procedures. The most obvious benefit, however, is the reduction of work on the part of METI. There are of course potential problems with relying so heavily on companies to regulate themselves, given their market-driven economic interest in bolstering exports, although so far these issues have not surfaced in an obvious way.

Government-academia relations

In recent years, government concern (specifically METI's and the Ministry of Education's concern) over the transfer of sensitive technologies and knowledge – also known as "deemed exports" or "intangible technology transfer" – has grown, as can be seen in their 2005 and 2006 requests for universities to strengthen their internal export control systems. Yet due to Japan's lack of arm exports and involvement in military affairs, many lament that Japanese people, especially academics, lack adequate security awareness. Furthermore, METI, with its greater business and security expertise, sometimes butts heads with the Ministry of Education on deemed export policies. It is, however, significant that export controls figure into Japan's first-ever National Security Strategy 2014 and its National Defence Programmeme Guidelines for FY2014 and beyond. Raising awareness about export controls in academia is an ongoing process underway in other countries including the United States.

CISTEC

CISTEC (the Centre for Information on Security Trade Control) is unique to Japan and key to the efficient functioning of Japan's export control system. Founded in April 1989 after the Toshiba-Krongsberg scandal, it is the only non-profit organisation dedicated to the promotion of export controls in Japan. CISTEC functions as a liaison between the government, industry, and academia, and provides a variety of export control forums where people get together, exchange information, and sometimes engage in debate. For more than two decades, CISTEC has been playing a pivotal role in making Japan's export controls efficient and effective through a wide variety of activities.

Despite its role in keeping the number of bureaucrats at METI devoted to strategic export controls small, CISTEC itself is by no means a large organisation. As of September 2012, it employs approximately 40 staff members and operates on an annual budget of roughly 6 million US Dollars, a little less than half of which comes from membership fees, and the rest from revenues of its own activities. As of March 2014, the organisation has 408 associate members including major exporting companies and research institutes.[16] CISTEC representatives claim their membership includes all major Japanese exporters of dual-use technologies.

Such a third party institution dedicated to forging ties between industry and the government is unique globally and therefore may provide a model

16 CISTEC, "CISTEC Associate Members List", available from http://www.cistec.or.jp/english/about/members.pdf (accessed 7 March 2014).

for countries in Africa and beyond, particularly as it is self-supporting and can reduce the government's burden associated with implementing export controls.

CISTEC's roles

CISTEC has two major roles. The first is *promoting export compliance*. CISTEC does this through, for example, a seminar series, of which they offer 34 a year (25 general export compliance seminars and 9 events on laws and regulations). They also offer a training and certification programme for professionals. As of 2012, there were 12,483 "associate" status holders, 147 of "legal expert" status, and 285 of "expert" status.[17] CISTEC also facilitates knowledge transfer through activities such as publishing journals and articles on current issues. CISTEC's other major role is *representing industry*, both before government and internationally, seeking to create a favourable environment for Japanese exporters.

CISTEC and industry

As part of its industry representation, CISTEC lobbies METI on behalf of its members. It submits comprehensive "letters" to METI that point out flaws and issues in the Japanese export control system and propose reforms. In 2010, CISTEC submitted a letter to METI on behalf of Japanese industries entitled "Request for a Comprehensive Review of Japan's Security Export Control Legal System", which they followed with a similar letter in 2012. CISTEC seeks harmonisation of export controls worldwide and to promote Japanese companies' export interests before METI and the international community.

CISTEC also works in cooperation with the industry groups Keidanren (the Japan Business Federation), the Japan Machinery Centre for Trade and Investment (JMC), and the Japan Foreign Trade Council, Inc. (JFTC).

CISTEC committees

Committees are at the core of CISTEC's activities. The Export Control Research Committee has two research boards – the Policy, Rules and Procedures Board; and the Goods and Materials Board – which each have various subcommittees established for specific research themes. Through the committees, CISTEC channels industry opinions and consolidates them into public comments and proposals to the government. Members of each committee are from private companies, and these active corporate members sustain CISTEC's activities.

---

17 I.J. Stewart, "Antiproliferation: Tackling Proliferation by Engaging the Private Sector", Harvard Kennedy School Belfer Center, November 2012.

Outreach to Asia

CISTEC also takes part in METI's international outreach activity in Asia, especially in countries like Malaysia and Thailand in Southeast Asia, which are still developing their export controls but with which Japan has significant economic and business ties. In collaboration with the authorities, CISTEC annually holds the Asian Export Control Seminar in Tokyo and Industry Outreach Seminars in various countries in the Asian region.

Another example of outreach is CISTEC's secondment of an official to Hong Kong's MTI's export control department. This seconding system transferred CISTEC's Model Compliance Programme (CP). The Hong Kong government now provides Model CP for local industry. The Japanese government also helped establish the liaison group, an informal group for exchanging information and providing Hong Kong industry feedback to its government.

Reforms in progress at CISTEC

Certain reforms that CISTEC had proposed to METI in its 2010 and 2012 letters are underway. One significant reform is matching Japanese control lists with the European ECCN system. Currently, the controlled items in Japan are identified by classification numbers that are specific to Japan and different from the European Export Control Classification Numbers (ECCN), which are now the international standard. CISTEC anticipates that rationalisation will have a number of benefits, including:

(1) For each controlled item, it will become easier to conduct one-on-one classification comparison between the Japanese list and the EU list.

(2) Japanese exporters can easily share product classification information with overseas companies with the same basis of understanding.

(3) It will become easier to check the differences between national control lists and between Japan and the international export control regimes.

(4) Classification of imported goods will become easier.

Another reform that METI intends to introduce is a system of Voluntary Self Disclosure in which a penalty on any self-disclosed violation will be mitigated under certain conditions. METI is already partially implementing this system as a trial.[18]

Reforms in progress at METI

18 "Overview of Japan's Export Controls", p. 44.

Moving forward, the biggest challenge for METI, and the ultimate goal of Japanese industry, is the establishment of a new single Export Control Act coupled with Export Control Regulations. This would mean breaking away from the current system built under the Foreign Exchange and Foreign Trade Act. CISTEC argues that the legal framework should be redesigned in light of a new reality, and that export controls should focus not on "item classification" but on "end-use screening", which it sees as critical in today's non-proliferation efforts.

Other fundamental challenges in Japan's export control system include Japan's lack of an intelligence-gathering service, although this may be changing with the recent development of its surveillance satellites. The lack of intelligence means that Japan has to rely on foreign countries for information on the actual end-use of its exports. Furthermore, Japan's system is highly reliant on private companies for its export controls. All governments rely on companies to conduct their exports legally, including the United States with its "Front Line of Defence" approach, but Japan is at the far end of the spectrum in delegating export control oversight to companies. While the Japanese government has prosecuted relatively few export control violations, this of course is not necessarily a measure of an effective system. Due to its lack of an intelligence service, Japan may not realize gaps in its system unless another country discovers illegal end-uses of Japanese technologies or goods.

Further challenges: rationalisation

Moving forward, the biggest challenge for METI and the ultimate goal of Japanese industry is the establishment of a new single Export Control Act coupled with Export Control Regulations. This would mean breaking away from the current system built under the Foreign Exchange and Foreign Trade Act. CISTEC argues that the legal framework should be redesigned in a new light of reality and that export controls should focus not on "item classification" but on "end-use screening", which it says critical in today's non-proliferation efforts.

Other fundamental challenges in Japan's export control system include Japan's lack of an intelligence-gathering service – although this may be changing with the recent development of its surveillance satellites. The lack of intelligence means that Japan has to rely on foreign countries for information on the actual end-use of its exports. Furthermore, Japan's system is highly reliant on private companies for its export controls. All governments rely on companies to legally conduct their exports, including the United States with its "Front Line of Defence" approach, but Japan is at the far end of the spectrum in delegating export control oversight to companies. While the Japanese government has prosecuted relatively few export control violations, this of course is not necessarily a measure of an effective system. Due to its lack of an intelligence service, Japan may not find out just how effective its system is unless another country discovers illegal end-uses of Japanese technologies or goods.

Conclusion

In recent years, both the United States and Japan have moved towards more rationalised export control systems. We should expect further changes in the coming years, and these reforms will likely reduce the burden on industry and government in applying for and implementing export controls, respectively. If both countries achieve their goals, they should become more economically competitive while still ensuring national and international security.

Japan recovered from a major scandal at the end of the Cold War to emerge as one of the most efficient export control systems in the world. CISTEC, a third-party organisation that interfaces between the government and corporations on the practice of export controls, may be useful to many other countries looking to reduce the government burden in conducting export control licencing, outreach, and enforcement.

Russian Dual-Use Trade Control

An Example to Follow?

Ekaterina CHIRKOVA

PhD Candidate – University of Liège

Introduction

The current system of export controls in Russia was established in the 1990s after the breakup of the Soviet Union in 1991. With the disappearance of the USSR, the gap in Russian export control laws created opportunities for some "grey market" sales and attracted States and non-state actors interested in acquiring sensitive technologies without having to comply with the restrictive export policies and regulations.[1] It raised fear in the international community and the Russian establishment of a potential accelerated spread of WMD. For Russia, an active member of the international nuclear non-proliferation system, it was vital to prove capable of respecting its commitments, maintaining its relations with other States and country's competitiveness.[2] These factors explain the Russian membership and active role in five out of the six major export control regimes (all but the Australia Group).

Non-proliferation export controls	
Zangger Committee	Member
Nuclear Suppliers Group	Member
Australia Group	
Missile Technology Control Regime	Member
Wassenaar Arrangement	Member
United Nations Security Council Resolution 1540 (2004)	Initial report submitted (26 October 2004) Second report (23 August 2005)

1 For more information see, for example: V.A. Orlov, "Export Controls in Russia: Policies and Practices", *The Non-proliferation Review*, 1999.

2 *Idem.*

The development of the system of export control and its main components

During the period 1992-1996 Russia has made significant progress in creating dual-use export control laws and regulations. To date, Russia has adopted approximately 50[3] documents related to export controls. Among them 5 federal laws, 16 executive decrees, 12 directives of the Government, 14 orders, a number of necessary amendments to the Criminal Code and Administrative Offences Code as well as related legislations such as an Environmental Directive.[4]

Finally, in July 1999, a new Federal Law on Export Controls (FLEC) was signed by President Yeltsin and entered into force, concluding the creation of a national legal system of export controls.

The Law on Export Controls and associated legal documents mainly concerns dual-use items while military items are covered by a separate set of laws. Among them is the federal law on "military-technical cooperation with foreign States" adopted on 3 July 1998, which sets out the regulatory principles. It is much more restrictive than the general export control regulations items and specifies that "only 'national negotiators', State-owned or partly State-owned companies which are authorised by the President of the Russian Federation to participate in military-technical cooperation, are entitled to ship military products abroad".[5] However, some dual-use items that were previously used for military purposes can be exported only by the State agents.

More precisely, FLEC (as amended in 2007) specifies the following controlled goods and technologies: "crude resource, materials, equipment, scientific and technical information, work, services, and the results of intellectual activity that could, by virtue of their distinctive features and properties contribute substantially to the development of weapons of mass destruction, their delivery systems, and other types of weapons and

---

3 The number mentioned in this article represents the documents specified on the official website of the Federal Service for Technical and Export Control: http://fstec.ru. According to different sources, the exact number varies. For example, A. Grave (2008) mentions 300 legal acts related to export control of nuclear materials, including international agreements and conventions signed by the Russian Federation. For more information see: A. Grave, A. Petrenko, "Export Controls in Russia and Security of International Nuclear Material Transportation", Security Index No. 3 (86), Issue 14, PIR Center for Policy Studies, Moscow, 2008, p. 86.

4 For more information see the official website of the Federal Service for Technical and Export Control of Russia at http://fstec.ru/en/.

5 I. Zotkin, C. Bastien, G. Mardian, "Chapter 10. Russian Federation", in Aubin & Idiart (eds.), *Export Control Law and Regulations Handbook*, Kluwer Law International BV, The Netherlands, 2007, pp. 261-287.

military equipment".[6] There are six lists of dual-use items to be regulated that correspond to the lists of the international regimes and should be approved by the President. The lists enter into force no earlier than three months after the date of their official publication. They cover:

- Nuclear materials, equipment, special non-nuclear materials and related technologies;
- Equipment and dual-use items and related technologies used for nuclear purposes;
- Goods and dual-use technologies that can be used to create weapons and military equipment;
- Equipment, materials and technologies that can be used to produce missiles;
- Chemicals, equipment and technologies that can be used to produce chemical weapons;
- Micro-organisms, toxins, equipment and technologies.

The main purposes of the control are to protect the interests of the Russian Federation; to satisfy the requirements of international treaties of the Russian Federation pertaining to the non-proliferation of WMD and their delivery systems and to the control of exports of military and dual-use products; to create the necessary conditions for the integration of the Russian economy into the world economy.[7]

The set of activities regulated by the Law is also quite comprehensive. It focuses on foreign economic activities in general which include "foreign trade, investment, and other activity, including cooperative production, in the international exchange of goods, information, work, services, and the results of intellectual activity, including the exclusive rights to them (intellectual property)".[8] Transfer of technology by post, e-mail or other communication means is also covered by the law and requires a special authorisation. However, comparing to the EU export control regulations, brokering is not well defined in the Law.[9]

All aspects of export control operations are under the exclusive jurisdiction of the Russian Federation. Chapter II of FLEC gives a legal basis of organisation of export control, specifying the powers of different governmental bodies and specially established agencies (such as Export Control

6 Federal Law on Export Control, Passed by the State Duma on 22 June 1999 and Approved by the Federal Council on 2 July 1999, Article 1 "Basic Terminology".

7 Federal Law on Export Control, Article 4.

8 Federal Law on Export Control, Article 1.

9 See, for example: Federal Law on Export Control, Article 20.

Commission and Federal Service for Technical and Export Control, FSTEC). The following scheme describes the sector organisation:

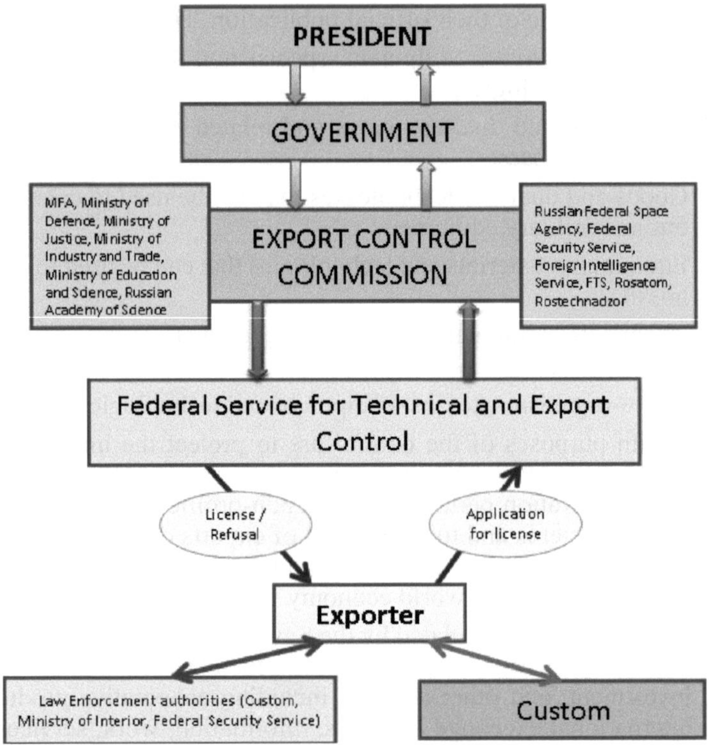

Original version (in Russian): S.V. Vladimirova (*et al.*)[10]

According to the Article 8 of FLEC, the different missions of governmental entities in the field of export control are:

> The President defines basic policy guidelines, ensures coordination between the various governmental agencies involved in the process of export control and approves the lists of controlled goods.
>
> The Government implements export control policy (including compliance with international regimes) and determines procedures for conducting foreign trade in controlled items.

10 S.V. Vladimirova (*et al.*), "Export Controls: Manual", State Scientific Center of the Russian Federation – Institute for Physics and Power Engineering named after A.I. Leypunsky (SSC IPPE), Obninsk, 2012, p. 41.

The (FSTEC) under the authority of the (Ministry of Defence) plays a prominent role; it issues licences for the export of dual-use and critical nuclear materials. The (FSTEC) has seven regional branches across the territory of the Russian Federation.

The Export Control Commission coordinates policy, implements legislation and settles disputes between different administrative bodies.

A series of ministries and federal agencies intervene in the licence delivering process: they receive the document package from the (FSTEC) and approve/disapprove the licence issuance. Their opinion is mandatory. In the event of a negative decision, the applicant will not be granted a licence. The applicant has, at this stage of the process, the opportunity to support its case by submitting explanatory documents. When deciding whether the licence should be granted, the bodies involved in the inter-agency review take into account several criteria. They consider the end-user, the technology and the item to be exported.[11]

According to this scheme and the different missions of governmental bodies, FSTEC is mainly responsible for the licencing procedure. Prior to an application for a licence at FSTEC, the exporter should obtain an obligatory certificate that classifies the item subject to an export. This independent classification procedure can be conducted through the exporter's intraorganisational export control programmemms or with a help of an organisation officially authorised to conduct this type of classification procedure (there are about 20 organisations of this sort in Russia). For the latter, the exporter "must provide a series of documents, which include evidence of the proposed end-use and guarantees that the exporter will abide by intellectual property rules, and the State's policy on official secrets".[12]

If the item is subject to export control according to the classification, the FSTEC examines the licence application within 20 days.[13] However, this period "can take up to three months, depending on whether the exporter is new to the process, the end-user is known, or the file is complete".[14] The most difficult cases are transferred to the Export Control Commission that coordinates the work of different above-mentioned governmental bodies in the field of export control.

There are two types of licences. An individual or one-time licence is issued for specific items within one contract specifying their quantity, end-user, seller and purchaser. Another type – general licence – specifies

---

11 I. Zotkin, *op. cit.*, p. 278.

12 *Ibid.*, p. 275.

13 Decree of the President of the Russian Federation No. 1085, 16 August 2004.

14 I. Zotkin, *op. cit.*, p. 276.

the quantity of goods without identifying the specific users. A general licence may be issued only to a Russian legal entity that has an intraorganisational export control programmeme (equivalent of internal compliance programmememe) and it obtains the official State certificate of its accreditation.

Transfer of technology is considered to be particularly sensitive. This is why "the Russian Federation has attempted as far as possible to subject to control as wide a range as possible of intangible technology transfer".[15] Both "data transfer" and any "technical help" may require a licence. However, technology and goods related to fundamental research are exempted from export control. Nevertheless, this does not facilitate much the export rules as it is rather difficult "to distinguish between fundamental science and applied science, and the boundary between the two is sometimes blurred and constantly moving".[16]

For temporary import/export, no licence is required on the condition that the goods and technology will remain under the direct control of the exporter and will be returned to the Russian Federation by the scheduled date. In this case, only a written authorisation letter from the Export Control Commission is needed. No licence is required for re-export or export of items/services for repair and technical support of airplanes or ships of the Russian Federation located abroad.

The transfer of certain products or technology to a foreign national in the Russian Federation – so called "deemed export" – is also covered by the export control rules.

There are also some differences in licencing procedures for particular types of items. For instance, nuclear items can have different export requirements if the contracts for their export were signed before 1992 or if there is an international agreement of the Russian Federation signed with other countries-importer about the civil use of nuclear energy. These conditions usually facilitate the export.

The Federal Law on Export Control also contains a "catch-all" clause. Article 20 "Comprehensive Control" of FLEC provides that Russian parties should renounce contacts with foreign parties "if these parties have valid reason to believe that these goods, information, work, services, and results of intellectual activity will be used by a foreign State or foreign party for the development of weapons of mass destruction and their delivery system".[17]

---

15 *Idem.*

16 *Idem.*

17 Federal Law on Export Control, Article 20 (1).

To classify the products as well as to comply with the export control regulations, Russian exporters can implement an intraorganisational export control programme with the assistance of Federal agencies of the executive branch of Russian government. Such programmes are "mandatory for organisations conducting scientific and (or) production activity for the satisfaction of Federal State needs in connection with the maintenance of the defensive capabilities and security of the Russian Federation and regularly earning income from foreign economic operations with controlled goods and technologies".[18] Once implemented, they should however receive an official accreditation from the Government.

In case of non-compliance, the exporter or an authorised organisation that conducted a classification procedure are liable. According to the Article 31 of FLEC, "the officials of organisations and citizens guilty of violations of laws of the Russian Federation in the sphere of export control will be subject to criminal, administrative, and civil legal penalties in accordance with laws of the Russian Federation".[19] There are different forms of punishment provided by the Russian legal system. In cases where the Criminal Code applies, usually the head of the legal entity is liable and can be sentenced for up to 7 years of imprisonment. However, there were only few cases where this measure was really applied. Organisations violating laws will be subject to a fine in the amount of the value of the exported tangible or intangible goods "representing the direct objects of the violations".[20] Furthermore, an organisation violating the law can be deprived of the right to conduct certain types of foreign economic activity for up to three years in case the violations result "in the infliction of considerable injury on the political and economic interests of the Russian Federation, national defence, and state security, or in the case of a repeated offense".[21]

Custom control: Eurasian Custom Union

The Russian Federation is a member of the Eurasian Custom Union (ECU) that was established in January 2010. Other members are Belarus and Kazakhstan. Armenia, Kyrgyzstan, Tajikistan and Ukraine could be considered potential members of the Union. Though, for instance the goods turnover of the Russian Federation together with the members of the ECU is lower than with the EU. According to the World Bank

18 Federal Law on export Control, Article 16.

19 Federal Law on Export Control, Article 31.

20 Federal Law on Export Control, Article 32.

21 Federal Law on Export Control, Article 32.

2013 Doing Business Survey,[22] "the three members of the ECU are ranked in the bottom third when it comes to trading across borders, with Kazakhstan ranked 182nd, Russia 162nd, and Belarus 151st in the world out of 185 countries".[23] According to the World Bank, "these rankings are due mainly to high costs (measured in US dollars per container), the time it takes to export and import (measured in days), and also the large number of necessary documents".[24]

The ECU had initiated efforts to harmonise the export control rules in 2011 but did not move far since. Moreover, the Russian Federation and Belarus have had a bilateral agreement since April 1999 calling for the development of a single procedure for export controls in both countries. Nonetheless, according to the expert data, "there remains (…) a significant lack of effective and compatible controls between the Russian Federation and Belarus (and among the Newly Independent States (NIS) in general), mainly because they have different perceptions of what poses a threat to their countries" as well as due to the rudimentary export control systems in certain NIS.[25]

The Draft Agreement on Common System of Export Controls (2011) of the ECU provides common definitions of import/export, foreign economic activities, export control, internal shipment, controlled items and technology, transit, etc. It also defines a single list of controlled goods that should be developed by the Custom Union Commission and then approved by the Intergovernmental Council of the Eurasian Economic Community (heads of the Member States).[26] Military items are not covered by this Agreement. Article 6 of the Agreement is a "catch-all" clause.

Licences are issued by a designated body of the State, on the territory of which the exporter permanently resides. Licences for import, export or transfer issued by one Member State of the ECU are valid on the territory of all other members according to the Draft Agreement.[27] However, a Member State of the ECU cannot issue an export licence for controlled items originated from another Member State without a written agreement of the latter, unless this Member State or any of its entities

22 See: http://doingbusiness.org/rankings.

23 World Bank, "2013 Doing Business Survey, in Carneiro, F.G., What Promises Does the Eurasian Customs Union Hold for the Future?", Economic Premise No. 108, World Bank, February 2013, p. 4.

24 F. Carneiro, *op. cit.*

25 I. Zotkin, *op. cit.*, p. 263.

26 Draft Agreement on Common System of Export Controls of the States-Members of the Custom Union, 9 December 2011, Article 4.

27 Draft Agreement on Common System of Export Controls (2011), Article 10.

has rights for these items or technologies according to the Agreement on common understanding of rights and regulations of the property relations of 9 October 1992.[28]

The Agreement also provides for the cooperation and assistance in export controls,[29] consultations as well as exchange of information between the Member States regarding the denials of export of those items that are not included in the single list. While the Member States would still have certain independence in the decision-making process, the Agreement specifies that any denials or limitations with regards to trade should not undermine the level-playing field between the members of the ECU and third countries.[30] Any disputes falling under this Agreement should be brought to the Court of the Eurasian Economic Community.[31]

According to the World Bank, harmonised rules for regulating trade should reduce production costs for exports and imports, eliminate trade borders within the Custom Union, reduce the bureaucratic load (amount of documents required for import and export), as well as reduce corruption and potentially help strengthen economic and political institutions.[32]

Russian export controls model: pros and cons

Recent assessments indicate that Russia has made significant progress in creating its export control system. According to the Nuclear Threat Initiative's (NTI) "Nuclear Materials Security Index", Russian implementation of United Nations Security Council Resolution 1540 ranks above average. The main focus of the index is on the security of nuclear materials. The factors that are taken into consideration are compliance with UNSC Resolution 1540 reporting requirements and implementation of UNSC Resolution 1540. Russia's score is 80 over 100 (same as USA).[33]

Russia offers general legal and implementation assistance with export controls to countries of the CIS and the EEC.[34]

There are still, however, certain problems and challenges of the system that continue to raise concerns over illicit trafficking from Russia. For instance, Russia has been slow to incorporate many of the relevant

28 Draft Agreement on Common System of Export Controls (2011), Article 8.

29 Draft Agreement on Common System of Export Controls (2011), Article 17.

30 Draft Agreement on Common System of Export Controls (2011), Article 15.

31 Draft Agreement on Common System of Export Controls (2011), Article 21.

32 F. Carneiro, *op. cit.*, p. 4.

33 See: http://ntiindex.org/countries/russia/.

34 "Offers from Member States – Russian Federation", in "Russia 1540 Reporting", Center for Non-proliferation Studies, NTI, 5 March 2013.

provisions into national law, which has minimised its intended impact. There is also a certain lack of will to enforce the laws that makes the enforcement mechanism lax and less transparent. Moreover, inefficient and infrequent communication among different agencies creates additional problems for check-and-balances.

Widespread corruption[35] is still a serious problem in Russia in many sectors, including export control. Lobbying by exporters "interested in maximum profit in the shortest period of time without due understanding of consequences that may result from illegal commercial activities"[36] creates an additional problem for the implementation of Export Control policies in Russia. Lack of a non-proliferation culture in general as well as financial and technical problems have also contributed to the gap between policy and practice. Russia's vast territory coupled with regional factors such as the neighbour's poor export control regimes create loopholes in the system.

Conclusions

The analysis of the Russian export control system shows many challenges in the implementation of the policies and enforcement of the regulatory directives. While Russia made a significant progress by the creation of its export control regime in the 1990s to prevent a growing threat of illicit trafficking in the country, its evolution is very slow. A straightforward approach chosen by the Russian government with the President on top of decision-making and implementation reveals many problems in the mechanisms of checks-and-balances as well as weak enforcement. The involvement of the exporters and of the Parliament is almost absent.

The Russian model of export control represents a well-developed "1st generation" export control system that, however, is significantly rigid and needs reforms and modifications. It contributed positively in the short term but its long-term added value could be significantly improved.

---

35 Russia ranks 127th among 175 according to the Corruption Perception Index 2013, Transparency International, http://cpi.transparency.org/cpi2013/results/.

36 *Voprosy Bezopasnosti*, No. 51, April 1999 in V. Orlov, *op. cit.*

EU as a Model, "Yes But"...

Ivana MICIC

Senior Researcher, University of Liège

The EU dual-use export control system[1] might be a useful reference to countries in the process of developing or updating their respective export controls system. However, it is important to stress that the EU system is not a "one-size-fits-all" model. States must simultaneously take their own context into account (political, economic and regional realities) when developing export control systems while also understanding the needs and dynamics of the larger international system and requirements. However some main elements could be taken away from EU standards and its EU Member States' implementation and enforcement. Indeed, their practice and experience could inspire other countries and could be used for the establishment or development of their own export control system. This chapter will highlight those potential elements by trying to depict in each case a brief picture of the practice of the different approaches across the EU.

Since the adoption of United Nations Security Council Resolution 1540 in 2004, many UN Member States are required to adopt or reform their export controls system as the Resolution places "binding obligations on all UN States to adopt legislation to prevent the proliferation of nuclear, chemical and biological weapons, and their means of delivery, and establish appropriate domestic controls over related materials to prevent their illicit trafficking" and asks States "to refrain from supporting by any means non-State actors from developing, acquiring, manufacturing, possessing, transporting, transferring or using nuclear, chemical or

1 "Export control" is commonly used terminology even if the scope is wider, controlling other activities such as import, transit, brokering, transhipment and financing. For some countries in order to encompass all activities above, the term "trade controls" is much more used. The name does not matter as long as there is a clear definition of which activities shall be controlled. This chapter will use the term export controls but it encompasses other activities too.

biological weapons and their delivery systems".[2] The Resolution goes beyond export controls per se and covers many more issues. This chapter will discuss only export controls and related activities to be controlled including penalties, as stated in point 3.d of the Resolution that each State shall:

> Establish, develop, review and maintain appropriate *effective national export and trans-shipment controls* over such items, including appropriate laws and regulations to control export, transit, trans-shipment and re-export and controls on providing funds and services related to such export and trans-shipment such as financing, and transporting that would contribute to proliferation, as well as *establishing end-user controls*; and establishing and enforcing appropriate *criminal or civil penalties* for violations of such export control laws and regulations.

Another relevant point for the chapter is point 6 calling States to "Recognizes the utility in implementing this resolution of effective national control lists and calls upon all Member States, when necessary, to pursue at the earliest opportunity the development of such lists".[3]

Following the resolution, many countries which are not significant exporters (or producers) of relevant items found themselves in a situation where they had to introduce or update their export control systems. UNSC Resolution 1540 provides the possibility to ask for assistance. One of the 1540 Committee functions is to facilitate and match requests of donors or seekers of the assistance.[4] Additionally, individual States offer support and several countries carry out cooperation programmes related to export controls such as the US Export Control and Border Security Program,[5] EU's Project of EU Outreach in Export Control of Dual-Use Items,[6] and a Japan and Australia support programme for countries' development of control systems in their region. International Organisations such as the Organisation for the prohibition of Chemical Weapons and the International Atomic Energy Agency also run some activities; as well as international export control regimes,[7] etc.

Many EU Member States' officials are active in various export control related capacity-building and assistance programmes with third countries. The EU export control system and some EU Member States' approaches

2 See: http://www.un.org/en/sc/1540/.

3 See: http://www.un.org/en/sc/1540/.

4 *Idem*.

5 See: http://www.state.gov/t/isn/ecc/c27911.htm/.

6 See: http://www.eu-outreach.info/.

7 The Wassenaar Arrangement, the Nuclear Suppliers Group, Australia Group, Missile Technology Control Regime and Zangeer Committee.

to it will serve as a reference for this chapter. During the capacity-building programmes EU Member States share their national experience in enforcement and implementation of provisions and of course the reference to the legal basis which is on the EU level.

The EU approach towards export control, i.e. EU export control system, is quite unique. The EU has one Regulation for dual-use export controls that is directly implementable in all 28 EU Member States.[8] The EU itself has updated its previous EU Regulation[9] in 2009 to upgrade the controls and update its EU Member States obligations to be in line with Resolution 1540. Controls of activities such as brokering, transit and transshipment were added as new provisions to be controlled in the new Regulation. While there is one EU Regulation on the EU level, there are 28 more or less different ways of implementing and enforcing it on the national level. Indeed, each EU MS has its particular way of approaching the enforcement according to its national policy, exports, industries, administrative capacities, transit points, etc.

Export control systems in EU Member States including implementation and enforcement were updated and adapted on a rolling basis due to the swift and continuous pace of technological development, geopolitical changes, some national scandals and shifting priorities on the national, regional and international levels. The current EU system has been evolving for more than two decades.

Trade of dual-use items "represents a significant portion of EU trade with strategic partners"[10] which reflects the importance of having an export control system in place. The purpose of establishing the EU system is also to enable the international trade of such dual-use items. Even if one country is not a big producer of controlled goods, it is important that the control system takes into general account the demands of international export control regimes or other international fora that determine this international trade. With the system established they can become a trustful trade partner and so enhance their competitiveness, credibility and trade generally. The system therefore should be a balanced system between the country's own political, national, economic and cultural features and tendency and international demands of export controls.

---

8 Council Regulation (EC) No. 428/2009 of May 2009 *setting up a Community regime for the control of exports, transfer, brokering and transit of dual-use items*.

9 Council Regulation (EC) No. 1334/2000 of June 2000 *setting up a Community regime for the control exports of dual-use items and technology*.

10 See: http://ec.europa.eu/trade/import-and-export-rules/export-from-eu/dual-use-controls/.

Export control introduction or updates – challenges

On the one hand, every country around the world should develop its export control system such that it appropriately reflects the regional, political and economic needs and realities. On the other hand, when one country is seeking to build up its own export control system, it is often confronted with donors or cooperation partners with a varying range of approaches and legislative traditions, making it challenging to determine the best way forward. EU countries have one regulation and share the same fundamental legal basis for controls of dual-use items, providing a framework for countries aiming to join the EU.[11] For other countries and regions the reference could be Resolution 1540 and some regional references, if any.

When an official from the EU Member States is giving support to a country in another region, the first thing one should be aware of is that the dual-use trade controls as understood in the EU is not understood uniformly around the world. Also, references to the EU system and the EU itself can be difficult for some countries to understand as the EU history, construction, integration and practices are not always clear. *Idem* when one refers to items to be controlled i.e. "dual-use items" which are usually perceived to be linked to weapons of mass destruction (WMD) proliferation only. All these terms and references need to be clearly explained to partner countries in need of support so they can understand the context and how the EU export control system functions. Other issues that EU MS officials might be confronted with are: that the reference for establishing export controls in the country is Resolution 1540 only – which is wider and encompasses activities beyond export controls only, and makes references to much broader issues in comparison to the EU Regulation. Indeed, Resolution 1540 refers to issues such as CBN weapons, border protection, non-state actors (interpretation of the Resolution could be that the focus is on non-state actors only), related material, production, use, storage, transport but also refers to terrorism threats and purposes, etc. Additionally, the scope and items under control can be interpreted differently than in the EU. The wider scope gives more room for different interpretations of what needs to be controlled. One interpretation could be that all items in question should be controlled, that most are hazardous or/and that all could have military or terrorist applications. From an EU perspective, all listed dual-use items are controlled but not all listed items are considered to be hazardous. Scope, items to be controlled, purpose and the terminology should be clarified from the beginning of cooperation to make sure that there is a

11 See below.

clear understanding and that the topic of discussion is understood to be the same for all parties involved. If the concerns of the one country lie in the area of import of chemicals which could be used for example for illegal production of various medications in illegal factories, the country's area of focus would be health and environment issues for its population and discussion might steer more in that direction rather than being on items that that the country might export and/or which could contribute to development, production or transport of WMD. A national system of export control that focuses on an import does not preclude also addressing export and WMD issues; one does not exclude the other. The point is that while no single system corresponds to all States' needs; elements of existing systems can be taken to help to establish the new or revised systems that reflect the States' realities and needs.

Potential elements for an export/trade control system

While there could be endless discussions about how exactly an export control system can or should look, some features seem to continuously emerge, setting common elements. These elements that one country should consider having in place are developed below; however, it should be kept in mind that these elements do not necessarily have to be all put in place and each country shall make use of them depending on its legal system, administrative capacity and national / regional priorities.

While EU Member States have a single dual-use export regulation at the EU level, they have some flexibility in national implementation of export control.

Based on the EU regulation, EU Member States intended to adapt their national system according to their needs and administrative capacities (which is not always easy to match). The advantage of the EU, when promoting export controls to a third country is that one country can pick from 28 different approaches while having in place one common umbrella (the EU Regulation) and see what would best suit its system.

Before delving into the details, one should stress that each country should have the political will to introduce or update its export control system, as well as clear national policy related to non-proliferation of WMD or/and CBRN controls. Without it, it will be difficult to introduce one functioning system. Even if they want to comply with Resolution 1540, some countries do not see export control as priority. They do not have proper resources, nor necessary capacity to implement or enforce such a system. In some regions export controls could be simply very low on a priority list. Usually, the Ministry of Foreign Affairs is coordinating such a topic on a national level because of the significance of export controls on an international level, in some countries of course other institutions might be responsible, but if it is not supported by the political will, it would be very difficult to enhance further the system.

Legal framework

If countries' officials consider drafting or updating export control law to comply with Resolution 1540, they can:

(a) Add controls of relevant items in already existing law (in a national conventional arms export law or another existing international trade law that considered that items should have similar controls), or

(b) Draft a specific separate law.

In the EU control of dual-use items and control of export of conventional arms are regulated by two separate regimes. While EU dual-use export controls is regulated by the EU Regulation[12] directly implementable in all EU MS; conventional arms export controls are outlined in a "Common Position defining common rules governing the control of exports of military technology and equipment", defining a set of criteria which are legally binding – but it is up to each EU MS' discretion to implement it into its national law as well as draft its law.[13] Even if two regimes are divided on the EU level implementation of legal basis among EU Member States are different.

(a) Some EU Member States have two separate laws, one controlling dual-use and other conventional arms exports. Dual-use law is outlining national procedures and responsibilities, including penalties and some other adds on as allowed by the EU rules.

(b) Some EU Member States have one law for controlling exports of dual-use items and conventional arms (and sometimes some other items). Usually the export control provision would be covered under the Foreign Trade Act, or Strategic Exports Control Act. Some EU Member States such as the Netherlands have an "Export control of Strategic Goods Law", which encompasses dual-use, conventional arms or items under embargo while in the United Kingdom in the "Export control order", strategic goods are also referred to and encompass dual-use, conventional arms, torture equipment and items under embargo.

12 And, additionally, the Council Joint Action of 22 June 2000 *concerning the control of technical assistance related to certain military end-uses* (2000/401/CFSP).

13 Common Position 2008/944/CFSP *defining common rules governing the control of exports of military technology and equipment.*

Among EU Member States the way the legal basis is set on a national level may differ but common elements and procedures to be encompassed in the law(s) are defined mainly as:

- Activities to be controlled,
- Actors involved,
- Items to be controlled (definition of lists and items to be controlled),
- Competent authority(ies) for licencing / prohibiting,
- Assessment / licencing procedures,
- Competent authority(ies) for enforcement of the law,
- In case of breach, administrative and/or criminal penalties in place,
- National and/or regional and/or international cooperation.

Activities to be controlled

One of the first things which should be defined is what types of activities should fall under controls (and clear understanding of why are they controlled). These include activities such as import, transit, brokering, transhipment, financing, etc.

As stated above, clear understanding of why those activities should be controlled seems to be clear from the EU perceptive and is also stated in Resolution 1540 (see above). In the EU the focus is on export and imports on dual-use items are not controlled. However, in some regions, internal or regional dynamics are much more difficult and complicated. Indeed, in some countries the non-state actors[14] could be "in the country" or in the neighbouring one. Borders could be insecure and difficult to control so the issues cannot be solved by licencing export procedures, but it creates a much more complicated reality than it seems. The purpose of control could be considered not to be only export but import which might be of more concern. One should take into account those arguments to make sure to understand how these challenges can be encountered in order to establish a system suitable for such an environment.

Actors involved

One should also define actors involved who should fall under control: exporters, producers, shippers, brokers, etc. It is of utmost importance if authorities can identify these country's potential economic actors that will fall under controls. Communication between authorities and actors is also important and the organisation of awareness raising events is crucial. Indeed, it is important to communicate to actors the legal obligations they

[14] See above and United Nations Security Council 1540(2004).

have in this regard, as many are not aware that controls of such items might be in place.

Items to be controlled

UN Security Council Resolution 1540 requests each country to adopt an "effective national control list" (see above) to control (or prohibit) items' exports. The choice of the number of lists and items is to be defined by each country in accordance with international obligations and relevant conventions and to the regional / national needs.

The EU controlled list is consolidated and encompasses items from all international export control regimes (including the CWC list of items). It also includes conventional arms and conventional dual-use items.[15] The one consolidated list is an advantage for a country and its economic actors. Some countries outside of the EU have introduced the EU list for that reason.

In countries across the globe, there is no clear understanding or consensus regarding the terms "dual-use items", "strategic" or "sensitive" items or "related material" (as stated in Resolution 1540); or what is to be considered as potentially military or hazardous, or items which could contribute to CBRN weapons. Some countries consider that the trade of dual-use trade items should not be as strict as conventional arms considering that the high percentage of dual-use trade items are mainly for civilian application and the potential military end use is assessed prior to granting (or denying) a licence. Additionally trade of conventional arms is perceived as much more political while dual-use items are considered to be mainly civil items and the balance between trade and security is sought. For this reason, each country while introducing or updating its export control system has to have a clear picture of what items should be controlled and list(s) should be established which match the most the possibility of proper implementation and enforcement.

Additionally each State could introduce the concept of a catch-all clause[16] (same or different from the EU) to have a possibility to control a broader range of items without having to deal with the complicated list(s) which is not relevant for national or regional trade or transfers. This is also an interpretation in Resolution 1540 which refers to end-use controls.

---

15 See: http://www.wassenaar.org/. and S. Bauer, "Arms trade control capacity-building: lessons from dual-use trade controls", SIPRI Insights on Peace and Security, No. 2, 2013, p. 8.

16 Possibility of control of non-listed items under certain conditions. See Article 4 Council Regulation (EC) No. 428/2009 of May 2009 *setting up a Community regime for the control of exports, transfer, brokering and transit of dual-use items.*

Competent authority(ies) for licencing / prohibiting

The scope of controlled items is wide and they derive from various sectors. The reasons of controls are their end-use by their end-users in destination countries. There are so many unknowns in this equation that it is a challenge when one wants to determine the responsible authority. There should be an institution(s) / unit in place responsible for implementation of set licencing procedures and the issuing of licences.

In some EU Member States one licencing body is responsible for issuing licences for both (dual-use and conventional) and in others different institutions are responsible for the export of the respective items; in each case the decision-making process can differ. Indeed, one possibility is that the decision is based on an interagency consultation process and the other is that the licencing body has most decision-making powers. Different practices exist within the EU Member States. In some countries an official interagency commission exists and usually is composed of ministry of economy and industry; ministry of defence, ministry of foreign affairs, secret services and customs administration as permanent members. Other institutions can be consulted on a need to know basis. Additionally to licencing authorities, most of EU Member States have specialised offices for chemical or nuclear safety, security, etc. In some EU Member States those offices are part of the licencing process or give their opinion in the licencing process; and in some they do not have an active role in the licencing process.

Generally speaking, in some countries outside of the EU, the office for chemicals for example could be also responsible for issuing the licences for import and export, and transit of chemicals. The ministry of defence, security, economy, industry or interior could be in charge for the export of conventional arms, etc. It is up to each country to decide according to the administrative capacities that are already in place on what would be the best way forward, to build on the already existing system and maybe merge some responsibilities in the already existing system rather than creating a parallel non sustainable system. One or five licencing authorities, that does not matter as far as the responsibilities and procedures are clearly defined.

Assessment and licencing procedures

Assessment during the licencing procedure should be based upon clearly determined criteria. The set of criteria should be composed of international obligations which a country must follow and national criteria which follow national economic and security policy. This set of criteria is unique for each country for its national specific and international involvement.

In order to implement the law and process all the above licencing, procedures should be defined in order to issue, deny, revoke the licences, etc. Different types of licences can be put in place. Across EU there are individual, global and EU general licences[17] and some EU Member States have national general licences. Once a decision is made on what items and activities should be controlled, assessment should be based on risk assessment, end user and end-use of items, risk of diversion, national, regional and international obligations (UN embargos and regional or national), national and foreign security policy, etc.

Competent authority(ies) for enforcement of the law

Depending on the system competent authority(ies) can have single, complementary or mixed responsibilities. The enforcement agencies would enforce the law:

- At the border points (export and/or import and/or transit) supported by risk management (which needs to be developed too); those controls could be enforced by customs administration and / or border agencies or border police. Responsible administration should have power to stop, detain and if necessary seize the items controlled.
- Pre- and post company audits on the premises could be done by customs and/or licencing authority.

In case of suspicion or discovery of breach of the law(s) during those controls, at least one administration should have investigative powers. It could be customs administration and/or police or other bodies with investigative powers.

Responsible body(ies) for controls of items during activities defined above should be appointed by national law. Most of the EU Member States have respective customs departments dealing with their traditional tasks and have additionally dual-use items to be controlled: clearance, risk management, foreign trade company audits etc., and it is important to have good intra-agency exchange of information. Additionally, some EU MS, such as the United Kingdom, Germany and the Netherlands, have specialised team(s) or department(s) in customs administrations dealing only with the enforcement of export control laws. In Germany, the German Customs Investigation Office (ZKA) has full investigative powers and runs the investigation. In the Netherlands a specialised customs team POSS (precursors, strategic goods and sanctions) with also investigative powers can initiate and/or run investigations. Complex investigation will

---

[17] See: Council Regulation (EC) No. 428/2009 of May 2009 *setting up a Community regime for the control of exports, transfer, brokering and transit of dual-use items.*

be passed to the Fiscal Information and Investigation Service (FIOD). In some other smaller Member States one official is responsible for coordination of all those controls related to export controls on the national level and within its administration.

Administrative and/or criminal penalties in place

As far as the penalties are concerned, the need for the establishment of civil or criminal penalties is stated in Resolution 1540 (see above). In the EU Regulation penalties are called to be effective, proportionate and dissuasive. It is up to every EU Member State to interpret what effective, proportionate and dissuasive means and adapt it in its system. Current practice is that administrative penalties are in the dual-use export control law and criminal penalties in the criminal code, thus this also depends on legal traditions. Penalties should be defined and also implemented as one territory could be used for illegal transit or export without risk of being able to enforce the breach of the law.

National and/or regional and/or international cooperation

Another common element which is important to have is good interagency cooperation. The effective implementation and enforcement of export controls is not possible without effective interagency cooperation on a national level (in many procedures). Exchange of information between the licencing authority and customs is crucial for effective enforcement; including with intelligence services. In some countries as explained above some licencing process is done with the consultation of other Institutions and an official Interagency Commission established for this purpose consisting of all relevant authorities dealing with issues connected either to the items, subjects or activities in question. Having such a Commission can strengthen interagency cooperation as all institutions are involved in a process since the beginning of the procedure and have all relevant information needed. However, the decision of setting of interagency commission can depend of the size of the country, administrative capacity, and institutions involved.

Additionally, on the EU level, there is intra-EU coordination which is also very important for more effective implementation across the EU. Partly, the cooperation is defined in the Regulation and is an obligation while additional exchange of information via working group meetings and other events strengthens EU controls as well as national controls of EU Member States.

The information exchange is also taking place in international export regimes as most of the EU Member States are participating States to all of them. The majority of EU Member States are members of the international export control regimes.[18] Attending plenary sessions or various technical, legal and licencing, enforcement working groups give the possibility to EU Member States officials to meet with other participating States" colleagues, strengthen networks and exchange information.

EU as a model, yes but...

As one can see from above, it is very difficult to refer to the EU as a model with so many variations of implementation and enforcement among EU Member States.

Over the years the EU has developed and adapted its economic policy, and as far as the dual-use export control system is concerned one can say that the system developed is very specific to the EU. It has: the dual-use Regulation setting up the system, e-system dual-use information and denials exchanges; monthly coordination group meetings chaired in the frame of European Commission and meetings of the Council Dual-Use working party; occasional joint meetings with licencing and customs, peer reviews, etc. Such a model could only be applicable to a similar regional set-up (or if they have customs or trade union) and it is difficult to implement some provisions which are only EU specific.

It could be considered as a model and there is a possibility to adapt a similar approach in the sub-regional/regional settings, to develop closer understanding of the issues and challenges within the region, to adapt a common denominator (such as the EU Regulation) to the regional needs and realities, to exchange information and have closer cooperation. The common denominator on the regional level by giving to each State the possibility of implementation according to its needs can further enforce its system. However, there should be some existing mechanism in place, cooperation and exchange of information and trust. Transposing the EU model in regions or countries might be confusing as the history and traditions are not the same. The concept itself could be used and would strengthen the region but should be adapted to the regional needs and realities.

When a country is seeking to set up an export control system and to comply with Resolution 1540 (and soon probably with ATT),[19] it should first make sure that there is a clear understanding of what exactly are we talking about and once definition is clear to discuss how other countries

[18] The Wassenaar Arrangement, the Nuclear Suppliers Group, Australia Group, Missile Technology Control Regime and Zangeer Committee.

[19] Many lessons learned from capacity building experience from dual-use could be used in future ATT activities. See: S. Bauer, "Arms trade control capacity-building: lessons from dual-use trade controls", SIPRI Insights on Peace and Security, No. 2, 2013.

or the EU has set up the system according to their needs. Once it is clear what is at stake, countries can do a proper needs' assessment of flows, exports, transit cases of such items, and identification of potential applicants. According to its traditions, system and administrative capacities one can decide if the controls should be added in the already existing law or a new law or two laws should be drafted and which activities and which items should be covered and which authorities should be involved.

As stated at the beginning, the decision to update or establish an export control system will probably be influenced by political priorities. For example, in the South East Europe (SEE) region, candidates and potential candidate countries to the EU[20] previously had one law controlling both conventional arms and dual-use items. SEE countries aspire to adopt the EU standards and they therefore try to adapt the same EU logic. Even if some EU Member States have one law in place, but the system is separated on the EU level, most of the SEE countries currently decided to separate their export control law into two (one controlling conventional arms and one dual-use items). Indeed, the EU Regulation is not applicable for them yet. In order to be able to implement properly requirements from the EU Regulation they decided to separate the laws for more clarity towards EU *acquis* and understanding, implementation and enforcement. However having one or two laws does not go against the EU logic. Having two laws helps administration and to explain to actors that control of conventional and dual-use have also differences; and to make sure that the implementation and enforcement are done properly. Some additional elements taken from the EU are also taking place in SEE, such as regional meetings, exchange of information, which reinforces national and regional export controls. One should keep in mind that this particular region is very specific as their aim is to be part of the EU, and therefore introduces as many EU characteristics as possible. It shows how policy and political will supports enhancement of export controls in the Region and how those can shape the system.

Some other regions have different political or economic priorities, and different needs on a national and regional level according to the level of exports, imports or transit. Even within the region, one country can have different needs and priorities. One region could be seen more as a transit zone and its system should be more adapted for transit or import than exports. If there is no regional similarities or cooperation a country can follow the rest of elements given at the EU level. If there is a prior regional

20 In this context the reference is to Bosnia and Herzegovina, Macedonia, Montenegro and Serbia.

cooperation, or customs union, the EU model can be a great example of how countries could exchange information and strengthen their national needs on the regional context and level. In the EU, the process was long and it is a process evolving, adapting to the needs and realities, constantly updating, while confidence has to be established for the system to work. EU integration is still in process and one cannot expect other regions to have the same level of trust and exchange of information on the topic which might not even be relevant for them so much.

The EU Regulation

Regime, Framework or Guidelines for Sub-Regional and/or National Regimes?

Dr. Laszlo STEFAN

Senior Counsellor – Authority of Defence Industry and Export Controls

Council Regulation 428/2009/EC: a regime?

The term "regime" refers to a system, a set of conditions and is widely used in a political context referring to governance. In the export control world the term is often used to express a particular framework: international political cooperation for common standards governing international trade of strategically controlled items, i.e. the Australia Group, the Missile Technology Control Regime, the Nuclear Suppliers Group, the Wassenaar Arrangement. The question arises whether the Council Regulation (EC) No. 428/2009 of 5 May 2009 which called for the setting up of a Community regime for the control of exports, transfer, brokering and transit of dual-use items (Recast),[1] i.e. the common legal instrument of the EU export control system for dual-use items, may and should be called a regime through which we express a certain claim for universalization of this act.

It may be argued that the Regulation may serve as a solid basis for a universal norm governing export controls of dual-use items. Certainly parts of the Regulation have been tested over time, as they were put together from elements that had already been applied to existing and functioning in some Member States of the European Union. Some of these Member States have a vast experience in export controls and also play a key role in shaping international export controls and export control regimes. Considering the fact that the Regulation as a common legal instrument implemented in a variety of countries,

[1] Here after "the Regulation".

has remained unchanged as to its principal elements since its adoption, this fact further underlines the test of time. Parts of the Regulation are used internationally as points of reference or even as *quasi* norms, like the catch-all clause, or the control list, just to name a few. Furthermore the Regulation includes all obligations stipulated in the United Nations Security Council Resolution 1540, as binding for all States. Not only are the generally described and thus rather vague obligations laid down in the Resolution covered but also guidelines adopted by the international export control regimes are more or less covered by the Regulation, as mentioned above. Just like these guidelines, legislation adopted by the European Union undergoes severe scrutiny and wide institutional debate. The EU Commission has the right of initiative in this field including proposing legislation, drawing its experience from being the focal point of the common policy on export controls. The Commission is the focal point of intra-EU and international coordination and cooperation: a horizontal-policy overview of strategic trade controls. Member States on the other hand may be considered as having a vertical-policy expertise, being responsible for implementing export controls, which includes taking the concrete decisions on transactions that may have security and economic effects beyond the individual Member State. Moreover, States participate in the different export control regimes, exchange experience, take decisions on control lists, policy guidelines, or even about contacts with third countries, where, absurdly enough, the Commission might not even participate at all. The Member States are gathered in the Council and as such are the legislators. A new co-legislator since the Lisbon Treaty is the EU Parliament, directly elected, it has a new angle as well as policy agenda, which undoubtedly enriches this triad. The differing positions of the Institutions (on proposed legislation) are clashed in so-called trilogues that serve the purpose reconciling the positions of the three institutions should they diverge on specific legislative proposals. Needless to say, before any Institution takes a position, there is a strict inter-institutional scrutiny of any proposal, including by the Member States and their decision makers – equally set up in an inter-institutional system. This expresses how complex and thorough the EU legislation is, and how many aspects have to be taken into consideration for any legislative act. On the other side many decisions concerning the concrete text of the Regulation reflects complex compromises, that could be temporary in nature (*hic et nunc*) and should be viewed in that angle. Any outsider may draw on this experience.

EC Regulation 428/2009 may also be viewed in the sense of a *Framework* implementing a universal norm which requires further detailed regulatory instruments. There are plenty of notions contained in the Regulation implying that it might be the result of EU specific premises, relying on higher norms and implementing legislation respectively The Regulation may thus be understood as a *Framework.* The Regulation reflects the integration of States, but also possibly its fragmentations. Common legal instruments are laid down, however provisions for common implementation, including enforcement is missing from the Regulation. Provisions setting up consultation mechanisms, information systems (e.g. denials) try to bridge these gaps. Though export controls of dual-use items are under the Common Commercial Policy of the European Union, as stipulated in the Treaties and affirmed later by the European Court of Justice, one cannot ignore the fact that many aspects thereof belong to the Common Foreign and Security Policy (with a very different institutional setup), and even more to the national foreign and security policies of each Member State. Especially the security policy is a delicate issue belonging principally to the Member States.

On the other hand the Regulation contains many EU specific solutions that are certainly of not of much interest to other regions. Taking the example of the EU general licences or the intra-EU transfer controls: they remain very EU specific with little or no use to other regions. Going further, the entire export control regime of the EU relies on the four freedoms and the customs union, the EU institutions having legislative and control powers laid down by the Treaties, which make the Regulation very EU specific.

These facts support conclusions as to the Regulation which fits the role of a regional framework with enough freedom and room for national interests and agendas to be asserted and exercised.

The last part of the exercise is the question whether the Regulation could be considered as a *guideline* in the meaning of a politically binding set of recommendations serving adherence to and implementation of a universal norm – which requires further detailed regulatory implementing instruments.

One could argue that the Regulation may fulfil this task due to the fact that it is a perfect expression of the principle of subsidiarity: common framework interpreted as a directive (or *guidelines*) serving higher norms, relying on adjustable and indeed varying national implementation due to national needs and political-economic interests. The author is not suggesting that this really is the case presently in the EU, as no comprehensive comparative study has ever examined the diverse implementation practices as suggested by some stakeholders.

The common framework, the Regulation, relies upon national implementation that not only includes decisions on licences, but also on the enforcement, furthermore on controls, specific to services relating to controlled goods, software and technology like brokering services or technical assistance. It is not surprising that a Coordination Group is set up by Article 23 of the Regulation: in order to coordinate and harmonise (possibly diverging) national practices. Obviously even among the EU Member States, different emphasis is laid on export controls depending on the national political interests, economic, legal or even social outset. This is even more true in different regions of the world.

Conclusions

Above we have considered different possible roles of the Regulation: it may be considered as a basis for a universal regime in the meaning of a universal norm. We have also reflected on the EU specific aspects and premises that make the Regulation to some more or less a *framework* or where others consider it to be a mere *guideline*.

The author has a clear preference for international and universal norms for export controls of dual-use items binding for all States, as these items are identified as capable of design, development, production or use of weapons of mass destruction. In the present circumstances the United Nations has the most appropriate legislative powers to create a universally binding international norm, if ratified by the States, as required. United Nations Security Council Resolution 1540 based on Chapter VII of the UN Charter lays down the fundaments, by listing a number of legal requirements that need to be in place for an effective export control system. Obviously, a taxation of relevant legal instruments lacks the precise content of a prescriptive norm; the Resolution thus remains in our understanding vague as regards to the concrete requirements. Some arguments consider that existing frameworks like the BTWC, CWC or the NPT have appropriate mandates in place or if not (yet), they should constitute the right fora for widening further their non-proliferation objectives, often just referred to as trade controls, referring to the value burdened term of non-proliferation. We see these international institutions as missing the overall and cross-sectoral objective of export controls for the sake of weapons of mass destruction (WMD) non-proliferation (or strategic trade controls) in a universal manner. The above-mentioned existing institutions however may well complement a universal norm on WMD non-proliferation, though they will have to consider some controversial issues in their own framework. Most of these treaties or conventions cannot be easily re-negotiated or amended as political consensus would be lacking and thereby risk total failure, thereby compromising achieved results.

Taking the experience of Hungary, the acceptance and "adaptation" of the EU's Regulation (EC Regulation 1334/2000) as a higher legal norm did not cause any major challenges in the course of our accession to the European Union. Our experts were acquainted with the world of export control regimes, their guidelines, and thus a legally tighter instrumentalisation of the requirements caused no essential concerns. Hungary was not present when the Regulation was drafted but this did not hinder its relatively smooth adaptation. Similarly, if a universal norm was created on trade controls of dual-use items, this would not pose an unsurmountable obstacle in our view to the international community. A deductive approach that universally binds all States to exercise export controls based on common stipulations have in our view a higher chance of general acceptance and universal support than the present legal-institutional state of play.

A universal norm – hypothetically a result of a common deductive legislative exercise – should be complemented by an inductive approach for levelling out differences in the concrete implementation. This takes us to the question of how much power should/will be delegated to an institution by a treaty? This is obviously interrelated with the political priority attached to the issue. Countries or future State Parties obviously face very different challenges, and circumstances; therefore implementation may differ to a high degree. Countries (State Parties) may well identify and asses their own needs for better implementation based on their factual experience. A universal norm should institutionalise a coordinating body helping to level out the playing field and assisting members in need. Without substantial coordination and assistance mechanisms we see the chance for improvement as being very vague in this envisaged context. If one considers the amount of money being spent today on outreach and assistance programmes, often running in parallel with each other, one may hope for better synergy in a future common framework. Assistance may well be provided in a regional approach facing similar challenges and additionally helping to network staff in charge of implementation. As harmonised implementation cannot preclude some sort of verification, it should only be put here as a question, whether this should imply a reporting scheme based on self-assessment or stricter modes as set out and implemented at some international institutions.

We have been considering the hypothesis notion of the Regulation serving as a draft for a universal norm implied in the term *regime*. We could not avoid considering the arguments suggesting that the Regulation would rather be just a *Framework* or just a mere set of *guidelines*. Our preference was expressed for a universal norm generally regulating trade controls of dual-use items with clear regulative content. As to the question whether the Regulation could serve as a basis for negotiation, the answer was affirmative.

Bridging the Gap

The Role of Regional Organisations in Developing Universal Export Controls

Sara DEPAUW

Researcher – Flemish Peace Institute

"I ask you to stop and think for a moment what it would mean to have nuclear weapons in so many hands, in the hands of countries large and small, stable and unstable, responsible and irresponsible, scattered throughout the world".[1]

President John F. Kennedy

Introduction

Export control is a policy field that entails both trade and international security. It concerns the imposition of trade restrictions to prevent an outside "enemy" from obtaining goods and technologies. Export controls have a long history dating back to the late 16th and early 17th centuries when treaties between countries were adopted to control certain goods (often referred to as "contraband") in times of war.[2] Currently, export control law is mostly aimed at preventing the spread of weapons of mass destruction (WMD) as well as of conventional arms.

Export controls also serve a general policy of economic containment. This was very clear when CoCom was set up during the Cold War, an informal group of Western countries which tried to avoid export of high-technology items to the former Soviet bloc and China. Governments have always searched for cooperation among like-minded States in developing export controls since coordinated action is more effective.

1 M. Willrich, "The Treaty on Non-proliferation of nuclear weapons: nuclear technology confronts world politics", in Joyner, D. H. *Arms Control Law*, Surrey: Ashgate Publishing Limited, 2012.

2 S.A. Evans, "Technological ambiguity & the Wassenaar Arrangement", University of Oxford, thesis submitted for the degree of Doctor of Philosophy, 2009, pp. 162-163.

After the dissolution of CoCom the geographical spectrum of export controls widened with Russia and other Eastern European countries entering as founding Members of the Wassenaar Arrangement and countries such as South Africa and South Korea also entering international control regimes.[3] Export control policies today are influenced by five international export control regimes which group a number of industrialised States that share a common basis for export controls on a range of goods and technology. These export control regimes set up a common framework for developing national export control policies.[4] Also, export controls moved away from blocks of countries opposing each other and evolved towards more specific end-use, end-user concerns, following perceived threats in contemporary security policy. No longer are there only entire States, or groups of States, that are seen as possible enemies but also specific individuals and groups (sometimes referred to as terrorist groups) within countries.

These trends are embodied in the adoption of UN Resolution 1540. Since 2004, dual-use export controls are binding by UN Resolution 1540 (see infra) upon all Member States of the UN not only the most industrialised ones. The nature of international law however requires translation into national legislation that usually is more precise. Since export controls are mostly initiated and developed by the most industrialised countries, which lay ahead of other countries, serious gaps in terms of means and capacity have to be bridged in order to achieve effective universal implementation.

This chapter points to the role that regional organisations could play to overcome the gap between national capacity and international goals. It focuses on the EU and the role it has played in streamlining national export control policies but also describes internal challenges in harmonising national export control policies, as they occur among like-minded industrialised States. Acknowledging the diverse nature of regional organisations worldwide, it is not the intention to look at the EU as a model or best practice as each regional organisation is embedded in its

---

3 Commission of the European Communities (1998), Report to the European Parliament and the Council on the application of Regulation (EC) 3381/94 *setting up a community system of export controls regarding dual-use goods*, COM (1998) 258 final, Brussels, 15.05.1998.

4 The Zangger Committee (1971) and Nuclear Suppliers Group (1974) focus on proliferation of nuclear items and its means of delivery, Australia Group (1985) focuses on biological and chemical weapons, Missile Technology Control Regime (1987) controls unmanned delivery systems of WMD, Wassenaar Arrangement (1994) is the only regime that focuses on conventional arms and dual-use technologies related to the development of military capabilities.

own history and institutional setting. Nevertheless, a closer look into the development of an EU export control regime, shows some dynamics, obstacles and opportunities that might be informative for other regional organisations that aim at contributing to the strengthening of dual-use export controls.

Resolution 1540[5]

In April 2004, the Security Council of the United Nations adopted Resolution 1540. This resolution aims at preventing proliferation of weapons of mass destruction and related items (main focus on nuclear weapons) to non-State actors, a risk that was not explicitly covered by existing WMD non-proliferation treaties.[6] Resolution 1540 was adopted under Chapter VII of the UN Charter and is binding for all UN Member States without ratification.

The initiative for drafting Resolution 1540 was launched during a speech by President George W. Bush to the UN Security Council in April 2003 where he pointed to the salience of the risk of proliferation of weapons of mass destruction after the attack on the Twin Towers in 2001. In the same year, the Khan network which smuggled centrifuges and other nuclear materials to countries such as North-Korea, Iran and Lybia was revealed.[7] This was the context in which the Resolution was approved by all Members of the Security Council, even though its legal basis – chapter VII of the UN Charter – caused discussion. During the public debate on the Resolution, three main critiques were voiced. First, there is no mention of disarmament (which means that no obligations are included to limit weapons of mass destruction in the hands of the have's, only to prevent their obtainment by the have not's). Second, some countries did not agree with Chapter VII as a legal basis to enforce a resolution on all UN Members without negotiations.[8] This was perceived (e.g. by India)

5 This section benefits from input by Joren Kippers, an intern at the Flemish Peace Institute, which is much appreciated.

6 T. Ogilvie-White, "UN Security Council Resolution 1540: Implementation Challenges", in *Presentation to the Workshop on Strategic Trade Controls*, Taipei, Taiwan, Augustus 2013, p. 1.

7 C. Ahlström, "United Nations Security Council Resolution 1540: non-proliferation by means of international legislation", *SIPRI Yearbook 2007*, Oxford: Oxford University Press, 2007, p. 460; W.J. Broad *et al.*, "A Tale of Nuclear Proliferation: How Pakistani Built His Network", *New York Times*, February 2004.

8 G.H. Oosthuizen, E. Wilmshurst, "Terrorism and Weapons of Mass Destruction: United Nations Security Council Resolution 1540", in *Chatham House Briefing Paper* 4:1, 2004, pp. 3-4.

as external coercive export control norms without having agreed to it on a multilateral basis.[9]

Asian mainly countries perceived Resolution 1540 as an attempt by the US and other Western countries to force the *war on terror* upon countries which have little to do with WMD or their proliferation.[10]

Third, critiques were voiced about the binding nature of the resolution as well as the vagueness of its definitions and language.[11]

Almost ten years after its adoption, difficulties in the implementation reveal some strengths and weaknesses of the resolution.[12] According to the most recent figures displayed by the 1540 committee, 168 countries have issued one or more implementing reports 24 countries did not. This reflects quite a substantial degree of support for the Resolution. The reports however do not shed light on the real state of affairs in terms of implementation, since they are often diplomatic documents declaring support without representing real measures of implementation. According to UNIDIR, evaluations and outreach activities of the 1540 Committee and NGO (such as the Stockholm International Peace Research Institute, the Verification Research or the Training and Information Centre) show that countries encounter serious problems in implementing the resolution. These problems are not longer driven by political disagreement with the document itself, but mainly by a capacity deficit and diverging policy priorities. South Africa for example, criticises complicated reporting requirements that are not adapted to the capacities of developing countries. Often, countries mention that they are dealing with more urgent needs than the implementation of 1540, such as flows of small arms and light weapons in and through their countries. Even though concise in its form, resolution 1540 is indeed quite demanding. All UN Member States should take extensive measures, broadly described in the resolution, including changes in their national legal systems, in order to combat ill-defined present and future threats.[13] Not only do countries have to

9 UNSC, Report S/PV.4950: p. 24, consulted via http://www.securitycouncilreport.org/atf/cf/%7B65BFCF9B-6D27-4E9C-8CD3-CF6E4FF96FF9%7D/Chap%20VII%20SPV%204950.pdf.

10 L. Scheinman (Ed.), *Implementing Resolution 1540: The Role of Regional Organizations*, New York and Geneva: UNIDIR, 2008, p. 46 and pp. 158-160.

11 A. Marschik, "The Security Council as World Legislator? Theory, Practice and Consequences of an Expanding World Power", in *IILJ Working Papers* 18, 2005, p. 15.

12 B. Finlay, "Meeting the Objectives of UN Security Council Resolution 1540: the Role of Civil Society", in *Stimson Center*, December 2012, p. 7.

13 D.H. Joyner, "Nuclear non-proliferation and the UN Security Council in a multipolar world", in D.H. Joyner (Ed.), *Arms control law*, Ashgate Publishing Company, UK, 2012, pp. 587-611.

adopt legal measures, they also need to foresee effective licencing procedures and border controls. Requirements include physical protection, effective border controls, law enforcement efforts, and "appropriate laws and regulations to control export, transit, trans-shipment and re-export and controls on providing funds and services related to such export and transshipment".[14]

Analyses of African responses to Resolution 1540 for example, have emphasised the relatively low numbers of reports and little detail as to implementation measures. Countries such as the Democratic Republic of Congo, export rough materials with proliferation risks such as uranium, but are less advanced in establishing technical demanding export controls foreseen in many industrialised countries. African responses generally seem to emphasise the need to avoid creating multiple and overlapping WMD-obligations (by existing non-proliferation treaties) that stretch already limited resources for implementation and enforcement.[15]

Resolution 1540 rightfully acknowledges the importance of global awareness and controls, but there is a wide gap to be bridged. Legally binding instruments originating from the UN and supported by industrialised countries are not tailored to be easily implemented in countries with diverging concerns, means and priorities around the world. Several studies have focused on the role of regional organisations to implement Resolution 1540.[16]

Development of an EU dual-use export control policy

This section focuses on the role of the European Union in implementing Resolution 1540 and in establishing a dual-use export control regime more generally. It describes how the EU gained competence in the field of dual-use, what motivated its Member States and how the EU contributes to enhance national capacity in dual-use export controls. It also points to a number of challenges the EU encounters and makes some suggestions to improve EU regional cooperation.

As stated in the Commission's report up until 1995, export controls in the European Union were implemented by national legislation only. Most EU Member States based their national export control policies on agreements in the international control regimes, and implemented these in

---

14 I. Antony, L. Grip, "Africa and the global market in natural uranium", in *SIPRI policy paper* No. 39, 2013.

15 *Idem.*

16 See for example: L. Scheinman (Ed.), "Implementing Resolution 1540: the role of regional organisations", UNIDIR, New York and Geneva, 2008.

their own administrative structure. Discussions on a common policy for exports of dual-use goods started in the European Commission in the early 1990s. The issue was raised in the context of the completion of the internal market: dual-use goods should move as freely between Member States as they do within each of them.[17] The EU figured that internal trade barriers for dual-use items could be abolished if a certain degree of trust among EU countries could be established. Therefore all Member States established effective controls based on common standards for exports to non-EU countries. From the perspective of the EU common commercial policy, the initial intentions of the EU had little to do with preventing proliferation of WMD, intra-EU free trade was the main objective. The Commission submitted a proposal for a Council Regulation in August 1992. On the basis of this proposal, the Council established on 19 December 1994 an arms export regime for dual-use goods. The regime entered into force in 1995. Since then, dual-use items circulate freely within the internal market, except for a list of sensitive items (e.g. products to be used for nuclear technology) for which stricter controls apply.

The Regulation did not create an EU licencing authority. Member States remain the implementing bodies that assess the technical and political aspects of export licences for dual-use goods. While successful in terms of intra-European trade facilitation and establishment of the internal market, the European Commission did acknowledge that the regime "largely failed to function as a credible common export control regime".[18]

In July 2000, the regime was reformed and replaced by Regulation 1334/2000 and in 2009 it was reformed again. Up until today, the EU is looking for ways to improve the EU dual-use export control regime. The EU dual-use regime is based on Article 207 TFEU (ex-Article 133 TEC). It forms part of the EU common commercial policy, even though it touches upon CFSP. According to the Article 3 of the TEU, this policy belongs to the exclusive competences of the EU, which means that the EU alone is able to legislate and adopt binding acts in these fields. The Member States' role is therefore limited to applying these acts, unless the Union authorises them to adopt certain acts themselves. The EU dual-use trade policy developed into a so-called "hybrid" system, where a common European legal framework applies but most executive measures are delegated to the Member States (see *infra*).

17 Commission of the European Communities (1998), Report to the European Parliament and the Council on the application of Regulation (EC) 3381/94 *setting up a community system of export controls regarding dual-use goods*, COM (1998) 258 final, Brussels, 15 May 1998.

18 *Idem.*

Content-wise, the EU dual-use policy developed along the lines that the European Commission already identified in 1998. The Commission foresaw three trends that would define the nature of dual-use export controls. First, export controls would move away from general containment (East versus West during the Cold War) to targeted controls with more specific controls on end-use and end-users. Second, the pace of technological development and their general availability leads to increasing pressure on EU exporters, to banalisation of certain goods and technologies and ultimately to a general tendency to release controls. Third, the Commission predicted an incremental influence of the European Union on national export controls of its Member States.[19]

The adoptions of EU Regulation 428/2009 and its amendments embody these trends. The Regulation keeps its targeted controls on the most sensitive items and even adds WDM-targeted controls on brokering and transit activities (in line with the requirements of Resolution 1540). At the same time the EU also releases controls on less sensitive trade by introducing Community general export authorisations (CGEA)[20] or updates in the control list which include de-control of certain items. In October 2013, the European Commission presented a report to the Council and the European Parliament on the implementation of Regulation 428/2009.[21] According to the report, the EU provides a uniform legal basis, but there are still some operational differences among Member States in its implementation. Stakeholders ask for a critical review of intra-EU transfers (annex IV of most sensitive items that require licences for intra-EU trade), more general licences for low-value shipments, a more flexible procedure to update the dual-use list, – these are all measures to decontrol less sensitive trade – but also ask for a better pooling of resources and exchange of information and increased transparency in order to enhance legal certainty.[22]

---

19 *Idem.*

20 CGEA cover most of the exports to the US, Canada, Japan, Australia, New Zealand, Liechtenstein, Switzerland and Norway, exports of certain dual-use items to Argentina, Iceland, South Africa, South Korea and Turkey, export after repair or temporary export of most dual-use items to a number of destinations, and export of telecommunications and chemicals to some destinations.

21 This report provides information on the implementation and impact of the Regulation since its adoption until the beginning of 2013 and covers activities in 2010, 2011 and 2012.

22 European Commission, Report from the Commission to the Council and the European Parliament on the implementation of Regulation (EC) No. 428/2009 *setting up a Community regime for the control of exports, transfer, brokering and transit of dual-use items*. COM (2013) 710 final, Brussels, 16 October 2013.

Challenges for the European dual-use export control regime

Even though the European export control regime can benefit from a network of strong and wealthy States compared to many other regions in the world, the EU faces a number of challenges.

Field of application: the reach of dual-use

Dual-use items include civilian items with military applications in both conventional weapons as well as chemical, biological and nuclear weapons. In the political debate, dual-use items are often associated with WMD alone. In the EU legislation, all dual-use items are dealt with together. There are technical linkages as some items and categories, such as machine tools and lasers, have both applications in conventional arms and WMD.[23] The European Commission strongly emphasises the risk of proliferation of dual-use items for WMD. This is in line with the trend to focus controls on the most sensitive items, while releasing controls for non-sensitive ones ("to build high walls around a smaller yard").[24] The question then is, what items are categorised as sensitive? In discussions about amending regulation 1334/2000 it became clear that the European Parliament does not easily agree with the classification of dual-use items as non-sensitive.[25] Since then, the debate has not disappeared from the agenda. Concerning dual-use, the role of the Parliament increased after the Treaty of Lisbon, since its legal basis (previous Article 133 TEC now Article 207 TFEU on the common trade policy) was amended. The ordinary legislative procedure (an equivalent to the co-decision procedure) now applies to the common commercial policy, which strengthened the role of the EP in decision making. Whereas the EP was not involved in adopting legislation in this policy field before the Treaty of Lisbon, the

---

23 S. Bauer, "Arms trade control capacity building: lessons from dual-use trade controls", SIPRI insights on peace and security, No. 2013/2 March 2013.

24 Obama's goal of the US export control reform, 2009.

25 European Parliament, Draft report on the proposal for a regulation of the European Parliament and of the Council amending Regulation (EC) No. 1334/2000 *setting up a Community regime for the control of exports of dual-use items and technology*, Committee on International Trade, 2008/0249 (COD) (COM(2008)0854 – C7-0062/2010 – 2008/0249(COD)).

European Parliament, Opinion of the Committee on Foreign Affairs for the Committee on International Trade on the proposal for a regulation of the European Parliament and of the Council amending Regulation (EC) No. 1334/2000 *setting up a Community regime for the control of exports of dual-use items and technology*, Committee on Foreign Affairs, 2008/0249(COD), (COM(2008)0854 – C7-0062/2010 – 2008/0249(COD)).

Council has to share powers now with the EP.[26] In the light of the Arab Spring, new discussions were raised on the need to control so called "digital arms" or "cybertools", civil technologies that might be used in connection with human rights violations in the countries of destination. It is clear that the European Commission's view – which generally guards economic interests of the EU – conflicts with the more ethically inspired arguments of (some) Members of the European Parliament. The question to what extent security technology and so called "digital arms" should be controlled, challenges the WMD-related approach to dual-use items and the demand from industry to increasingly liberalise trade in dual-use items. To what extent use/misuse of technology should lead to trade restrictions will continue to be subject of debate in the coming years.

Institutional friction

Even though the EU has strong institutions and solid competences, the institutional setting on EU-level is complex and the division of power within the EU hampers a coherent development of the EU dual-use export control regime. First, there is an overlap as well as a split between CFSP and common commercial policy on the EU level. Secondly, national competences restrict the capacity of the EU in developing a common policy.

Dual-use export controls falls under the EU's commercial policy but is also linked with the EU's policy to prevent the spread of WMD, which is part of the EU's common foreign and security policy. Since the Treaty of Lisbon, it is the High Representative for foreign affairs and security policy and the Council of ministers who determine what level of priority to assign to non-proliferation and export controls, and the ways in which the European External Action Service are dealing with these issues.[27] Without elaborating on the content of the EU non-proliferation and disarmament pillar within CFSP,[28] it should be clear that these two policies potentially strengthen, but may also weaken each other. Since there is a clear common ground within CFSP to combat proliferation of WMD (there is much less common ground in the field of conventional arms, security equipment or cybertools), the EEAS could strengthen the sharing of information, making use of the diplomatic services of the EU for instance, strengthen export controls of third countries by outreach

26 The detailed procedure is to be found in Article 294 TFEU.

27 S. Bauer, I. Micic, "Controls on security-related international transfers", in *SIPRI Yearbook 2010*.

28 For more information, see: S. Bauer, I. Micic, *op. cit.*; I. Anthony, L. Grip, "Strengthening the European Union's future approach to WMD non-proliferation", SIPRI Policy Paper No. 37, June 2013 and http://www.eeas.europa.eu/non-proliferation-and-disarmament/wmd/index_en.htm.

activities or adopting embargoes under CFSP. These are but a few examples. Actions within CFSP however mainly support outreach activities and "effective multilateralism", while the role of EEAS in strengthening the internal capacity of the EU and its Member States (inreach) to prevent destabilising exports lags behind. The economic focus of the EU commercial policy in the implementation of Regulation 428/2009 is reflected in the documents of DG Trade of the European Commission. Most attention goes to the liberalisation of the internal market, and incrementally also to markets outside the EU. More efforts to help the Member States in assessing the risk for proliferation in licencing assessments would strengthen the EU policy against the proliferation of WMD. DG Trade of the European Commission however is not tasked with tackling proliferation of WMD. Other bridges will have to be built to overcome institutional impediments to strengthen the EU effectiveness and transversal coherency in both trade and CFSP.

Recently, the High Representative of the EU has established a new body in between the Commission and EEAS, the service for foreign policy instruments (FPI). FPI acts as the bridge between the CFSP structures in the EEAS and the central services of the Commission. FPI is responsible, under the authority of the High Representative of the Union for Foreign Affairs and Security Policy in his/her capacity as Vice-President of the Commission, for the operational and financial management of the budgets for Common Foreign and Security Policy (CFSP).[29] In addition, it is also responsible for the implementation of foreign policy regulatory instruments such as "sanctions", the Kimberley Process on conflict diamonds, and the "anti-torture" Regulation. In practice, FPI represents the European Commission in sanctions-related discussions with Member States at the Foreign Relations Counsellors Working Group (RELEX) and prepares proposals for Regulations on sanctions for adoption by the Council of the European Union. In its management plan, the FPI adopts support to the implementation of the strategy on non-proliferation of WMD (including the implementation of UN Resolution 1540) as one of its objectives.[30]

It is worthwhile to explore if this service could be meaningful in bridging EU Commission and Council policies related to control on trade in dual-use items.

---

[29] The service is also responsible for the Instrument for Stability (IfS), Industrialised Countries Instrument (ICI), Election Observation Missions (EOMs) and press and public diplomacy (PPD).

[30] European Commission, Service for foreign policy instruments 2013 management plan, consulted via: http://ec.europa.eu/atwork/synthesis/amp/doc/fpi_mp_en.pdf.

Economic versus ethical aspirations of the EU

Building on the former section, the elephant in the room is the underlying contradiction between support for economic development of the EU in the dual-use sector and ethical considerations in relation to the risk of proliferation of WMD, conventional arms and other technologies that might contribute to violations of human rights. The EU aims for both, in separate institutions and governed by different bodies, with cross-references that mainly exist on paper.

Small States versus large Member States in the EU

There are strong differences in capacities around the globe, and also in Europe resources available to small and large Member States differ substantially. It is plausible that small Member States have more to win with closer EU cooperation, and less to lose. More to win because of lack of capacity. Although licencing officers of smaller Member States generally have fewer licences to process, they are as dependent to central services like intelligence or diplomatic services as other countries. Less to lose because their voice on the international fora is too weak alone, and gains by EU representation. Strong Member States are more keen to keep their sovereign powers on the international scene. The UK and France as permanent Members of the Security Council is a case in point, also in bilateral relations or in the international regimes their leverage is much stronger.

From the perspective of a small Member State, it is worthwile to examine how the EEAS could play a role in strengthening the capacity of its own Member States (not only of third States) to govern dual-use export controls. In the first review of EEAS, two years after its creation, the EEAS points to its global coverage "of all geographical and thematic issues" with its network of 139 EU delegations in 163 third countries and international institutions. "Collectively the EU can achieve things that no Member State individually is able to do". EEAS reaches places where hardly any EU Member State is represented, and in places where national embassies are present, the EEAS can increase effectiveness in partnership with national diplomatic services. In its review the EEAS acknowledges that close cooperation between the EEAS and the Commission is vital on the various global issues where the external aspects of internal EU policies have a growing foreign policy dimension.[31] Also for proliferation of WMD, a more elaborated role for EEAS in supporting Member States could make a difference.

---

31 European external action service (2013), "EEAS Review", consulted via: http://eeas.europa.eu/library/publications/2013/3/2013_eeas_review_en.pdf.

Room for improvement in the EU dual-use export control policy

Little exposed in the EU Regulation, are measures to strengthen the common outcome of export controls. One way to do this would be the creation of an EU licencing body. In the development of the European dual-use export control regime, a proposal to install a body to process all dual-use licences of all Member States was never put on the table. Such a licencing body could be meaningful for two reasons; first, in guaranteeing equal trade restrictions (a level playing field) to all EU companies. Second; it could contribute to the development of a comprehensive EU policy in the fight of proliferation of WMD and conventional weapons by pooling and sharing all expertise and intelligence information.

The EU has the competence to create a European licencing authority. The principle of subsidiarity (can this task be sufficiently fulfilled by the Member States) is not applicable to the EU's exclusive competences (see Article 5 TEU). But still, changes to the legislation require approval by the European Parliament and the EU Member States represented by the Council (according to the ordinary legislative procedure). Given the history of export controls, the role of EU Member States in the international control regimes, the link with intelligence and its interconnectedness with international security, it is unlikely that the EU Member States will transfer the control over licencing decisions to the EU. When it comes to sensitive cases, integration in the field of CFSP is not strong enough to be delegated to an EU body.

Moreover, outreach to industry is essential to export controls and EU Member States are much better placed to reach them. Export controls are also embedded in national licencing procedures and cooperation with national customs services. It is therefore worthwhile to look for alternatives. The EU solution of liberalising less-sensitive trade while maintaining strict controls on sensitive trade (EU general licences, flexible changes to the lists) and establishing administrative cooperation among national licencing officers, seems to be at this stage of EU integration the more realistic option.

The EU already developed an electronic system for dual-use exports to share information on denied exports, it coordinates discussions among licencing officers in the coordination group Article 23 on specific situations of concern. The EU also tries to strengthen best practices by publishing EU guidelines and organising workshops. The EU could however provide more guidance on Article 12 which describes the assessment criteria that national licencing officers should take into account. When it comes to interpretation of the EU-list, the EU installed a pool of national experts to advise EU Member States on a voluntary basis when they encounter difficulties with interpreting the technical descriptions of items on the EU-list.[32]

The EU control regime would benefit from more guidance in establishing challenging dual-use controls on e.g. intangible technology transfers. Apart from clarifying assessment criteria to be used according to Article 12, the EU could evolve towards a better use of trade restrictions where deemed necessary. The EU implements all UN embargoes, but could go further in adopting independent restrictions. Binding advices of the European Commission on the interpretation of the EU-list would take the idea of a pool of experts to a higher level in order to ensure a common implementation. Last but not least, the EU should aim for a high level of transparency, which allows democratic control. Parallel to the yearly report on conventional arms, it would be helpful if the EU would report to the European Parliament not only on its general policy but also on the licences that have been issued and that are being used. These data should be based on national reports – which should be required by the EU Regulation – with data on exports of dual-use items that should be produced in all EU-Member States. Not only would this allow for democratic control, it is also essential to gather these data in order to inform future policy developments.

Conclusion

Export controls are regulated on several policy levels, from the most global one (the UN) to local levels of governance. The higher the policy level, the more abstract the language of the legal document. The merits of Resolution 1540 are its global reach and its focus on non-State actors. States are legally bound to create export controls. International support (both financially as in terms of expertise) is raised to support them in this task. Many challenges lay ahead however in implementing the resolution and developing effective national export controls. Reports of the implementation of Resolution 1540 reveal that there are major gaps between different regions. Regional institutions might serve as a stepping stone and help to strengthen the capacity of their Member States in developing the necessary controls. This chapter took a closer look to the European Union. Although the EU devotes substantial resources for outreach activities to non-EU countries, the chapter focuses on what the potential benefit

32 European Commission (2013), Report from the Commission to the Council and the European Parliament on the implementation of Regulation (EC) No. 428/2009 *setting up a Community regime for the control of exports, transfer, brokering and transit of dual-use items*. COM (2013) 710 final, Brussels 16 October 2013.

of regional support is to its own Member States, and what challenges the EU still encounters.

What the story of the EU dual-use export control policy may learn, is that the development of a regional policy is an incremental process, with lots of institutional stumbling blocks, both to overcome division of competences between the regional level and its Member States as between different degrees of integration of related policy fields (trade and foreign affairs). From a regional point of view, its weaknesses are shown in the unfinished harmonisation of export controls, meaning the assessment of risks and its outcome. No public information is available however to assess the degree of divergence, which is another deficiency in the EU control system (the lack of public data). The most prominent advantage of regional cooperation is to be found on the economic level. Despite the necessary trade controls, trade restrictions can be substantially limited to a minimum in liberalised custom unions such as the EU. Free trade in most dual-use items amongst EU Member States appeared to be the main driver behind EU integration. The prevention of proliferation of WMD is the other objective, for which cooperation and integration is less advanced, as is more generally true for the EU's Common Foreign and Security Policy and Justice and Home Affairs. Even though there are limits to what one can expect from the EU's CFSP, there is some room for improvement. With a view to the prevention of proliferation, it is recommendable to further develop cooperation among licencing officers by stimulating exchange of information, to guarantee a common interpretation of EU-dual-use lists, to develop best practices to face dual-use challenges, to makes use of trade common restrictions when necessary, to balance economic and ethical considerations with regard to new technologies, and to strengthen transparency to allow for democratic accountability. As such, the EU can further contribute to the strengthening of Member States' capacities in the prevention of WMD and conventional arms.

The EU Export Control Regime

Standards for the Walloon Region?

Anne-Valentine RENSONNET

University of Liège

Introduction

Since the adoption of United Nations Security Council Resolution 1540, export control has undergone an increased development around the world and export control regimes have been particularly developed in certain countries, notably in the United States of America, Japan and the European Union. This paper will show how the export control regime is developed in the Walloon Region in Belgium. We will try to see if the European Union dual-use export control regime constitutes a real model or only a set of prescriptions.

In order to answer this question, different aspects of the export control regime implemented in Belgium and particularly in the Walloon Region will be analysed. First, the existence of different levels of authority in the export control regime will be examined. Second, the authorities in charge of implementing export control regimes will be analysed. Third, the role of customs in the export control regime will be examined. Fourth, we will draw attention to awareness procedures for economic actors, and, finally, we will list the penalties applying in the case of non-compliance with the relevant laws.

The European Union competence: from theory to practice

In Belgium, four levels are involved in the definition of the export control regime: the international level, the European level (regional level), the national level (the federal level) and finally the subnational level (the Walloon region). These levels influence the implementation of the export control regime.

Export control of dual-use items is an exclusive competence of the European Union and is legislated under the Common Commercial Policy.

The main instrument is the Council Regulation 428/2009 of 5 May 2009 (the Regulation) *setting up a Community regime for the control of export, transfer, brokering and transit of dual-use items*. By this Regulation the European Union complies with its international obligations. The United Nations Security Council Resolution 1540 sets forth obligations for States, but not their practical implementation. Nevertheless, this document constitutes the basis for adopting national instruments in implementing an export control regime "(...) with criminal or civil penalties in place for violations of export control laws".[1]

Implementation of Regulation 428/2009 has been a regional competence since 2003. In the European Union, it constitutes a Belgian specificity. Belgium is the only European country that has federalised its export control competence. The Regions are competent for trade in military equipment and dual-use items that originate from their territories.[2] There is, however, a notable exception as concerns the import and export of such materials for the army and the police where the Federal government remains competent. The ministerial decree regulating export and transit of dual-use items of 28 September 2000[3] provides that Regulation 428/2009 is applied in Belgium but enumerates exceptions concerning the Benelux. These regions are not only competent for the implementation of the control of trade in strategic goods but also holds the legislative power to draft regulations in the field of export control, in accordance with their respective competences. This competence is nevertheless limited by the international obligations of Belgium.

The principal legal tools are federal legislations because the Walloon region has not adopted new legislations since 2003. The principal legal tools for the implementation of the dual-use Regulation are the Law of 11 September 1962 on the import, export and transit of goods and associated technology[4] and its implementing Royal Decree of 30 December 1993 regulating the import, export and transit of goods and associated technology.[5]

---

1 A. Wetter, "Enforcing European Union law on exports of dual-use goods", *SIPRI Research Report* 24, Oxford University Press, 2009, p. 3.

2 Loi spéciale du 8 août 1980, Article 6 Paragraph 1 VI, (4).

3 Arrêté Ministériel *réglementant l'exportation et le transit de biens et technologies à double usage* du 28 septembre 2000 (Moniteur Belge of 20 October 2000), amended by Arrêté Ministériel of 12 April 2002.

4 Law of 11 September 1962 *on the import, export and transit of goods and associated technology*, Belgian Official Journal, 27 October 1962.

5 Royal Decree of 30 December 1993 *regulating the import, export and transit of goods and associated technology*, Belgian Official Journal, 2 February 1994.

The different legal tools in the international, European, federal and regional levels are legally binding. Belgian authorities are complying with the international obligations. Furthermore, Belgium is also a member of different international export control regimes like the NSG, the Australia Group, the MTCR and the Wassenaar Arrangement. The tools adopted by these informal regimes are not legally binding but States party to these regimes conform generally to their decisions.

Licencing authorities: the need of collaboration

In Wallonia, the competent authority is the Arms and Dual-Use Licencing Directorate (*Direction de la gestion des licences d'armes et de biens à double usage*) which forms part of DG06 Economy, Employment and Research (for the administrative analyses); the Service licence control, is concerned with external affairs and human rights (*Service Contrôle Licence, analyse politique étrangère et droits de l'homme*) which belongs to *Wallonie-Bruxelles International* (for the international political analyses of sensitive demands).[6] The political decision of granting or denying licences is an exclusive competence of the Minister-President of the Walloon Region. The Minister-President of Wallonia bears the political responsibility.

The licencing authority is competent for the control of all dual-use items, for weapons control and chemical weapons control. Nevertheless, the trade in nuclear material[7] to non-EU Member States is subject to an additional opinion of the Committee of advice on non-proliferation of nuclear weapons (CANVEK / CANPAN).[8] This Committee collaborates with regional licencing authorities. Regional licencing authorities participate in this Committee with an advisory vote. Furthermore, the regional authorities submit, on their initiative, the licences requested from them. This particularity is based on the Law of 9 February 1981 *establishing the conditions for export of nuclear materials and equipment as well as technological data*[9] and, the Royal Decree of 12 May 1989 *on transfer of nuclear materials, equipment and nuclear technological data and their derivatives*. The law states that a federal authorisation is required

6 Gouvernement Wallon, "Rapport au parlement wallon sur l'application de la loi du 5 août 1991, modifiée par les lois du 25 et du 26 mars 2003 relatives à l'importation, à l'exportation et au transit d'armes, de munitions et de materiel devant servir spécialement à un usage militaire et de la technologie y afférente", 2011, p. 20.

7 Nuclear material listed in the Nuclear Suppliers Group List.

8 Commissie van advies voor de niet-verspreiding van kernwapens/Commission d'avis pour la non-prolifération des armes nucléaires.

9 *Belgian Official Journal*, 23 December 2010.

for trade in nuclear material. This authorisation has been challenged in Constitutional Court by the Flemish Region.[10] In its Decision, the Court stated that authorisation granted by the Committee of advice on non-proliferation of nuclear weapons is parallel and complementary to the licencing procedure provided by Regulation 428/2009 and implemented by the regions.[11]

At European level, there is an obligation to exchange information between individual EU Member States and the European Commission. Article 19 of Regulation 428/2009, states:

> Member States, in cooperation with the Commission shall take all appropriate measure to establish direct cooperation and exchange of information between competent authorities.[12] The Dual-use e-system became fully operational in June 2012. This system is a secure electronic system hosted by the Commission for exchanging information among Member States. Member States have (…) the possibility to enter information concerning denials on dual-use items, to exchange documents in a library or to perform full data exports.[13]

At the national level of Belgium, a cooperation agreement[14] was adopted in 2007 between the Federal authority and the three regional authorities. This agreement is the basis of a sincere cooperation principle between the federal authority and the regional authorities in conformity with the international and European obligations. This agreement concerns the exchange of information between the federal authority and the regional authorities, notably the designation of a point of contact within the services for the cooperation with the others by the Foreign affairs minister and the competent minister of each regional authority. By this agreement, mechanisms of international consultations and the representation of Belgium in the international export control regime are organised. The Walloon region maintains informal collaborations and consultations

10 Constitutional Court, Case 168/2011 of 10 November 2010.

11 Q. Michel, "Le contrôle du commerce des biens à double usage: 10 ans après la regionalisation", conference, 23 October 2013.

12 Council Regulation (EC) No. 428/2009 of 5 May 2009 *setting up a Community regime for the control of exports, transfer, brokering and transit of dual-use items*, Article 19.

13 European Commission, "Report to the Council and the European Parliament on the implementation of Regulation (EC) No. 428/2009 setting up a Community regime for the control of exports, transfer, brokering and transit of dual-use items", 16 October 2013. 17 p.

14 Accord de coopération entre l'Etat fédéral, la Région flamande, la Région wallonne et la Région de Bruxelles-Capitale *relatif à l'importation, l'exportation et le transit d'armes, de munitions et de matériel devant servir spécialement à un usage*, 17 July 2007.

with different federal services as the justice service, the customs and the defence services.

Concerning the regional level, a new informal structure of concertation among regional authorities was created in 2007. This structure permits the exchange of information on different fields linked to the management of competence, to improve synergies among regional authorities and to define a common working method concerning specific matters.[15]

The control by customs authorities: a federal competence

The Customs have a role of verification in the export control regime. Article 16 of Regulation 428/2009 provides that Customs are Allowed – without prejudice to the powers granted them and pursuant to the Community Customs Code – to suspend or stop the export of dual-use items for which a valid export licence has been issued (by their own or another Member State) if there is a reasonable suspicion that:

- Relevant information was not taken into account when the licence was granted;
- Circumstances have materially changed since the licence was granted.[16]

In such case the authorities of the Member State that issued the licence shall be immediately consulted. The consequence is revocation, suspension or annulment of the licence.[17] In the case of maintenance the licence, a notification shall be sent to the other Member States and the European Commission.[18]

The Community Customs Code established an electronic information exchange system between Member States and customs administrations. The exporter must notify customs authorities information on items prior to their import in or export from the EU via an electronic pre-arrival and pre-departure declaration. Furthermore, exporters can be granted the status of authorised economic operator, which provides facilitations regarding customs controls relating to security and safety considerations.

---

15 Gouvernement wallon, *Rapport au parlement wallon sur l'application de la loi du 5 août 1991, modifiée par les lois du 25 et du 26 mars 2003 relatives à l'importation, à l'exportation et au transit d'armes, de munitions et de materiel devant servir spécialement à un usage militaire et de la technologie y afférente*, 2011, p. 32.

16 Council Regulation (EC) No. 428/2009 of 5 May 2009 *setting up a Community regime for the control of exports, transfer, brokering and transit of dual-use items*, Article 16.

17 *Ibid.*, Article 13.1.

18 S. Depauw, "The legal framework for the control on trade in dual-use items in Flanders", Flemish Peace Institute, Background Note, 2011, p. 29.

There is no agreement relating to cooperation between the Walloon licencing authority and the Belgian customs authorities. In practice, however, this cooperation takes place and all authorities are in contact with one another based on their respective competences.

Awareness raising: collaborations between the public actors and the economic actors

The awareness of companies concerns the information that economic actors have about the existence and content of the dual-use export control. Different mechanisms are developed to help companies.

At European level, the European Commission organises meetings between economic actors and the Dual-Use Coordination Group, established by the Article 23 of Regulation 428/2009. The website of the European Commission provides information on trade of dual-use items. The European Commission has also organised different conferences on export control as well as a relevant "Green Paper" on the subject. At the European level, stakeholders are consulted on export control policy. The Green paper illustrates the will of the European Commission to include the concerns of stakeholders in the review process of the Regulation 428/2009.

At the regional level, the Walloon region organises different seminars and information sessions for the economic actors, An annual report on trade of arms and dual-use export control is presented to the Walloon parliament. This report is publicly available and can be consulted on Internet. Moreover, the website of the Walloon region provides useful information.

Penalties in case of non-compliance

Non-compliance in implementation of provisions of Regulation 428/2009 can be sanctioned. Article 24[19] of the Regulation states that each Member State shall take measures to ensure proper enforcement of Regulation 428/2009 and shall lay down the penalties applicable to infringements of the Regulation. In Belgium, the penal provisions are set in three legislations adopted by the Federal authority.

---

19 Article 24: "Each Member State shall take appropriate measures to ensure proper enforcement of all the provisions of this Regulation. In particular, it shall lay down the penalties applicable to infringements of the provisions of this Regulation or of those adopted for its implementation. Those penalties must be effective, proportionate and dissuasive".

First, the Law of 11 September 1962 on the import, export and transit of goods and associated technology, particularly the articles 10 and 10bis, state that a penalty could be decided in the case of importations, exportations and transshipment without a valid licence or in case of certain infringements.[20] The penalty may consist in the denial of any import, export or transit licence for a period ranging from one to six months.[21]

Second, the Law of 18 July 1977 on customs and taxes enumerates penalties particularly in articles 231, 249-253, 263-284. Article 231 states that the goods will be confiscated and, in addition, a fine will be imposed. The amount of the fine corresponds to the value of the said goods if the declaration is submitted with a licence but not in conformity with the conditions of the licence.

Third, the Law of 9 February 1981 *establishing the conditions for export of nuclear materials and equipment as well as technological data*, and particularly Article 6, states that attempts of evasion of declarations, declarations acquired on the basis of wrong information and falsely acquired licences may be punished with a term of imprisonment ranging from four months to one year and from one month to five years if it concerns nuclear trade.

> Supervision and control of compliance with all mentioned obligations are, in practice, chiefly the task of the Customs and Excise Administration officers. Nevertheless, the authority of the judicial police enforces compliance with the applicable legislation: i.e. verification as to whether the declaration made corresponds to the transported goods and as to the required import, export, or transit licence. This means that federal officers verify the licences issued by the regions. For this verification the customs officers can in turn call upon the expertise of the licencing authorities. They have to inform the licencing authority about infractions or attempts of infractions without delay. Every public administration has the duty to inform the licencing authority about useful information regard infractions or attempts to infractions. In particular with regard to import, export, and transit subject to licencing, including trade in military or dual-use goods, the officials of the Economic General Inspection and the officials or officers appointed to that task by the competent Minister are also authorised to track down and establish violations.[22]

20 For example: trade in prohibited arms, collaboration in the circumvention of the commercial traffic, submission incorrect or incomplete information in order to obtain a licence, refusal to cooperate in a control or investigation.

21 Q. Michel, *Sensitive trade. The perspective of European States*, Brussels, P.I.E. Lang, 2011.

22 Depauw S., *op. cit.*, p. 29.

The penalties are defined in specific laws with regard to dual-use and nuclear trade control and customs. The common criminal law does not enumerate these penalties.

Table 1: Summary of penalties

Law of 11 September 1962 on the import, export and transit of goods and associated technology	**Law of Law of 18 July 1977 on customs and taxes**	**Law of 9 February 1981 establishing the conditions for export of nuclear materials and equipment as well as technological data**
Articles 10 and 10 Bis	Articles 231, 249-253, 263-284	Article 6
To any person: – Who imports, exports, or trans-ships – or attempt to do this – without a valid licence, – Who trades in prohibited arms, who collaborates in the circumvention of the commercial traffic – Who submits incorrect or incomplete information in order to obtain a licence, – Who refuses to cooperate in a control or investigation.	– The declaration is submitted with a licence, but not in line with the conditions of the licence, – Extenuating circumstances or the acceptance that the violation is because of oblivion or committed by mistake may lead to a settlement.	Attempts of evasion of declarations, declarations acquired on the basis of wrong information and falsely acquired licences
Possible denial of every import, export, or transit licence for a period ranging from one month to six months	– Confiscation of goods – Fine	– Imprisonment: one month to five years – Fine – Confiscation of goods

Conclusion

The aim of this chapter was to illustrate the implementation of the export control regime in the Walloon region with regard to international and European obligations. It demonstrated that the Belgian export control regime is complex due to the intervention of different legal levels. According to our analysis, the European Union dual-use export control regime could not be considered as a real model but is, however, more than a set of prescriptions. The Member States have indeed the possibility to implement widely or restrictively the provisions of Regulation 428/2009.

The case of Belgium illustrates typically this difficulty. The consequence is that the export control regimes are different in each Member States and therefore lead to an "asymmetrical implementation" of EU export controls which creates distortions of trade and sometimes results in a fragmented market affecting the equal treatment of European companies.[23] To prevent the proliferation of WMD it would be beneficial to have a more uniform set of regulations within the European Union.

23 Commission Staff Working Document, "Strategic export controls: ensuring security and competitiveness in a changing world – A report on the public consultation launched under the Green Paper", 17 January 2013, p. 24.

Export Control Systems: a Bulgarian Perspective

Velislava ZHIVKOVA

PhD Researcher, International Institute of Energy Policy and Diplomacy, Moscow State Institute of International Relations

It has been a long way for the Bulgarian export control system to evolve to its current state. Until 1989 and especially during the period 1978-1988, Bulgaria was characterised by a strong military-industrial complex, which was of a dominant importance for its national economy. The "complex" was specialised and export oriented (around 90 per cent of its production) within the Warsaw Pact and the COMECON.[1]

The transitional period after 1989 had a strong impact on the military industry in the country. Bulgaria lost many of its traditional markets[2] and the industry was concerned with the introduction of further export controls, which would lead to further loss of markets and income.[3]

However, in 1991 the Government laid down the foundation of an export control regime, as the first set of legislation had only covered military products.[4] Dual-use goods and technologies were included in the law at the end of 1992.[5] Finally, a comprehensive set of legal instruments consisting of a law[6] and an implementing regulation was adopted in 1996.

---

1 P. Gounev, E. Tsenkov, B. Mariani, L. Attree (eds.), *Weapons under scrutiny: Implementing arms export controls and combating small arms proliferation in Bulgaria*, Centre for the Study of Democracy (CSD) and Safer world, p. 19-27.

2 *Idem.*

3 See further: Mladenov N.E., *The emerging Non-proliferation Export Control Policy of Bulgaria after 1990*, NATO Research Fellowship Report 1999.

4 Council of Ministers Regulation No. 13, 12 February 1991.

5 Council of Ministers Regulation 114 (amended by CoM Regulation 224).

6 Law on the Control of Foreign Trade Activity in Arms and in Dual-use Goods and technologies, State Gazette No. 102, 1995.

Legal basis

Currently, the Bulgarian legal system for export controls is aligned with the European and international standards, due to its membership in the European Union and adoption of the international export control regimes. The law covers certain categories of conventional weapons and the associated equipment and their means of production,[7] as well as a range of dual-use items. Technology and software related to controlled items, as well as technical assistance associated with them are also subject to control. An important feature of the system is that it is being regularly revised and updated in order to respond to contemporary challenges.

The latest amendment of the comprehensive Export Control Act – the *Defence-Related Products and Dual-Use Items and Technologies Export Control Act*[8] came into force in June 2012. The Act introduces rules and procedures transposing into national law the relevant provisions of Directive 2009/43/EC of the European Parliament and of the Council of 6 May 2009 so as to simplify procedures and conditions of dual-use transfer within the Community. The Act also introduces new types of permits for dual-use transfers out of the territory of Bulgaria. There are now four types of export authorisations – individual, global, national general and EU general.

Implementation of Regulation 2009/43 requires companies applying for authorisations and/or registrations[9] to present a description of their established internal compliance program and the management system.

Pursuant to Directive 2009/43/EC, the law establishes a procedure for the certification of recipients of defence-related products from other Member States by which the certified recipients can benefit from a simplified inclusion in the general authorisations for transfer, published by the suppliers' Member State.

The list of military products as well as the list of dual-use goods and technologies that are subject to import controls were also updated in 2012 (Decree No. 158 of the Council of Ministers 2012).[10]

---

7 For example, missiles, military vehicles, radioactive materials, military electronic equipment, military technologies, technical assistance for maintenance, repair, modification and modernisation of weapons.

8 Promulgated, State Gazette No. 26/29.03.2011, in force 30 June 2012, Amended State Gazette No. 93, 27 November 2012.

9 Include licences to export, import and transport, certificates for recipient of defence-related products, registration certificates for transfer, and certificates for registration for brokerage of defence-related products.

10 Annual Report of the Interministerial Commission for Export Control and Non-proliferation of Weapons of Mass Destruction with the Minister of Economy, Energy

Licensing procedures

The Interministerial Commission for Export Control and Non-proliferation of Weapons of Mass Destruction, the Interdepartmental Council on the Defence industry and Security of supply and the Minister of Economy and Energy are the governmental bodies with primary responsibility for export controls.

In addition to the above-mentioned institutions, the Minister of Interior, the Chairperson of the National Security Agency and the Director of Agency "Customs" of the Ministry of Finance also have controlling functions over the implementation of the national export control policy.[11]

The Interdepartmental Council authorises the export, import and transport of defence related products, issues the certificate for the recipient of the products related to defence, and the certificate for registration for the transfer, as well as the registration certificate for brokerage. Co-chairs of the Council are the Minister of Economy and Energy, and the Minister of Defence. The Council also includes representatives of the Ministries of Economy and Energy, of Defence, Interior, Foreign Affairs, Finance, Transport, Information Technology and Communications, of Regional Development and Public Works, Education and Science, the National Intelligence Service, the State Agency "National Security", and the State Agency "State Reserve and War-Time Stocks".

Chairperson of the Interministerial Commission is the Minister of Economy and Energy; its members are representatives of the Ministry of Foreign Affairs, the Ministries of Economy and Energy, Defence, and Interior, and the National Security Agency.

The Interministerial Commission reviews applications for individual and global authorisations for export, import and transfer from and to the territory of Bulgaria, transit, transportation, exhibition of defence related products and dual-use items, and brokerage transactions.

The Commission also considers applications for certificates for registration for production, processing or use of substances of applications of the Chemical Weapons Convention.

The Commission also publishes national general authorisations for transfer of defence related products, and for export and transfer of dual-use items. It also receives the general EU export authorisation declarations.

---

and Tourism for the implementation of the Defence-Related Products and Dual-Use Items and Technologies Export Control Act, 2012.

11 *Idem.*

The Minister of Economy and Energy is authorised to issue registrations for export and transfer of dual-use items and brokerage, imports of goods and dual-use technologies covered in Annex 2 of the Decree No. 158/24.07.2012 on the adoption of a list of products related to defence, and the list of dual-use items subject to import controls.

It also registers transfer of defence related products for the territory of Bulgaria,[12] as well as export, import and transfer of defence related products from the territory of Bulgaria to the entities listed under Article 5(2) of the Law.[13]

In terms of cooperation, in addition to the specific provisions of the Community regarding the common security policy, Member States of the EU undertake additional coordination and collaboration commitments. It is the responsibility of the Member State under Regulation 428/2009 to consider valid refusals to identical transactions before issuing a permit for brokerage/export of dual-use items and technologies, and to conduct consultation with the competent authorities of the Member State notified of the refusal in the case of coincidence.[14]

Moreover, as the EU activities in the field of export control and non-proliferation are closely related to the work of international export organisations and regimes, they are subject to discussions in three specialised working groups:

- CONOP – Council Working Party on Non-proliferation (EU External Action);
- WPDU – Working Party on Dual-Use Goods (EU Council);
- DUCG – Dual-use Co-ordination Group Meeting (chaired by the Commission, in 2010 a project for conducting peer visits in the Member States for identifying and sharing best practices was launched).

Customs

A significant role in the verification of export control implementation is attributed to the National Customs Agency, a centralised administrative

12 For entities under Article 5 Paragraph 1 of the Law – individuals and legal entities registered under the Commercial Law.

13 Structures of the central administration of the executive power led by the Ministers, the State Agency "National Security", the National Reconnaissance Office and the National Security Service. Obligation of those persons is to declare the planned transfer for the territory of the country.

14 The exchange of information on refusals made by Member States is carried out through a secure electronic system, developed and maintained by the European Commission.

structure within the Minister of Finance.[15] In addition to its role in verification, there is a specialised unit within the Agency,[16] which supports and controls the activities regarding the area of investigation and combating illegal trafficking of dual-use goods and technologies.[17]

An example of the verification work of the Agency is the procedure for granting delivery verification certificate:

- If the foreign exporter requires a delivery verification certificate, the importer submits to the customs office a filled delivery verification certificate in three copies, and a copy of the relevant import permit at the time of customs clearance of the goods;
- The presented delivery verification certificate is verified again at the customs office, which authorises the transaction;
- The first copy of the certificate is provided to the importer, the second copy within fifteen working days from the date of validation of the certificate is sent from the Headquarters of the Customs Agency to the Ministry of Economy and Energy, and the third one remains in the Headquarters of the Customs Agency.

Given the nature of the activity of dual-use export control, the Customs Agency has been trying to pursue a consistent policy in this area the last twenty years. Although the export control law was in a process of preparation at the beginning of the 1990s, cooperation with institutions like the National Academy of Sciences, the Ministry of Energy, the Nuclear Energy Regulator and the Institute for Nuclear Research contributed to the overall training of customs officers in controlling the transfer of dual-use goods and technologies.

Moreover, a number of training programmes were conducted through international cooperation during the years. The Customs Agency, jointly with representatives of the Department of Energy of the United States. conducted training programmes on the identification of dual-use items and technologies from 1991 to 2013 inclusive.[18] The curriculum in the last several years has been harmonised and is consistent with the EU requirements. The country's commitment for export controls at the external borders of the EU increased the requirements for the Bulgarian customs administration. Instructions and exercises were held through EU

15 Official website of the National Customs Agency: http://www.customs.bg/en.

16 Directorate "Customs Intelligence and Investigation".

17 Customs Agency Rules of Procedure (in Bulgarian): http://www.customs.bg/bg/page/234.

18 *Idem.*

programmes in order to enhance the customs officers' expertise in the EU export control requirements.[19]

In addition, courses such as "train-the-trainers" are organised for Bulgarian instructors so as to keep and manage the knowledge and experience in the country. Attendees to these programmes are customs officers, as well as representatives from the Border Police, the National Security Agency, the Military Information Office, the Military Police and others.

Awareness raising

Close collaboration between the competent authorities and the representatives of industry, and the academic and science communities is a necessary condition for the proper functioning of a national export control system.

Due to the long experience in military trade in the country and the willingness of the national companies to be in conformity with the national, EU and international requirements, there is an overall good knowledge of the rules among the well-established companies in Bulgaria.[20]

However, not only in Bulgaria, attention should be directed towards new, emerging companies, small companies and companies, which are expanding their list of production. Such companies could be potential law-breakers due to understaffing, little familiarity and understanding of the sensitive nature of some goods and technologies in their scope.

One way of managing this issue is the requirement for internal compliance programmes to be established in every company applying for authorisations and/or registrations. Such provisions, as already mentioned, are included in the current version of the Bulgarian export law, in compliance with Regulation 2009/43/EC.

In order to discuss and clarify the contemporary challenges and issues, a series of activities related to awareness raising have been initiated in the past several years.

Two workshops were organised in 2010:

- Government-industry on current European and national legislation on export control of dual-use items. Internal corporate compliance and control systems;
- Government-academia on export controls the transfer of technology;

19 Website for Customs-related information: http://info.mitnica.com/index.php?p=archiv&page=23&src=4171.

20 From communications with several representatives of the industry.

- Two workshops devoted to the partnership "Government-industry" were held in 2011;
- Current European and national legislation on export control of dual-use items. Internal corporate compliance and control systems;
- Best practices of export control of dual-use items and technologies.

The Bulgarian Industrial Association and the "Internationally Controlled Trade and Security" unit with the Ministry of Economy and Energy organised a seminar in 2012 in connection with the latest export control legislation and aiming at raising the awareness of the industry of the new authorisations and requirements of the Regulation 428/2009.[21]

Sanctions

Breaches and related penalties for breaches of rules governing export control of dual-use items and technologies are set forth in the comprehensive export control law and the Criminal Code of Bulgaria.

The Export control law contains administrative and penal provisions – a fine or a property sanction amounting from BGN 1,000 to BGN 500,000 (approximately 500-250,000 Euros) depending on the type of violation, natural/legal persons, repeated violation (in case the deed is not a crime).[22]

The Criminal Code provides for dual-use export control rules breaches in two chapters – crimes against the economy, Section "Crimes against individual economic sectors" and dangerous crimes, Section "Crimes committed in a generally dangerous way or by hazardous devices".

The first chapter envisages imprisonment of up to six years and a fine up to BGN 200 000 (approximately 100,000 Euros):[23]

- For particularly serious cases, the punishment is imprisonment of three to eight years and a fine of up to BGN 500,000 (approximately 250,000 Euros);
- In minor cases the punishment is a fine of up to BGN 20,000 (approximately 10,000 Euros);

---

21 Annual Report of the Interministerial Commission for Export Control and Non-proliferation of Weapons of Mass Destruction with the Minister of Economy, Energy and Tourism for the implementation of the Defence-Related Products and Dual-Use Items and Technologies Export Control Act, 2012.

22 See Article 72, 73 and 74 of the Defence-Related Products and Dual-Use Items and Technologies Export Control Act.

23 See Article 233 (1) to (4) of the Criminal Code Promulgated State Gazette No. 26, 2 April 1968, effective 1 May 1968, amended and supplemented 27 September 2013.

- Weaponry or goods, or technologies with dual application, which are the object of a crime are confiscated by the State notwithstanding their ownership, or, if the above items are missing or have been appropriated, the equivalent of their value shall be adjudicated, as determined by the Foreign trade contract.

The second chapter provides for imprisonment of three to ten years and a fine of up to BGN 200,000 (approximately 100,000 Euros).

Law on extradition[24] (including European arrest warrant) and bilateral agreements for extradition may be applicable to cases of export control violations concerning Bulgaria.

Extradition could be agreed in cases of criminal offenses punishable in Bulgaria by imprisonment or detention for not less than three years under the Criminal Code. Such cases include illicit trafficking of nuclear or radioactive materials, terrorism, illicit trafficking of weapons, munitions and explosives.

Conclusion

Following this discussion on some elements of the national export control system, it appears that some of the features fully or partly set out in the Bulgarian system could be considered as being practical and applicable to a "model" export control system.

It is first the existence of one only comprehensive export control law, set in one legal document that covers both defence related products and dual-use items. This minimises the risk of confusion among the industry and also facilitates the work of the competent authorities to ensure compliance with the rules.

Second, a centralised competent authority with ultimate responsibility for explicitly dual-use (and possibly military products) transactions might lead to better communication among all parties concerned – industry, other involved authorities, academia, scientific community.

More outreach activities and a good communication with the industry lead to increasing the understanding of the issues by both sides and encourages the companies to contribute more than just obeying the letter of the law.

Interdisciplinary trainings organised collectively for representatives of different bodies involved in the export control, help to harmonise and clarify the collaboration mechanisms between the institutions.

---

24 Law on Extradiction in force 4 July 2005 amended State Gazette No. 49/2010.

The European Union has the potential to increase its role in dual-use export control facilitation (good level of expertise and experience in ensuring compliance with dual-use rules i.e. during the process of enlargement). Cooperation and assistance activities with third countries evolved in the past less then ten years and a number of projects have been implemented in different regions of the world. Currently, there is not a designated EU body for dual-use export controls outreach activities with third countries, but the Federal Office of Economics and Export Control (BAFA) is mandated to implement projects in this field. One step further in the EU export controls evolution may be the establishment of such body.

EU Regulation + French Regulations = An Exportable Control Model?

Sylvain Paile-Calvo

Senior Researcher, University of Liège

Though it is not easy to qualify the European Union dual-use trade control system set by the Regulation 429/2009 as a "stand-alone" regime, the question of its efficiency as a "copy-paste" model of set of rules or simply as a philosophical construction aimed at preventing the undesirable proliferation of weapons of mass destruction must nonetheless be addressed.

Similar to the international export control regimes, the European Union's set of rules contained principally in the Regulation 428/2009 does not address all the aspects of a comprehensive control of sensitive trade. For instance, it does not properly create a licencing authority, nor does it create infringements or sanctions. Unlike the international export control regimes, however, it establishes legally binding and enforceable rules. The European Union built a set of incomplete prescriptions which, it is assumed, cannot be seen as a perfect "model" *per se* with view to be reproduced in any part of the world.

In order to fulfil its function of proliferation-risk mitigation, such a system in place must be completed by additional prescriptions, which organise the controls and implement the European principles for a daily application. In the European Union, this must be proceeded by the Member States inside their national legal *apparatus*. Hence, similar to the structure of the customs legislation, the trade control system shaped by France is different from the 27 – and more – other systems that coexist under the umbrella of the European principles. The subsidiary – "French" – system is the product of the French constitutional organisation and the French administrative culture and organisation.

The interdependency between the European principles – though legally and directly enforceable – and the national implementation of these principles leads to asking if the combination of these two levels, and not alternatively one or the other, can be seen as an efficient and exportable model or approach of dual-use trade controls which could potentially be reproduced at different levels of decision – regional, sub-regional, national – outside the Union's borders. Subsidiarily, the lessons learnt from the European experience shall lead to ask which of these levels, including the universal one, is the most suitable level for designing such trade controls.

An objective answer to these two fundamental questions necessarily requires emphasis and analysis of both the gaps left by this combination and the caveats used by a Member State such as France for building the optimal trade control system. This will be covered in this chapter through studying the elements that, in the framework of the Outreach actions[1] for assistance to third countries, constitutes the pillars of an effective and efficient trade control system: the existence of a legal framework organising the controls, of licencing mechanisms and structures, a coordination with the missions of the customs authorities, the existence of mechanisms aimed at raising the awareness of the stakeholders and of sanctions in case of infringement of the established rules.

Structuring a model

Notwithstanding the force of the law as a legislative act, especially in the Common Law tradition's countries, all the prominent national export control systems sit on acts that have a legally binding strength. In the context of the European Union, three levels of definitions of rules are met: the international level, the EU regional level and the national level. Though the international rules in dual-use export control are mainly adopted in the framework of the six main international regimes, with the exception of the United Nations (UN) Security Council Resolution 1540 adopted according to the UN Charter' Chapter VII, from an organic viewpoint they do not legally bind their members.[2]

The European Union level is unique in comparison with the hierarchy of norms that exist worldwide. In the area of the dual-use trade control, the EU has the legislative power. The Regulation 428/2009 shall thus be seen as a law, directly applicable as a norm and enforceable as a sovereign source of legal constraint on the Member States and their legal and physical persons. The European Union Court of Justice is thus competent for examining cases of infringements of the Regulation by the Member States. However, since the European Union Member States are almost all members of every regime, the EU does follow the lists adopted by these

1 Long-Term Programme of the European Union.

2 France is a full member of these six main international fora: Nuclear Suppliers Group, Zangger Committee, Australia Group, the Chemical Weapons Convention, Wassenaar Arrangement and Missile Technology Control Regime.

regimes as if they were binding and it modifies its own Regulation when the international guidelines are amended. Though not legally binding, the international rules are in practice. Substantially, the EU legislation is comprehensive. It encompasses in one list the scopes of all the main international trade control regimes an in one text all the rules that are applicable to the items contained in this list.

The role of implementing the law through detailed prescriptions and running the licencing of the dual-use trade belongs to the Member States, according to the principle of subsidiarity that is enacted in the EU "constitutional" corpus.[3] According to this principle, the most adequate level must be the one made responsible for providing the guiding principles or rules. Though the Member States have internal administrative organisations for applying the export control rules on a daily basis, which the EU does not, and have a thorough knowledge of their industrial and commercial realities, they shall be responsible for the implementation of the European legislation. In the French constitutional system, this legislation is higher in the hierarchy of norms than the national ones and does not need, being a monist system, prior inclusion in national text to take effect. Nonetheless, everything that is outside the constitutional scope of the law[4] or that is applying or completing the law may be ruled by the different regulatory acts in the hands of the executive power: decrees, arrêtés and, in the framework of dual-use trade controls more specifically, notices and avis. Substantially, though the French national regulations implement the EU legislation, the final legal picture is comprehensive. In principle, the "legislation" – understood in its broadest meaning does not make a difference between the categories of weapons of mass destruction that found the respective competences of the international regimes.

When looking at the organisation and articulation of the legal structures, one may state that the French acts alone are insufficient for being considered as a directly exportable model. The EU rules cannot stand alone either though they have the legal strength required. They need the national ones to become effective. The international principles are too generic and do not have the legal strength for founding an exportable model. However, when studying the original connections that exist between these three levels specifically, one must state that the European regional level acts as a legal philosopher's stone, turning international soft law to national hard law. *De facto*, the French industrial and commercial operators are legally accountable for the application of the international principles set by the regimes, endorsed and enacted by the European

3 Treaty on the European Union, Article 5.

4 Article 34 of the French Constitution, *Constitution du 4 Octobre 1958*.

Union, completed and implemented at the national level. This suggests that the international level, using the form of a universal and binding treaty, might be adequate for founding a trade control model.

Organising the licencing

In the French picture, the main competence for the dual-use items' trade licencing is in the hands of the Dual-Use Goods Service (SBDU).[5] The SBDU, created within the structure of the Directorate General for Competitiveness, Industry and Services (DGCIS), is placed under the authority of the Minister of Industry. Its mission is to review the applications and to deliver the authorisations under the authority of the Minister, who acts through the SBDU, on behalf of the European Union for the EU general export authorisations and on behalf of the French Republic for all other authorisations. In addition, the SBDU is also responsible for the export of explosive powders designed for civilian purposes. Other authorities exercise their missions in the formal control of the dual-use trade in support to the SBDU. The Ministry of Economy and Finances formally publishes a list of countries subject to restriction on exports and technical ministries, such as that of Defence or Environment, and the Ministry of Foreign Affairs, must be consulted by the SBDU when a decision is to be taken on the export of particularly sensitive items or to sensitive destinations. In order to favour and formalise the communication in this area, a Dual-Use Items Inter-Ministerial Commission (CIBDU)[6] was created within the Ministry of Foreign and European Affairs. Its mission is to provide opinions with regard to the export, brokering, transit, and classification of dual-use items when an application regarding competences of several ministries is received or, more generally, on aspects of the applicable legislation.

Though not specifically related to one category of items in the meaning of the international regimes (nuclear, chemical, bacteriological, etc.), the licencing of the dual-use items' trade in France is not comprehensive. For the authorisation of the export of items of category 5 of the European Regulation ("telecommunication and information security"), for example, an expert agency, the Information Systems Security National Agency (ANSSI), provides opinions to the SBDU. In addition, the External Trade Titles Service (SETICE), which is an organ of the Directorate General for Customs and Indirect Taxation (DGDDI) placed under the tutorship of

5 Arrêté du 18 mars 2010 *portant création d'un service à compétence nationale dénommé "service des biens à double usage"*.

6 Décret No. 2010-294 du 18 mars 2010 *portant création d'une "commission interministérielle des biens à double usage"*.

the Customs Minister, is the licencing authority for the export of military items, of items listed in the "Torture Regulation"[7] and, together with the customs, and the import documents. Finally, France uses the possibility given the European Regulation to subject to prior authorisation the trade of items not listed for imposing controls over the international trade of helicopters and their spare parts as well as some tear gas and riot control agents

Despite the fact that the European Regulation 428/2009 establishes in its Article 19 that the Member States shall take the appropriate measures for "establish(ing) direct cooperation and exchange of information between competent authorities", notably as it relates to denials as foreseen by the international regimes' guidelines, and that its Article 23 creates a Dual-Use Coordination Group, the French regulations do not provide legal tools for organising the practical coordination of the authorities with foreign ones. On a day-to-day basis, France relies on the connections and dialogue between diplomatic and intelligence services and on the informal communication between the export control authorities of the other Member States with a view to avoid potential undercut conflicts.

The regime set by the European Union for itself and its Member States does not appear, after the review of the licencing structures, self-sufficient. Though its efficiency is not challenged here, it is not monolithic. It provides margin for too many differences – and thus inconsistence – between the Member States. As it relies on the pre-existence of national licencing structures, and possibly licencing cultures, it cannot be qualified as a directly exportable model. The national level, in this specific area, seems to be the most adequate one for setting trade control rules.

Defining the role of customs

Similar to the licencing-related rules, the principles and rules of the involvement of the customs services in the control of the dual-use trade are double layered. At the European regional level, the Union Customs Code[8] provides the fundamentals of the legislation that is applicable to customs, in the absence of European customs services. Nonetheless, it does not include any reference to dual-use trade in particular. At the national level, these rules are given a practical form, which in France,

7 Council regulation (EC) 1236/2005 of 27 June 2005 *concerning trade in certain goods which could be used for capital punishment, torture or other cruel, inhuman or degrading treatment or punishment.*

8 Regulation (EU) No. 952/2013 of the European Parliament and of the Council of 9 October 2013 *laying down the Union Customs Code* (O.J. 10 October 2013, L.269/1).

notably takes the form of a national Customs Code. If the French dual-use regulations contain few references to the customs' role in the area, the customs' national rules contain clear references to the dual-use trade controls, highlighting the applicable rules.

Beyond the limits of articles 16 to 18 of the European Regulation, the – French – customs services do not act in the licencing *per se* of the export, brokering, transit or transhipment of dual-use goods. However, the customs are represented at the CIBDU, which reviews the most sensitive licence applications and decides on such cases. The licence is then formally granted by the SBDU. In addition, they are charged with the verification of the shipments, of the documents that accompany these shipments and which must contain copies of the authorisation, of the reality of the information contained in these documents.[9] This includes the capacity for the customs services to ask for the presentation of all necessary documents even ex-post, since the licenced companies have the obligation to keep record of their dual-use goods' transactions. For military explosive powders, the customs services are also the authority which formally authorises the export. They also have the central role of formally investigating and characterising infringements to the trade control provisions, including both the European and French ones.

On the other hand, the other trade control authorities may be called to play a role in the missions of the customs, although this coordination is not always foreseen by the legislation. For instance, the SBDU may contribute to the investigations of the customs with view to characterise an infringement, if so required. Intelligence, police and gendarmerie are also meant to support the customs services in their missions.

Finally, neither the French customs legislation nor the European one make specific reference to coordination between national customs services in the area of the dual-use trade controls. These aspects shall thus be seen as covered by the common law of the customs, which includes the contribution of the French services to the activities of the World Customs Organisation.

Keeping in mind that the role of the European customs in the application of the dual-use trade controls is the product of the European customs union and the existence of a single market within its borders, one may state that nothing prevents this area to be ruled at a sub-regional or regional level when designing an exportable model or approach.

---

9 Bulletin officiel des douanes No. 6590 *règlementation relative aux biens et technologies à double usage*, 26 janvier 2004.

Raising the awareness of the industrial and commercial operators

Although the European and French public authorities are well aware of the dangers of the proliferation of weapons of mass destruction and set controls on the dual-use items' movements, the challenge lies with the information of the industrial and commercial operators. It is assumed that the main industrial and commercial operators that are active on the French territory are aware of the applicable rules, since France has many big companies and even world leading companies in the production and trade of all categories of dual-use items. These operators are clearly identifiable and their trade control internal structures are regularly convened to promotion and information events on the relevant rules and practices by the authorities and are regularly in contact with these authorities on their own exports. However, it is presumed that, with regard to the number of items and technologies covered by the control lists, that smaller companies, which often propose a handful of dual-use products only and have little staff, are less aware of the applicability of these rules to their own situation. This is asserted by the relatively low number of individual authorisations that is delivered annually by the SBDU (approximately 3,500 as of 2013) and the large recourse that is made to national general licences. Raising awareness to these operators, which count for an important share of the national economy, is thus challenging.

The French legal corpus, like the European one, does not give a specific importance to the role of economic actors in pursuing the objective of preventing non-proliferation beside the obligation to implement internal compliance programmes with a view to obtain global licences. Their involvement in the policies pursued by the authorities, notably through informal contacts, inreach activities, exchanges of information and best practices, is growing more important but not reflected yet in the legal instruments. A system of authorisation, for example, prevails on a possible alternative based on prior registration of the operators. In Europe, and especially in France where lobbying is not seen favourably in the political culture, it is difficult for private actors to promote their views to the legislators unless they organise themselves. Even then, the smaller operators may be under-represented.

Efforts are made by the European and French authorities for informing and raising the awareness of the relevant actors, notably through "exporters' conferences", about the exiting rules. Specific efforts are made, taking into account the structure of the European regime, by the SBDU at the national level for exchanging best practices and touching smaller companies, which are more challenging. However, the limited awareness of these latter actors suggests that this information may still be improved, notably in relation to the possible sanctions in case of infringements. Though these aspects are highly national, at least in the European regime, it can be assumed that awareness may be better, but not exclusively, raised at such level.

Defining sanctions

According to the Article 24 of the Regulation, the European Union clearly assigns to the Member States the responsibility to "take the appropriate measures to enforce" the rules, i.e. define the infringements and sanctions. Those shall therefore be found in the French national legislation, mostly enacted in codes, and are not specific to the dual-use goods.

The two main references to the infringements of trade control measures are in the Customs Code and the Penal Code. Exporting without a licence is considered as an offence in the Customs Code[10] and may be sanctioned by a maximum three-year imprisonment, the seizure of the good, the means of transportation and all items used for hiding the fraud as well as a fine amounting once to twice the value of the fraud. If the criminal intent is established, meaning that there is an actual intention for trafficking, the Penal Code foresees in its chapter on "the fundamental interests of the Nation" that the "exporter" be punished with a ten to thirty months imprisonment and a 150,000 to 450,000 Euros fine. A case law has been established along the long-standing French experience of the dual-use export control rules.

Other infringements may be characterised besides the illicit export, such as that the exporters must legally set a system of accounting for, and archives of all their dual-use exports that must be kept available to customs services for at least a three-year period, or in other texts. The Law of 26 July 1968,[11] which can be seen as anticipatively implementing the Article 5 of the European Joint Action,[12] states in its Article 3 that, notwithstanding more severe punishments contained in the legislations, infringements of the interdiction to communicate on secrets of "economical, commercial, industrial, financial or technical nature" may be sanctioned by a six-months imprisonment term and a fine up to 18,000 euros.

Owing to the – necessary – organisation of the means of enforcement of the legal rules, which a State is assumed to take responsibility for, the

10 Code des Douanes, articles 38 and 414.

11 Loi No. 68-678 du 26 juillet 1968 *relative à la communication de documents et renseignements d'ordre économique, commercial, industriel, financier ou technique à des personnes physiques ou morales étrangères.*

12 Council Joint Action of 22 June 2000 *concerning the control of technical assistance related to certain military end-uses* (2000/401/CFSP) (OJEC L159 of 30 June 2000).

national level seems to be the most adequate one for designing the trade control related sanctions.

Conclusions

After reviewing the existing three levels of design of dual-use trade control rules, it appears that, in the French case, none of them can constitute a stand-alone and directly exportable model, not even considering the terrain of import. The international regimes suffer from a lack of legal consistency, though they design only principles. The European Union regime *per se* is a set of rules and principles which must be, at least, detailed with a view to their practical application and, at the maximum, necessarily completed with a view to enforcing them. The French national regulations are, by definition, adapted to the French situation and the product of the evolution of the French rules, cultures and traditions in trade control.

However, when looking at the backbones of a model, or at least of a philosophical approach for the construction of a system, as defined along the Outreach practice of the European Union, options, though not consistent from one vertebra to another, can be found. The legal structure of a model would ideally be designed at the international level and the rules consigned in a universal treaty. The licencing process would ideally be organised by national legislation if the licencing authority remains national. The role of the customs, on the example of the European Union, would ideally be defined at the regional level. The industrial and commercial operators would be better made aware of and familiarised with the trade control rules if this was organised by the authorities at the national level. Finally, owing to the absence of supranational enforcement, infringements and sanctions should be defined nationally as well.

Based on these statements, a number of prospective assumptions can be made. If the licencing authority became regional, for example, the European Union would become the model for implementing not only the licencing of the dual-use trade but also for raising the awareness of the European industrial and commercial operators. The European Union could thus be considered as a model which could be exported for designing trade control rules at a regional – or sub-regional in the case of pre-existing customs cooperation – level.

In addition, if a trade control model becomes robust when it is able to guarantee that everyone will apply the same rules consistently and that it simultaneously fits the national specificities, then the regional level may be the adequate ground for designing a regime, or at minimum addressing the foundations of such regime. By nature, regional or sub-regional integration aims at conciliating trust and efficiency, which trade controls are about.

The EU Dual-Use Trade Control System for Greece

Christos Charatsis

PhD Candidate – University of Liege Scientific Officer in Export Controls and Non-Proliferation – Joint Research Centre (European Commission)

Is there a common EU trade control system?

Giving a "yes or no" answer on such a question is like answering if the glass is half empty or half full. There are some scholars arguing that there is no common export control system without a single European authorising body. There are others saying that a common system does exist, though with a fragmented implementation. Whichever answer one may give one thing is certain; the EU system stands out as a distinct sui generis regional model. For the purpose of this year's seminar, three questions will be addressed:

- How "common" is the EU trade control system (by providing a brief evaluation)?
- How is this European model implemented in the Greek context (by focusing mainly on the weaknesses of the system)?
- Could the European system function as reference model for other regional or national systems (based on the findings ascertained in the previous questions)?

To begin with, the EU trade control system constitutes a distinct model because it has been devised by Europeans for Europe in a way to address and serve in the first place European needs taking into account the peculiarities of the European endeavour as well. Moreover, the EU export control regime is governed by common principles, definitions and obligations for all Member States as specified in the cornerstone of the European export control regime, the Regulation 428/2009 (hereinafter mentioned as dual-use regulation or regulation).[1]

[1] The consolidated version of the dual-use regulation – including the latest amendments – is available at: http://eur-lex.europa.eu/LexUriServ/LexUriServ.do?uri=CONSLEG:2009R0428:20120615:EN:PDF.

Apart from the common legal framework, the EU export controls function as a means to implement common EU policy initiatives such as the EU strategy against the proliferation of WMD[2] and constitute an integral part of the EU's Common Commercial Policy (CCP), demonstrating the intention of the EU Member States to further common security and trade objectives. It is thus not surprising that the EU export control system reflects common obligations and commitments of the Union and its Member States *vis-à-vis* international law (e.g. the Non-Proliferation Treaty) as well as politically binding agreements (e.g. international export control regimes). The non-proliferation regime is clearly an international effort rather just a European matter and thus, the EU system is guided and inspired by rules and principles established at international level, as well.

Describing the EU export control regime as a perfectly common regime is like telling the half-truth. The legal provisions framing the EU system are implemented at national level: there are potentially 28 different interpretations of and approaches to the application of the European export control Regulation.

Generally speaking, export controls function as a trade measure serving security imperatives, and trade policies involve quite often foreign policy options.[3] From a European point of view, this can be quite challenging. Member States may have different national interests either in the high politics realm of foreign and security policy or in the lower realm of trade/economy. This is quite evident if one reflects on the intergovernmental character of the Common Foreign and Security Policy and the known weaknesses of the EU to assert its role as a unified international actor.[4] Acknowledging this reality, the EU trade control system leaves space to national considerations by providing or acknowledging national measures and controls.

An atmosphere of mutual recognition and trust among the MS has not been fully attained. It is characteristic that the EU export control system

2 The "EU Strategy against the proliferation of WMD" adopted by the Council in 2003 declares the resolve of the Union to use all instruments and policies at its disposal, to prevent, deter, halt and, where possible, eliminate programmes for the proliferation of weapons of mass destruction (WMD) and missiles and, sets out an action plan towards this target. The document is available in: http://europa.eu/legislation_summaries/foreign_and_security_policy/cfsp_and_esdp_implementation/l33234_en.htm.

3 The interconnection between CFSP and CCP has been explored by different scholars: indicatively see: S. Keukeleire, J. MacNaughtan, *The Foreign Policy of the European Union*, New York, Palgrave Macmillan, 2008.

4 For the role of the EU external relations in the post-Lisbon era see indicatively: S. Duke, "The Lisbon Treaty and External Relations", Maastricht, EIPASCOPE 2008/1, pp. 13-18.

envisages intra-EU controls in the case of the most sensitive items mentioned in Annex IV of the Regulation, undermining indeed the principles of the single internal market.

Areas of convergence and divergence

Answering the question how common is the EU trade control system provides evidence with regard to the degree of harmonisation of the system and vice-versa. A common legal framework along with the existence of harmonised policies for enforcement and monitoring is of considerable importance for providing a level playing field for the EU exporters and at the same time promoting the EU and international security.[5]

What do Europeans have in common *vis-à-vis* export controls? Apart from the generally common principles and goals such as the free movement of goods and the fight against the proliferation of WMD, Europeans have established a common dual-use list (Annex I of the Regulation) adopted and regularly updated according to the controls foreseen by the international export control regimes and other related arrangements. A catch-all mechanism targeting non-listed items is also available to Member States when certain conditions are met (e.g. sensitive end-use and end-destination as specified in Article 4 of the Regulation).

They do also share a common administrative language. The regulation provides for common types of authorisations valid throughout the EU, standard models of export and brokering authorisations and even a European Union general export authorisation (EUGEA) for exports to certain countries, directly available to all exporters conforming with the conditions specified in Annexes IIa to IIf (Article 2.9).

In terms of administrative cooperation, there are again a number of provisions linking the EU system. The MS are required to notify the Commission and other MS of any prohibition or modification of an authorisation as a result of an export, transit, brokering or catch-all control. MS shall also review denials of authorisations within three years from their notification and shall exchange data regarding important risk assessment parameters such as details of violators and data on sensitive end-users and routes taken (articles 13.1, 13.2 and 19).

---

5 The necessity for both a common legal framework and a harmonised implementation is clearly mentioned already in the preamble of regulation: "It is desirable to achieve a uniform and consistent application of controls throughout the EU (…) for the EU exporters" (Recital 18). "The existence of a common control system and harmonised policies (…) is a prerequisite for establishing the free movement of dual-use items inside the Community" (Recital 4).

Ultimately, the overall monitoring and coordination of the EU trade control system lies with the European Commission, which in collaboration with the Member States has the responsibility to oversee the effective implementation of the regulation. The Commission is responsible to review the implementation of the Regulation every three years and to report on its progress to the European Parliament and the Council (Article 25). Further clauses guarantee the transparency and effective coordination of the system (e.g. the national authorities empowered to grant/prohibit authorisations in each country are published in the official Journal of the EU). The set-up of a Dual-Use Coordination Group (DUCG) – chaired by the Commission – to meet regularly and examine questions regarding the implementation of the regulation as well as the draft of EU-wide guidelines are key tools towards the construction of a common and harmonised system.

Which are then the areas of divergence undermining a common EU system? First of all, as the Commission's Green Paper points out the implementation of the common legal framework is left almost entirely to the Member States. There are therefore different interpretations especially on what concerns the grey areas of the regulation.[6]

The regulation itself does leave room for the expression of national considerations. Already the preamble (Recital 12) enshrines the right of MS to impose intra-EU controls on grounds of public policy or public security considerations.[7] Member States may also pursue national controls of non-listed items *for reasons of public security or human right considerations* (Article 8). It is not therefore strange that some Member States maintain national lists based on such considerations. It is also enlightening that during the negotiations for the update of controlled lists in the international fora the EU does not speak with one voice since Member States do not necessarily form a unified front notwithstanding that the Union is not a member in most of the regimes.[8]

6 European Commission, "Green Paper, The dual-use export control system of the European Union: ensuring security and competitiveness in a changing world", Document COM(2011) 393 final, Brussels, 30 June 2011, available at: http://trade.ec.europa.eu/doclib/docs/2011/june/tradoc_148020.pdf.

7 Article 22 specifies the particular instances where intra-EU transfers shall or might be under control.

8 The EU is a founding member of the Australia Group; the Commission has the status of observer in the Nuclear Suppliers Group while there is no official representation of the EU in the Wassenaar Arrangement and the Missile Technology Control Regime (MTCR). In addition, eight MS are not members of the MTCR including Cyprus which is not a member of the Wassenaar Arrangement either.

Most interestingly, the imposition of an authorisation requirement as a result of a catch-all control is only valid in the issuing Member State which shall, where appropriate, inform the other Member States. This vague wording – "where appropriate" – might practically mean that the other Member State remains unaware of such controls unless the involved State ends up in issuing a denial.

From an administrative point of view, there are further discrepancies; all Member States are entitled to make use of national general export authorisations (NGA), for instance in case they wish to enhance their relationship with specific third countries. Naturally, different Member States may pursue close trade relations with different countries while not all of them have an aspiration to resort to such national authorisations. In addition, each Member State may require different criteria to be satisfied by the exporters prior the issuing of a licence.[9]

It must be said that a number of mitigating provisions intending to remedy the effects of national provisions and the potential conflicts of interest within the EU system are clearly stipulated in the regulation. It is mainly about information exchange requirements with the Commission and other Member States on any measures adopted pursuant to national concerns. Reasonably, the regulation also spells out a requirement for national authorities to examine all valid denials prior to granting an authorisation for an essentially identical transaction (Article 13.5). Further consultation procedures are provided in the case of an export involving more than one Member State (Article 11). The most interesting provisions relating to consultations procedures are mentioned in the table below.

Mitigating provisions	
Immediate notification of the Commission after resort to Article 8 (Article 8.2)	"*MS shall notify the Commission of any measures adopted pursuant to public security or human right considerations*"
Communication to the Commission of any NGEA issued or modified (Article 9.4(b))	"*MS shall notify the Commission immediately of any NGEA issued or modified*"

[9] Prior the granting of an authorisation either individual or global the competent national authorities are obliged to take into account some conditions (e.g. obligations they have each accepted as members of the regimes, EU/UN/OSCE sanctions and foreign policy considerations including those referred to the Council Common Position 2008/944/CFSP governing the control of exports of military technology and equipment (Article 12)). Apparently, such conditions including considerations of national foreign and security policy leave space to the expression of national interests.

Mitigating provisions	
Exchange of information on exporters deprived of the right to use an EUGEA (Article 9.1)	*"The competent authorities of the MS shall exchange information on exporters deprived of the right to use an EUGEA, unless they determine that the exporter will not attempt to export dual-use items through another MS"*
Consultation procedures under article 11 when more than one MS are involved in an export (Article 11.1)	*"In the case of an application concerning dual-use items which are or will be located in one or more MS other than the one where the application has been made, the fact shall be mentioned in the application and the MS shall immediately consult the competent authorities of all MS involved"* *"any objections of all MS engaged in an export shall bind the MS in which the application has been made"*

The exchange of information may take place through different channels depending on its nature and the obligations set in the regulation. For instance, the Member States are obliged to notify the Commission for the imposition of any intra-EU controls on the basis of Article 22. The Commission in turn shall publish such information in the Official Journal of the EU. Most sensitive exchanges of information regarding for instance denials and sensitive end-users take place during the meetings of the relevant EU committees (Dual-Use Working Party and DUCG) and through DUeS, the EU secure and encrypted electronic system for the exchange of information on export controls of dual-use items. Reasonably, part of the information exchanges takes place also informally or through the mediation of intelligence services.[10]

Identifying gaps in the legislation

Having broadly described the areas of convergence and divergence within the EU trade control system, an appropriate question could be whether we really need a perfectly common system; or, to what extent a common and harmonised system is required. However, for the scope of this study it is preferable to shed some light on the least elaborated areas of the regulation and on missing elements.

Although Recital 8 and Article 2 make clear that the transfers of technologies through any electronic means must be also under scrutiny,

10 Meetings and negotiations taking place at international level, for instance, in the framework of international export control regimes provide another avenue for exchange of views and information on most and least sensitive issues. In fact, the non-binding nature of negotiations in some of the fora and the high level of confidentially assured, make Member States keen to share their experiences.

important questions and related practicalities remain rather obscure causing in some cases undue hindrances to the EU industries; Such issues may relate to intangible transfers of technology (ITT) involving cross-border movement of persons, intra-EU industrial collaborations and usage of cloud computing services.[11] On what concerns the transfers of technology and knowledge as a result of academic activities, the situation is equally ambiguous; the recent Council Conclusions on the "New Lines for Action (NLA) in combating the proliferation of WMD and their means of delivery" commits anew the EU to adopt a package of measures including codes of professional conduct, awareness raising programmes towards the scientific community and enhanced cooperation in terms of consular vigilance.[12] However, the regulation does not provide any stimuli for such measures. It is instead confined to clarify that the basic research and the information falling in the public domain is excluded from the controls. But do Member States share a common approach on what basic research might mean? Furthermore, awareness raising activities and internal compliance programmes are rather overlooked by the regulation. Apart from few direct obligations set for the exporters (the suspicion clause and a record keeping obligation in articles 4.5 and 20 respectively), only Article 12.2 implies the importance of compliance measures.[13]

Another issue raised quite often by customs officers is the lack of the enforcement perspective. Despite the collaboration between the licencing and customs authorities at national level, enforcement needs and approaches are not generally taken into consideration in both stages of policy-making and policy monitoring. This is probably due to the fact that customs and trade control policy discussions take place in different fora at both international and European levels. It is indicative that in

---

11 Some recurring questions pending for clear answers have as follows: Shall the competent authorities ask for an authorisation from every EU employee accessing sensitive info either through his USB key or his company's intranet during his stay in a third country and, if yes how practical this might be? How the transfers of sensitive data through cloud computing services should be regulated? What should be applicable for those EU projects involving intra-EU transfers of Annex IV items and technologies or, is the introduction of a general export authorisation for intra-EU transfers an appropriate solution reducing the administrative burden of asking numerous authorisations for a single collaboration?

12 The NLA in combating the proliferation of WMD were first adopted in 2008. However, the period for their implementation has been repeatedly extended. The Council renewed recently the EU's commitment to ensure the continued pursuit of an effective EU policy on the new challenges presented by the proliferation of WMD and their delivery systems. The press release is available at the following address: http://www.consilium.europa.eu/uedocs/cms_data/docs/pressdata/EN/foraff/139067.pdf.

13 The national authorities shall take into account the applications of compliance mechanisms by the exporters while assessing an application for a global export authorisation (Article 12.2).

the meetings of DUCG monitoring the implementation of regulation the representatives of Member States are mainly licencing officers and rarely their counterparts from customs. This disconnection risks leading also to inconsistencies between customs law and export control law. For example, the differing definitions of the transit referred to in the Community Customs Code and in the dual-use regulation is a good example of the potential consequences of this mismatch between policy-making and practical implementation.[14] The organisation of an annual joint meeting gathering customs authorities and licencing officers is toward the right direction but could not change the situation on its own. In addition, the customs procedures specified in articles 16 and 17 of the regulation are of general character without bearing a real impact on this problem.

An effective enforcement demands also the establishment of penalties either administrative or criminal depending on the gravity of the infringement. The Member States are free to structure their prosecution approach, on the basis of the triptych for effective-proportionate-dissuasive penalties (Article 24). Hence, differentiations amongst Member States might be considerable. Contrary to other areas (e.g. competition and environmental law), the EU law does not go far enough to set what penalties might bring certain export control law breaches.

The Greek export control system as a test case

Given the analysis of the overall EU system provided above, it is useful to examine how the EU export control law is implemented in the Greek context.[15] Instead of carrying out a comprehensive analysis of the Greek system, for the purpose of the study it is useful to focus on those elements differentiating somehow the system.[16]

---

[14] A more detailed commentating of this inconsistency between customs law and the regulation 428/2009 can be found in Q. Michel, "The European Union Dual-Use Items Control Regime, Comment of the Legislation article-by-article", European Studies Unit, University of Liege, February 2014, p. 25. available at: http://local.droit.ulg.ac.be/jcms/service/file/20140210135832_Vademecum-DUV3Rev1.pdf. As it is explained, the operation of transit controls is an area demanding close collaboration between the customs and licencing authorities. Therefore, differing approaches and diverging definitions do not accommodate a more harmonised implementation of the EU trade control system.

[15] For an introduction to the Greek export control system see: C. Charatsis, "The Greek Experience", in O. Jankowitsch-Prevor, Q. Michel (eds.), *European Dual-Use Trade Controls: Beyond Materiality and Borders*, Brussels, P.I.E. Peter Lang, Coll. Non-Proliferation & Security, No. 28, 2013, pp. 105-114.

[16] This brief analysis of the Greek system relies mainly on the conduct of telephone interviews with both licencing and customs officers, in December 2013.

Greece as a law-abiding member of the international community conforms to legally binding provisions and politically binding agreements stemming from international and European law.[17] For instance, an inter-ministerial committee has been established aiming at monitoring and reporting on the implementation of the United Nations Security Council (UNSC) Resolution 1540 and connected activities (e.g. the Proliferation Security Initiative).

With respect the national implementation of export controls, the legal framework builds on the Ministerial Decision 121837/E3/21837/09 and the National Customs Code 2960/20001. One could expect that the national provisions clarify the grey areas of the regulation and specify further measures for its smooth implementation. Indeed, the ministerial decision contains some supplementary provisions; it clarifies the practicalities of post-shipment controls and the required documentation for an application, sets the obligations of the exporters (including record keeping requirements) and specifies the legal basis for the imposition of penalties. However, the ministerial decision is mainly confined in repeating the provisions of the regulation without adopting an enlightening and modern framework with regard the most sensitive issues such as the controls in ITT and compliance measures. This reluctance of the regulator to deal with the most uncharted areas of the regulation might be a recurrent issue for other Member States – especially the smallest ones – due to various reasons such as the limited resources available and the restricted negotiating power in the related international and European fora.

Generally speaking, the Greek legal framework is restrained from introducing national measures. However, the country aspires to further both trade and foreign policy interests when it is deemed particularly useful and advantageous. To that end, Greece has established NGA for exports to specific partner countries (Argentina, South Korea, Russia, Ukraine, Turkey and South Africa). Global export authorisations are also available under the specific criteria mentioned in the EU and national law.[18] Last, in just one case Greece has invoked Article 11.2 claiming its right to prohibit the export of a commodity originating from an EU State and passing through Greek territory to a third-country destination for public security reasons.[19] In this specific case, the requested Member

---

17 Greece is member in all export control regimes and party to all related international treaties.

18 Among the conditions for granting a global export authorisation lies an obligation for the exporters to provide the competent authorities every six months with data on the destinations and the exported commodities under GEA.

19 As stipulated in Article 11.2, a Member State may request another Member State not to grant an export authorisation or, if such has been granted, request its annulment in the

State examined the considerations of Greece and decided not to allow the export of the item in question. That not being the case, the decision of the requested State to grant an authorisation should have been notified to the Commission and other Member States through DUeS.

A further point raised frequently by the Greek export control professionals is the degree of flexibility characterising the system. The legal framework can be easily amended since no parliamentary approval is required and informal procedures mobilising different agencies and ministries can be easily applied if a case demands so. The coin has two sides though; this lack of formalised procedures can lead to ineffectiveness and problems relating to accountability and transparency.

A look at the numbers of authorisations issued and denials imposed during the first three years of the implementation of the regulation reveals a tendency of both customs officers and licencing authorities to refer a high number of cases to pass through the authorisation process.[20] It is characteristic that Belgium, a similar Member State than Greece – in terms of size and population – but with stronger industrial base issued between 2010 and 2011 considerably less authorisations (approximately 30%) than Greece and a double number of denials.[21]

Years	No. of authorisations		No. of denials	
	GR	BE	GR	BE
2010	551	325	4	10
2011	626	320	3	9
2012	388	469	6	10

case where an export might prejudice its essential security interests. In such a case, the State involved shall engage in consultations of non-binding nature.

20 Data provided to the European Commission by the Member States for the preparation of the report to the Council and the European Parliament on the implementation of the dual-use regulation. Member States have agreed upon the use of data by the author.

21 The corresponding figures provided to the European Commission by the Member States for the preparation of the report on the implementation of the dual-use regulation are not publicly available. It must also be noted that the percentage of authorisations reflects the total of the authorisations issued, meaning that the total volume of applications may be higher. As the Commission's report on the implementation of the regulation indicates, the increasing number of applications submitted and authorisations granted in contrast with the decreasing number of denials notified, represent a general tendency in the EU. This might be inter alia due to the increasing awareness of undertakings and the imposition of sanction regimes. See: European Commission, "Report to the Council and the European Parliament on the implementation of Regulation (EC) No. 428/2009, setting up a Community regime for the control of exports, transfer, brokering and transit of dual-use items", COM(2013) 710 Final, Brussels, 16 Oct. 2013, p. 12, available at: http://trade.ec.europa.eu/doclib/docs/2013/october/tradoc_151857.pdf.

There are two interrelated factors explaining these figures.[22] The first one is the "administrative cultural environment" and the predominant behaviour patterns dictating generally the unwillingness of the competent authorities to take a decision at the lower level and in the fastest mode. The second factor concerns the diagnosed lack of technical expertise to decide on a particular transaction. This means that a support team readily available to assist the licencing or customs officers is not available. Thus, they have to ask for the time-consuming and cost ineffective assistance of other agencies or ministries spending more time and unduly hindering, in some cases, the smooth conduct of trade. The imposition of an authorisation requirement used to function in the past also as an "awareness-raising tool" towards the exporters who could potentially export controlled technology in a future transaction. In some instances, the competent authorities may decide to release a commodity or prohibit its export based on the decisions of other Member States, for a transaction concerning identical items and exporters. This possibility functions as a remedy to the aforementioned lack of technical expertise speeding up the export of items with technical parameters close to the controlled ones.

In terms of enforcement, the Greek authorities make use of the common tools and practices available at national and international levels. The internationally recognised practice of authorised economic operators, the EU based e-customs procedures and the use of an EU correlation table linking the customs combined nomenclature with the dual-use classifications are indeed useful tools. A further practice intending to facilitate the work of the customs officers in the ground is the publication of national guidelines on the implementation of EU law. The objective of such circulars is to inform about the applicable legislation to certain transactions and to recommend the way to implement the relevant provisions. In any case, the customs and licencing policy departments do collaborate closely at a national level in all different phases of the export control process (documentary checks, risk analysis, post-shipment control and investigation/prosecution).

However, as previously mentioned, enforcing export controls effectively demands the engagement of customs authorities from the policy-making phase as well as keeping a close eye on their needs and problems concerning the practical enforcement phase.[23] To that end, a closer collaboration

[22] This opinion has been shaped on the basis of discussions and interviews with officers from both customs and licencing services routinely dealing with the implementation of the dual-use export controls.

[23] This argument is supported by the opinion of a senior Greek officer working for the policy department of the customs administration in the field of dual-use export controls.

between custom officers and licencing authorities in the first place at the European level could facilitate the adoption of more harmonised customs procedures. In addition, a closer collaboration between customs and licencing authorities could be also pursued at the international level as an effective implementation of export controls is the ultimate goal.[24]

As concerns the applicable penalties, the Law 936/1979 providing for tough administrative and criminal penalties for the violators of export control law, has been recently abolished. The competent authorities can still rely on the sanctions predicted in the National Customs Code 2960/2001 or on other pieces of the civil and criminal law for imposing dissuasive penalties. There is no specific provision though for sanctions incurred from export control breaches in the trade of dual-use goods.

Towards a universal trade control system?

It is rather far-fetched to speak out for a universal trade control model at the moment when a global governance system is not envisaged.

It is probably quite straightforward to adopt commonly agreed principles and establish broadly defined obligations for the members of the international community, as the UNSC Resolution 1540 indeed does. It is vastly more difficult to set out a particular model to function as an international standard. It might also be unnecessary.

As the European case shows, even in the highly converging EU environment there are different aspirations and concerns in either economic or foreign policy areas. An enhanced collaboration between Member States through an intense exchange of information could soften the edges and lead to a greater harmonisation of the system. The exchange of best practices, the adoption of practical guidelines and the central coordination/monitoring enforced in the EU system set the example of how a universal system could function.

As the Greek experience testifies, even at European level there are to some extent different needs and limitations. There are for instance, different technical capabilities and human resource capacities. The establishment of the dual-use pool of experts to provide technical assistance to licencing authorities intends to remedy such weaknesses although it is still in its infancy. As the example with the administrative mentality

24 For an analysis of the relation between trade control and national enforcement see: R. Chatelus, "The Role of Customs in Strategic Trade Controls: Challenges and Potential. Taking a States' Enforcement Perspective, Center for International Trade and Security", University of Georgia (not dated), available at: http://cits.uga.edu/pdf/chatelus_customs.pdf.

demonstrates, varying administrative cultures might have different explanations and in any case should not be underestimated.

To conclude, the EU trade control system is justifiably considered among the most elaborate worldwide. Despite its weaknesses such as the fragmented implementation, it proposes a best practice for almost every area of the export control process. The international community could probably use the EU case as a model in order to be inspired and avoid shortcomings of the system, with a view to defining norms and essential elements for an effective implementation of export controls globally.

From Models to a Model?

Lia CAPONETTI

Researcher – European Studies Unit, University of Liège

Exploring the possibility of a unique dual-use export control system

At present the European Union dual-use export control regime is the most comprehensive in the world but there is still a lot of work to do to make it fully effective.

The EU dual-use export control system is regulated by the EU Regulation 428/2009.[1] Although EU regulations are directly applicable in all EU countries, some provisions, in order to be implemented, need an integrating legislative action by the Member States. If the principle of subsidiarity could be invoked to justify this (at least) two-level legal system, on the other hand, disparities arising from different degrees of implementation and different legal systems among Member States may lead to disfunctionings of the entire system, affecting its efficiency and, in some cases, even its credibility.

Aside from these aspects, there should be a pragmatic reason for the existence of a two-level dual-use export control system, that is to point to the undeniable fact that the EU is not a single State nor a Federation, and therefore lacks the necessary instruments, especially for implementation and compliance. In this sense, the two-levels system is an imposed option, although greater effort could be made at the EU legislative level to harmonise the entire system.

At present, Member States have too much space to manoeuver, which prevents the application of the term "model" to the EU dual-use export control system, but rather to apply this term in plural as "models".

---

1 Formally amended by Regulation (EU) No. 1232/2011 of the European Parliament and of the Council of 16 November 2011 amending Council Regulation (EC) No. 428/2009 seeting up a Community regime for the control of exports, transfer, brokering and transit of dual-use items.

The EU dual-use Regulation sets common guidelines on the basis of which each Member State has established its own system.

Under these conditions, it is rather difficult to imagine a world-level model dealing with dual-use export controls. If there are disparities among States sharing institutions and procedures as integrated as is the case for the EU, this would be a far more difficult task to achieve where these conditions are lacking.

Further to such difficulties, there are specificities of each State and different needs: not all States are exporters of dual-use items or, at least, not in the same manner (in particular, in terms of quantity). These are some of the reasons why a tailored system would be preferable being more feasible and less time and money consuming.

In this chapter, some elements of the EU dual-use system in particular, the Italian system being part of the EU regime, will be considered and reconstructed in order to "design" some models of dual-use export control.

An export control system revolving around the Customs Agency

A valid model for States with low import-export flow of dual-use items, such as Italy,[2] should be as simple as possible.

In that system, the Customs Agency is the main actor who, through a centralised data system, performs a double function. The first function is to categorise items (in order to establish if they are dual-use or not); the second function is to deliver and work as recipient of licences request formats. When an economic operator needs to export a given item, he will check with the Customs agency database if this item is subjected or not to a dual-use regime. If this is the case, he will submit his licence application and the necessary documents[3] to the Customs Agency, which will forward the request to the policy decision-makers.

At the political level, the composition of the decision-making body changes according to the type of authorisation requested. In the case of general authorisations (European or national), it will be up to the competent national political authority to decide about the granting or denial of the licence whilst, in the case of an individual specific authorisation[4] and

2 See table 1.

3 According to the category of items different documents are requested to accompany the licence request. The Customs Agency's database provides potential exporter with required information.

4 The individual specific authorisation is granted to a single exporter for dual-use items or categories of dual-use items and for a specific end-user. The request for this kind

individual global authorisations,[5] the competent national political authority will consult a Consultative Committee before taking any decision. The inclusion of this "preliminary" phase in the decision-making process is the called for by the more sensitive nature of these two types of authorisations.

The composition of the Consultative Committee, may vary from one State to another,[6] but the main principle is that it includes the Ministries that are most concerned by the topic as well as technical experts in dual-use matters.

Any decision concerning the licence application (both granting or denial) is communicated to the Customs Agency. The feedback between the political and the technical level is very important for the Customs Agency since it allows Customs to gather all data concerning authorisations (granted or denied) with related informations concerning the transaction, which is useful for the verification phase.

---

of authorisation has to be subscribed by a legal representative of the exporter and it has to be accompanied by an end-user declaration reporting all the details about the object of the export operation and the involved subjects as well as an explicit declaration to not use these items for military purposes, nor in civil nuclear activities in facilities which are not covered by IAEA safeguards, nor for use in connection with the development and/or production of WMD or other nuclear explosive devices or the development and/or production of missiles capable of delivering such weapons and, finally, to not re-export, transfer or divert the imported items.

5 The individual global authorisation has to be accompanied by an explicit declaration, subscribed by the legal representative of the exporter and binding the exporter to use the authorisation granted only for the dual-use items and countries of destination indicated in the document. Once the exporter's request has been accepted, the exporter has to ask the end-user and/or foreign buyer to provide him/her with a declaration stating the engagement of the end-user to not re-export, transfer or divert the dual-use items part of the contract and their use only for civil purposes.

6 The Consultative Committee is composed of: a general director of the Ministry of Foreign Affairs who assumes the function of President; a general director of the Ministry for International Trade Policy within the Ministry of Economic Development as Vice-President; two representatives of the Ministry of Economy and Finances (one of which is from the Customs Agency) and a representative for the Ministry of Foreign Affairs, Ministry for International Trade Policy within the Ministry of Economic Development, Ministry of Defence, Ministry of Interior, Ministry of Communication, Ministry of Education, University and Research and Ministry of Health. Four technical experts on dual-use items controls participate take part in the Consultative Committee's meetings, but without voting right. For particular reasons or upon request by the competent national authority or the President of the Committee, also some representatives who can take part in the meetings without voting right: public security, customs, fiscal and monetary. Some experts, who are not from the administration, are also welcome (within the limits of the budget). The Committee is renewed every five years and its members are nominated by a decree of the Ministry of Economic Development, the competent national political authority in Italy.

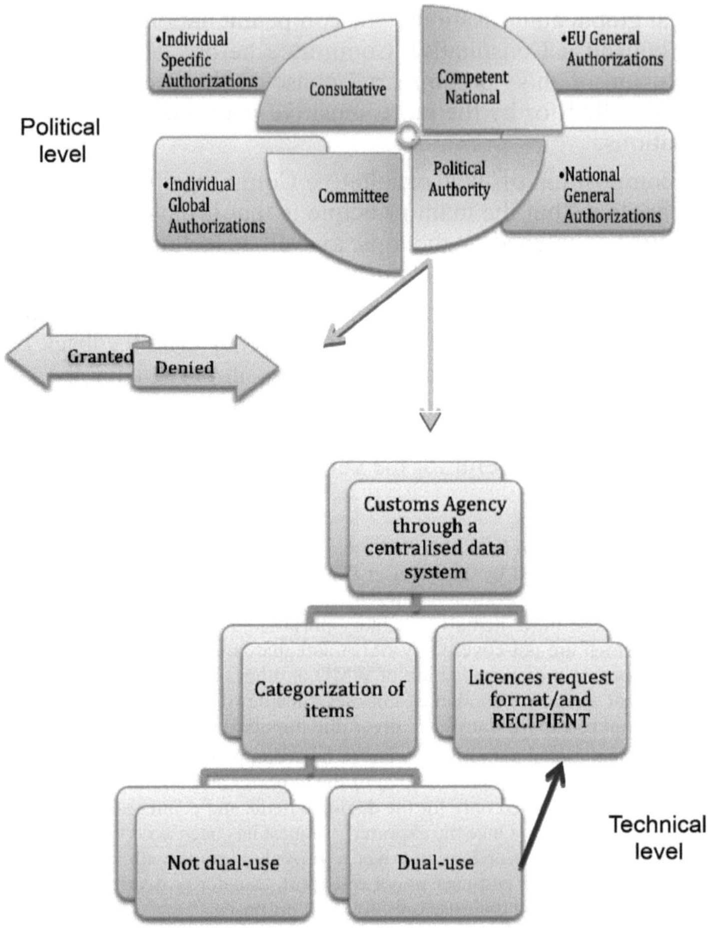

Figure 1: *Export control system revolving around the Customs Agency.*

Summing up, the system is divided into two levels: the political level deciding about the granting/denial of the authorisations and the technical level, managed by the Customs Agency and playing a central role in the main phases of an export control process; in the pre-shipment phases:

- Raising awareness to economic operators through the categorisation of dual-use items;
- Authorizing activities, working as "licence-filter";
- And, in the post-shipment phase, verifying activities through the export declarations control.

The main advantages of the model are, first of all, its feasibility due to the fact that Customs Agencies are already in place everywhere, a fact that allows for considerable savings, and second, the simplicity of the structure which makes it a valid model for States with low import-export flow of dual-use items.

Table 1: Licences granted by the Italian Ministry of Economic Development from 2006 to 2009

Licences	2009	2008	2007	2006
Individual Specific	365	437	346	313
Individual Global	23	28	7	14
National General	68 since 2003			
Community General	139 since 2003			

Source: Reports of the Ministry of Economic Development on the export activity of dual-use items to the Presidency of the Council.

Would the status of authorised economic operator work for dual-use trade?

On the basis of Regulation (EC) No. 1875/2006, European companies may require local customs authorities to issue a certificate that allows them to speed up and simplify customs controls in all international trade: the authorised economic operator (AEO).

Obtaining such status allows economic operators to qualify as "reliable" towards other economic operators and towards customs authorities (European and non-European); referring to the customs authorities, the status allows for the application of appreciable simplifications in customs and security controls for all goods coming in and getting out the establishment.

There are three possible certifications:

- AEOF: customs simplifications and security checks;
- AEOC: customs simplifications;
- AEOS: simplifications of security controls.

It is very important to clarify that the possibility of obtaining the AEO status for dual-use items exporters is not considered by Regulation (EC) No. 1875/2006. However, there is no provision that would impede it.

Possible advantages of the proposition and benefits coming from an internal compliance programme-AEO direct relationship

This wider application of the AEO certificate could have considerable advantages.

One of the main benefits would come from an internal compliance programme (ICP)-AEO direct relationship, as it could contribute to wider use and implementation of ICP among industries. The proper implementation and the effectiveness of an ICP within the industry would be a *conditio sine qua non* for industries to obtain the AEO certificate. Moreover, by building on an "unbreakable" bond between ICP and AEO, there is a possibility to create a single EU ICP (maybe on the model of the Wassenaar Arrangement's "Best Practice Guidelines on Internal Compliance Programmes for Dual-Use Goods and Technologies"), which, in turn, would provide several advantages.

The first consequence of an EU internal compliance program would be the possibility for all EU industries to be evaluated on the same basis, making competition for the acquisition of a AEO certificate more equal.

A second positive consequence would be to strengthen compliance at the EU level through a legally binding instrument, in this specific case a regulation.

A third advantage may be achieved if an EU ICP was created that starts from a model existing in an international regime (such as the Wassenaar Arrangement's "Best Practice Guidelines on Internal Compliance Programmes for Dual-Use Goods and Technologies"). In this case, the advantage would be to contribute to the international regime's credibility and efficiency by conferring binding forces to such instruments of international regime(s).

One of the consequences resulting from the application of the AEO mechanism to dual-use trade that could be considered an advantage is the fact that the approach to responsibility is inverted; it is no longer a matter of the State making rules and industries "passively" applying them but, instead, it is in the interest of the industry to comply with the rules and even to be the best because the reward is worth the investment. By creating an industry-centred responsibility approach, industry would be sensitised and made responsible for aspects relating to non-proliferation.

The proposal is also attractive from an economic point of view, for industries and national and European economies, as it would mean more efficiency in trade transactions as well as less costly and time-consuming for competent authorities.

The main risk of creating such mechanism would be the fact that the process could start a "black market" of certificates, causing a lack of control on the side of competent authorities on real transactions.

The particularity of the EU case

The EU dual-use Regulation set some common guidelines on the basis of which each Member State established its own system. However, though it appears unlikely, at the present time, to put in place a unique EU dual-use export control model, it would be feasible to adopt some measures in this direction and allowing for greater harmonisation among models of EU Member States. In particular, it would be advisable to strictly regulate on an EU basis, licencing conditions for dual-use items that are not listed in Annex I of Regulation 428/2009, rather than allowing Member States to freely apply or not apply stricter conditions, in order to avoid "market distortions" among EU Member States. In the same spirit as well as for international security, it would be recommended to exclude the possibility for a Member State to grant an authorisation that has been previously refused by another Member State. For this purpose, a European information data system could be created,[7] maybe on the model of the computer information system of the Italian Customs Agency (AIDA). Also, in the field of sanctions, greater harmonisation would be possible by stating, at the EU level (in a Regulation) which penalties should apply to which violation. However, these are "palliatives" for such a strategic sector in which industries hold a considerable bargaining power "against" weaker national governments, hampered by security concerns and international commitments on one side and on the other financial crisis and unemployment. A stricter EU-level management of the issue is required to overcome the national particularisms.

Final Remarks

Seeking to draw some conclusions, it appears that the possibility of establishing a unique dual-use export control system at the world level, does not seems to be feasible, mainly because of the specificities of States and their different needs. Moreover, all States are not exporters of dual-use items, and even among exporters there are different degrees of "importance". It is mainly for these reasons that a tailor-made dual-use trade control system has to be preferred to the "one size fits all" approach which risks to be too inefficient: in particular insufficient for countries with a strong flow of dual-use trade and too heavy and invasive for country with a low flow of trade in dual-use items.

7 Article 19 (4) of Regulation 428/2009. A secure and encrypted system for the exchange of information among Member States and, whenever appropriate, the Commission may be set up by the Commission, in consultation with the Dual-Use Coordination Group set up under Article 23. It should be amended by substituting the formulation "A secure and encrypted system for the exchange of information among Member States and whenever appropriate the Commission may be set up" to "A secure and encrypted system for the exchange of information among Member States and whenever appropriate the Commission shall be set up".

For the latter category of countries, the option of developing a system revolving around the Customs Agency has been envisaged and considered feasible due to the simplicity of its structure.

For the EU the high degree of integration and existing legislation cannot be ignored; however, to make the system work, some adjustments are required. In general it could be said that Regulation 428/2009 has to become more binding for the Member States, leaving less space to manoeuver but, on the other hand, a more *à la carte* approach could be applied. Another option that has been explored to regulate dual-use trade is the extension of the AEO status to industries of the dual-use sector in order to implement ICP among industries, providing more efficiency to trade transactions and inverting the responsibility approach so as to make industries more responsible and the governmental structures less overcharged. Potential additional benefits could come from an ICP-AEO direct relationship, especially at the EU level with the establishment of an EU ICP with the legal binding force of a regulation.

A Portuguese Point of View

Miguel Sousa FERRO

Guest Lecturer – University of Lisbon Law School Counsel – Eduardo Paz Ferreira & Associados

Introduction

The questions underlying the issue raised by the organisers of this book are so numerous and so complex, that they become almost overwhelming. It is, therefore, comforting that the requested contributions are so limited in size, as it makes one feel more comfortable about presenting merely broad considerations and thoughts on the relevant issues. In so doing, I shall focus on the topics which proved to be most relevant and controversial at the workshop that preceded the drafting of these considerations, at Chaudfontaine, in December 2013.

A special word of thanks to Quentin Michel, Odette Jankowitsch and their team, for their continued efforts in successfully bringing together an international group of experts to discuss an often neglected topic in an environment that allows for a candid and fruitful exchange of views, with the common goal of thinking ahead and looking for the best solutions for the most pressing problems in this field.

Naturally, I will not avoid making an initial reference to the situation in my country of origin, particularly considering that much of my perspective on the issues to be discussed is, of course, framed by this national experience.

The situation in Portugal

Portugal's industry and exports do not raise a very large number of concerns relating to trade control rules. Compared to countries such as Germany or France, the number of licences issued each year is quite small. The staff assigned to export licencing, both at the Ministry of Defence and at the Customs Authority, is minimal, and while their efforts are meritorious, namely in what concerns industry outreach programmes, there seems to be little political attention or support for a deepening of regulation and supervision in this area. One consequence of this state of affairs is that no special legislation has yet been adopted to regulate export control of dual-use items, even though a draft has been in the pipeline for quite some time.

And yet, both in what concerns defence items and dual-use items, there are clearly significant risks, in this field, associated to national economic activity which cannot be ignored. The level of concern is made all the greater by Portugal's inclusion in the EU internal market, which has justified the imposition of a uniform and directly applicable regime to all the Member States.

The adoption of EU regulations in this area has significantly limited the negative consequences of the relative passiveness of the national legislator.

And this may, perhaps, be one of the most important lessons to be learned from the Portuguese experience: one of the great advantages of a regional model is that it dispenses with the need for a country by country legislative intervention, extending to States where such concerns are not so prominent the benefit of the protection of legal regimes that are developed and pushed forward by countries with more experience and knowledge in tackling the relevant issues.

When such a regime is directly applicable, with no need for transposition into national law, the advantages are even greater, as this prevents delays that derive from different priorities being awarded by different States to the subject at hand.

The bottomline is that, if it weren't for the EU, Portugal might not presently have an export control regime for dual-use items at all, or it might have an outdated version of one.

Do we have an EU model?

There is clearly an EU model, but not a complete one. EU rules allow for significant discretionary margin in the interpretation and enforcement of several provisions. Experience shows that, at the end of the day, one Member State's regulator may prohibit exports that another Member State deemed legitimate and admissible.

This is an unacceptable state of affairs within the context of the functioning of the internal market, as it leads to competitive distortions between Member States. Indeed, this framework creates an incentive for regulatory competition between Member States, who may be tempted to adopt interpretations within their discretionary margin that favour their national economic interests. Ultimately, this might even lead, at least on a case-by-case basis, to a race to the bottom. On the flipside of the coin, a State should not see its economic interests damaged because it implements, in a certain instance, a greater level of prevention when it comes to international security than fellow EU Member States.

A full and effective EU model can only be achieved through the creation of an EU wide regulator, who would ensure a uniform treatment of requests for licences from all the Member States.

Aside from ensuring an absence of internal market distortions, this solution seems essential to implement a common commercial policy in this domain, and may have other significant advantages, which require further study and consideration.

Thus, for example, it may be the case that a common regulator would create regulatory efficiencies that would decrease administrative and enforcement costs in the public sector, as well as reducing compliance costs for companies. Centralisation in a single authority might also allow for a greater level of access to information and to a reduction in enforcement gaps.

A fundamental argument against the creation of such an EU regulator is that the decision to grant export licences involves a component of political decision-making that is still very much within the sphere of sovereignty of the Member States, not having been transferred to the EU.

However, from a first glance at the legal side of the argument, it seems entirely possible to accommodate such new powers within the framework of the existing treaties, even if, in the most restrictive interpretation, consensus might be required for some issues.

Secondly, it is not entirely clear that licencing decisions should be allowed to rest on political considerations, beyond those that derive from the criteria for authorisation or prohibition foreseen in the applicable legislation. It may indeed be argued that it is at that level, when the legislator still has control of the process and the criteria are set in a public and scrutinisable manner, that a political judgment is required, and that a political judgment by an administrative authority at the moment of granting licences carries the risk of regulatory distortion or even abuse of process.

Do we have a universal model?

UNSC Resolution 1540, and the documents associated thereto, are certainly, to some extent, a universal model, and a mandatory one at that. But it is, in my humble opinion, a misguided attempt at international legislation. The Security Council was not meant, nor is it prepared, to be a global legislator, at least not when it comes to adopting such specific provisions.

The content and language of Resolution 1540 is too close to the traditional thinking and structuring of UN Resolutions to be an adequate approach to a binding source of law, even one that still requires an intervention by national legislators.

Do we really believe that every single Member State of the United Nations needs to include in its legislation all the prohibitions foreseen in that Resolution, including all their specific elements and variations, in order to guarantee the attainment of the objectives of this measure? Do we expect the UNSC to take action against States who have not integrated the entirety of those prohibitions into their national law, even if in the absence of any demonstrable effect on international security? Possibly not.

I would argue that, in reality, for what is probably a majority of the countries throughout the world, export control rules could be far more modest and limited in scope than what is foreseen in the global model. And, indeed, in practice, it actually is quite more modest and could not be otherwise.

That being the case, one may question the very justification for a global model, at least one with a level of detail as the one that has been adopted. If the objective is merely to guarantee that national law includes provisions which guarantee that, when necessary, there is an appropriate legal basis to intervene in defence of national or international security, then a more general phrasing of prohitions might, in some cases, suffice, and may even be easier to comprehend and to enforce.

The existence of "a" global model – not necessarily the present one – does have obvious advantages. For one thing, by ensuring regulatory harmonisation across borders, transaction costs and companies' investments in regulatory compliance would be reduced, but only to the extent that harmonisation is actually achieved.

Above all, international peace and security is a pressing issue which cannot be ignored, and the global "model" must therefore always be understood, first and foremost, as a mandatory minimum for the sake of that goal.

At the end of the day, it would seem to be less important to have a detailed export control regime, identical or very similar, in every single State around the world, than to have (at least) a basic export control regime everywhere, as long as, given the characteristics of the legal order in question, that basic regime would suffice as a foundation for the national government to intervene when needed.

This is one instance where, quite clearly, a global uniformised regime will be neither realistic nor suitable. What works and makes sense for the USA and for Germany will be entirely out of place in Mali or in East Timor.

This picture is made worst by the approach of the 1540 Committee, who has taken what is an already "Westernised" view of how to go about defining an export control regime and has proceeded to specify its obligations from an "Americanised" point of view, deriving from the Resolution requirements that have little, if any, correspondence in the letter of the law, and whose necessity or relation to the spirit of the law is quite arguable. To be clear, in my view, an American interpretation of how to implement Resolution 1540 is not necessarily the right interpretation, and it should therefore not be used to build the template on the basis of which compliance with this Resolution is assessed.

Should we have a regional model?

It is safe to assume that it is settled that a region that has undergone a process of economic integration, particularly one that has led to the creation of a common commercial policy and to an internal market, requires some kind of harmonisation of export control rules. Thus, it is not in dispute that the European Union should have a regional model. In the EU, what can be discussed – as we have already mentioned – is the level of harmonisation, the degree of transfer of sovereignty to the supranational bodies in this regard.

Elsewhere in the world, however, regional models may also be useful and justified. Many African nations, including those grouped together in international organisations that pursue goals of economic integration (even if at an early stage), or Pacific island nations, to name a few examples, may find that their domestic industries and security concerns are quite similar.

In such cases, coming together to find a common solution may be a far more efficient way of drafting optimum export control rules that meet the needs and fit the reality of the respective region, thus best pursuing the ultimate goals of the international regime.

Such an option brings with it the added advantages of cost reduction for companies operating within that region, incentive to trade by reduction of information barriers, and greater ease of cooperation between national authorities.

The role of Customs

It seems to be often the case that too much weight is placed on Customs as the main agent for export control enforcement. Although Customs are a crucial ingredient in the recipe for success of export control, it can never be responsible for the greater part of the actual "control".

Control of dual-use items will always be a tough sell for customs officials. It is difficult to fully grasp, the items are difficult to identify and the psychological and financial rewards are far smaller than if their efforts were aimed at detecting other illegal shipments, such as narcotics.

What's more, Customs controls are a deterrent, but a small one. Only a very small percentage of shipments will ever be controlled in such a manner as to allow for the identification of illegal exports of dual-use items. Finally, exports of intangible items circumvent Customs altogether.

Thus, without neglecting the training of Customs officials in these subjects, far greater attention needs to be paid to awareness-raising campaigns and, above all, to dissuasion through sanctions and *ex post facto* enforcement.

The objective must be to create a regulatory environment such that exporting companies will have every economic incentive to cooperate with authorities and to avoid carrying out an export which may subsequently be deemed a violation of export control rules.

In order to achieve this result, high financial penalties are important. But just as important can be other types of sanctions with drastic economic consequences, such as the suspension of rights to export licences, by the company in question and any of its subsidiaries or parent companies, for a certain period following the detection of an infringement of a certain gravity.

Furthermore, an effective mechanism of company audits needs to be created. A company may not be concerned about its exports being thoroughly controlled at the borders, or it may be entirely unconcerned if its exports are of an intangible nature. But if it knows that, sooner or later and periodically, the export control authorities will inspect its transaction records to detect infringements of export control rules, it may think twice before taking a chance, and it may put more care into prevention and internal compliance programmes.

Thus, a body of trained inspectors within the borders, in periodical dialogue with companies, may obtain more promising results than a body of trained inspectors at the borders.

A list, my kingdom for a list?

Finally, too much emphasis is placed by some on the importance of creating a list of items subject to control.

It is true that the EU's list has proven quite useful. It makes it easier for European companies to know which of their activities fall under the scope of export control rules, allowing for greater legal certainty and cross border harmonisation. Such a list is crucial in the context of highly complex trade involving an extremely diversified set of industries. Also, that list has tended to be used as a reference even beyond the EU's borders.

But this does not mean that other States should simply copy the list. In a country that has only a very small fraction of the industries that generate items included on the list, the reproduction of it in its entirety is not only superfluous, it can be counterproductive, as it dilutes the information and makes it more difficult for companies in that country to identify the items of concern.

It is true that, thanks to transit or imports and exports, any country may need to apply export control rules to virtually any item. But these exceptional situations can be safeguarded through a catch-all provision, possibly accompanied by non-binding reference to foreign or international standards.

Let us not lose sight of the fact that even the EU list does not pretend to be exhaustive. The European solution was – simplistically – to automatically subject to licencing the listed items, and then to allow for a case-by-case assessment of exports of non-listed items.

If any list must, necessarily, contain only examples of the items subject to authorisation, why should countries with domestic industries that produce only a limited number of items of concern be bothered with reproducing a more complete list, the objectives of which could just as easily be achieved through a general clause?

A tailor-made country or regional approach to lists would have the added advantage of requiring an initial effort of dialogue with stakeholders, so as to allow for the identification of the items of concern produced domestically. In other words, national rules would be built in dialogue with national industry, in a partnership that could greatly contribute to both transparency and awareness raising. Also, this initial identification of areas and companies of concern should make subsequent enforcement efforts less burdensome for the administration.

Naturally, such "specialised" lists would have to be periodically revised to keep track of new industries and new technological developments. But that is equally true of a European-style extensive list.

Conclusion

Quentin MICHEL

Professor – European Studies Unit, University of Liège

It is commonly accepted that pursuant to the adoption by the UN Security Council of the Resolution 1540 (2004), States have committed themselves inter alia to strengthen their national dual-use export control systems. Acting under Chapter VII of the UN Charter the Security Council by this Resolution decides that "all States shall take and enforce effective measures to establish domestic controls to prevent the proliferation of nuclear, chemical, or biological weapons and their means of delivery, including by establishing appropriate controls over related materials".[1]

In subparagraph 3(d) the Resolution detailed the main elements that a national system must incorporate. That includes, in particular, appropriate laws and regulations to control export, transit, trans-shipment, re-export of dual-use items.

The 1540 Committee created by the Resolution and in charge with monitoring the implementation of the Resolution has identified a list of measures that a State shall consider to encounter an effective and appropriate compliance of the Resolution. Those measures relate to elements like border control measures, licencing, control lists, end-users controls, and extraterritorial applicability.

Looking at the wording of the Resolution and the list of measures detailed by the Committee, the approach appears to be inspired by somewhat similar provisions defined by international dual-use trade control regimes. Notably, the Wassenaar Arrangement and the Nuclear Suppliers Group adopted guidelines defining elements that a national trade control system should include.

The conformity of national measures to the principles of the guidelines is an essential element assessed by the regimes in deciding on eligibility for membership of a candidate State. No African State with the

1 United Nations Security Council Resolution 1540 (2004) Paragraph 3.

exception of South Africa is a member of an international export control regime and, even if their national dual-use trade control system were to be positively assessed by the members States, they might not fulfil the second condition for membership, i.e. to be a potential exporter of dual-use goods. Most African countries have a very limited number of dual-use items related activities, and their exports are essentially limited to certain raw materials, like uranium ore.

If African States are not members of the regime most of them have however signed and ratified international non-proliferation treaties and conventions applying trade control of dual-use items and in particular treaties regarding nuclear and chemical weapons. These treaties as the Non-Proliferation Treaty (NPT) include general provisions constraining participating States not to provide dual-use items for peaceful purposes unless certain principles are met. Two of them – the Chemical Weapons Convention (CWC) and the NPT – require specific verification and safeguarding measures to be carried out respectively by the Organisation for the Prohibition of Chemical Weapons (OPCW) and the International Atomic Energy Agency (IAEA). Others – like the Hague Code of Conduct against Ballistic Missile Proliferation – include peer review mechanisms to guarantee the respect of the obligations by the Member States.

African States have incorporated in their national laws their safeguards and verification commitments as set forth by those treaties and conventions. Safeguards agreements have been concluded, initial and annual reports have been drafted and submitted for verification in due time to the respective organisations. Therefore, States might consider being in full compliance with their weapons of mass destruction (WMD) non-proliferation commitments and, consequently, may also consider that they comply with the obligations of UNSC Resolution 1540, particularly as they have "taken and enforced effective measures to establish domestic controls to prevent the proliferation of WMD" in line with international treaties and conventions. It is recalled that if export control regimes define transactions, criteria, conditions or lists of items for the purpose of control as set forth in Resolution 1540, these are in fact only soft law instruments and their principles cannot be considered as binding international norms. Moreover, the guidelines of the Nuclear Suppliers Group (NSG) or Australia Group' are politically binding only for their respective members.

Considering that African States are in compliance with their commitments under UNSC Resolution 1540, it is necessary to identify specific purposes and political motivations to encourage these States and convince them of the necessity to review and develop their national export control systems beyond what is required by their international commitments.

This might not be an easy task, as most African States are confronting difficult economic situations and moreover have to take into account the limited financial resources available to their governmental authorities. The elaboration of a comprehensive national dual-use trade control system might not constitute a political priority.

The need for global security, assuming that no country could be sheltered any longer against the risk of a WMD used by non-state actors, might be a credible factor for convincing African authorities to review their control systems. There is a further convincing argument that there are certain dual-use items of essential use for "ordinary" governmental programmes such as the import of radiation sources for cancer therapy and export of the used source or, chemicals for pest control in agriculture. To import such items and related technologies, supplier States – usually members of international trade control regimes – might condition the transfer of these items to the requirement of an efficient trade control system in the end-user State, in line with the principles of relevant regimes rather than only with general principles of treaties. Thus, this demonstrates the necessity of defining what such a national system should be and whether a simplified system could be envisaged for countries with few activities involving dual-use items. Lastly, the question arises as to whether a regional system could constitute an option for these States.

From model to essential principles

The Chaudfontaine Group meeting and subsequent debates, made it quite clear that the concept of a "universal model" for a national trade control system for dual-use items could not be considered a valid option. In light of the diversity of legal systems (Common Law, Civil Law, combined systems) as well as the diversity in the volume of economic activities related to dual-use items, it would seem to be quasi impossible to define a single model that could be universally applied. Moreover such "one size fits all" approach might even be counterproductive as it would result in a model too small for large supplier States and oversized for States with few dual-use transactions.

Moreover, the safeguards and verifications systems required by the NPT and the CWC are both adapted to the level of activities of the State concerned.

The OPCW conducts data monitoring and on-site inspections based on declarations made by the State specifying activities taking place in its chemical industry. The Organisation verifies that the relevant activities are in conformity with the obligations under the Convention as well as consistent with the declared information.

The IAEA has adopted a specific model safeguards agreement for small quantities (SQP) to reduce the burden of safeguards' implementation for States with little or no nuclear material or activities, while retaining the integrity of the safeguards system.

Therefore, bearing in mind that non-proliferation treaties have adapted their level of safeguards and verification requirements of the relevant material and activities of the State, it might be interesting to apply a similar approach to the requirements requested by the Resolution 1540 and its indirect sources of inspiration, i.e. the international trade control regimes.

States that have very few dual-use activities, as is the case for most African States, might be more forthcoming if the level of requirements for a national trade control system were proportionate to their economic and political reality.

In the following paragraphs, we will attempt to define first what are the elements that shall be analysed and considered when drafting a dual-use trade control system and, second, the essential provisions that such systems should include for States with limited dual-use activities.

Elements to consider when drafting a national trade control system

The first conclusion resulting from the recent discussion in the frame of the Chaudfontaine Group, is that any national dual-use trade control system should respond to three essential questions ("3W"), namely "why", "what" and "ways" to control dual-use items.

The *why* control does not refer to the reasoning on the need to control dual-use items, but rather to the factors that should rule controlled transactions. It shall determine conditions to be fulfilled by the end-user (the State and the operators) and by operators in the end-user country. This shall also include criteria to be assessed by the competent authority.

The control *what* covers the entire scope of the national trade control system. This includes the list of dual-use items, specific provisions for items not listed and trade operations to control (export, import, transit, transhipment, financing, etc.).

The *ways* to control would focus on the different procedures that the State intends to develop so as to conform its policies to its international non-proliferation commitments. This would include control procedures and regulate the movement of dual items, covering also authorities and their respective roles in the process, as well as relevant interagency coordination and cooperation with other stakeholders (within and outside the State).

Elements of a dual-use trade control system for States with few dual-use trade activities

The list of elements mentioned in the preceding paragraph may be considered as being potentially applicable to a State with few dual-use activities. This however does not constitute a "model" of a trade control system, but rather intends to provide some essential components that such system could include in drafting process.

It has to be noted that dual-use trade of States with few relevant activities might reflect a completely different situation for which the appropriate system might require completely different answers. For example, Niger is assumed to have extensive uranium mining activities but almost no other trade activities in dual-use items. The appropriate national approach might favour a system that combines global export authorisations with the requirements of an internal compliance programme. In a different case, a State with no specific dual-use items activities but a land – locked, and thus potentially a transit State for such items, e.g. Burkina Faso, might favour a system of individual authorisations completed by a catch-all mechanism.

Based on the 3W approach as defined above a national trade control system might be organised as follows.

"Why controlling":

- Conditions to be fulfilled by the end-user (State and operators):
  - Condition to be fulfilled by operators within the country:
    - Registration. Considering the type of operators acting in the country it might be useful to link it to an ICP requirement.
  - Conditions to be fulfilled by the end-user (State and operators):
    - Integration of commitments imposed by international treaties. Example: the NPT requires States Parties not to supply nuclear materials to another State unless that State (the end-user) has concluded a comprehensive safeguards agreement with the IAEA.
    - Integration of binding requirements set forth in bilateral formal and informal agreements. Example (1): Items to be exported are manufactured by a facility that is submitted to certain conditions requested by the initial supplier. Example (2): Implementation of US extra-territorial export control commitments.

- Criteria to be assessed by the authority:
  - Integration of binding commitments contained in international treaties. Example: the CWC requires Member States to not assist, encourage or induce, in any way, anyone to engage in any activity prohibited to a State Party under this Convention (Article 1(d)).

What to control

- Define the dual-use items under the scope of the legislation:
  - Adopt a broad definition of the term dual-use with a view to cover all dual-use items (goods and technology).
  - Control list to contain a small number of items that are:
    - Regularly imported and used in the country. Example: radiological source for medical uses
    - Exported, manufactured, mined, in transit in the State
    - Produced by the neighbouring countries.
  - Three catch-all clauses ("operator has been informed", "is aware" and "has ground for suspecting") with a broad end-use scope. Example of scope: items in question may be intended, in their entirety or part, for use in connection with non-peaceful activities.
- Defining movements under the scope of the legislation:
  - The system shall include the control of tangible and intangible transfers,
  - Export and import of listed items shall be submitted to authorisation/licencing requirement,
  - Possibility to control transit, transhipment, brokering, financing, shipping, re-export.

Ways to control

Procedures to control and regulate the movement of dual-use items:

- Custom central implementing authority:
  - Authorisation application management
  - Delivering, suspending and retrieving licences
  - Verification and post-shipment control (operators record keepings control)
  - Prosecution (reference to specific law)

- Delivery of licences to be subject to political authorisation granted by:
  - Ministry of Foreign Affairs
  - Committee composed by different Ministries (representatives):
    - Foreign Affairs, Economy, Interior.

Regional system

The possibility to establish an African regional system of dual-use trade control has been investigated. However, the adoption of a regional dual-use trade control regime similar to the EU dual-use Regulation or with an even higher level of integration appears to be somewhat premature and not easily adapted to the present status of African regional integration. The necessary conditions for the establishment of a single market among concerned African States headed by a regulatory authority, do not appear to be met even by the most integrated custom unions i.e. the East African Community Customs Union.

An analysis of African regional governmental organisations shows that these institutions do not appear to have yet the appropriate legal and political infrastructure required for hosting such a system.

The possibility of adopting specific "soft law" instruments – guidelines or best practises – in the mode of what has been achieved by international export control regimes could be a valid option for African regional organisations dealing indirectly with sensitive items, notably arms. Such is the case of the International Conference on the Great Lakes Region (ICGLR). The ICGLR has set up a number of sub-programmes, notably the "Joint security management" of common borders, disarmament and repatriation of all armed groups in Eastern Republic of Congo, development of border zone and promotion of human security as well as fight against the proliferation of small arms and light weapons.

Nevertheless, although most African States have few dual-use activities only, the respective national situation and the challenges regarding control of these activities are not identical and therefore a common regional approach might appear to be more cumbersome than useful.

The drafting of regional general dual-use trade principles, politically or legally binding, could also be an option for some African regional organisations like the African Union but the added value of such processes compared to similar principles that could be deduced from non-proliferation treaties for which African States are member seem to be rather negligible.

About the Authors

Yacine Amara is a Nuclear Lawyer in the Algerian Atomic Energy Commission, at the Treaty and Cooperation Department, providing advice and assistance on the AIEA TC Programme and nuclear regulatory framework; he has been involved in the conclusion of many of cooperation agreements for the development and peaceful uses of nuclear energy.

Lia Caponetti is a researcher in the European Studies Unit of the Department of Political Science at the University of Liège (Belgium). She holds a double master degree in Political Sciences focus on European Politics and Euro-Mediterranean Relations. She did her master thesis on the European Union's WMD non-proliferation policy, focusing on the competence-sharing between the EU institutions.

Christos Charatsis is a research fellow at the European Commission's Joint Research Centre providing policy support with regards to the implementation of the dual-use regulation. He is currently preparing a PhD study on compliance with export controls law from the standpoint of research organisations in collaboration with the University of Liège.

Renaud Chatelus is a senior scientist at the EC Joint Research Centre in Ispra (Italy). He was customs export control investigator, IAEA inspector and safeguards analyst, and border control trainer for many international assistance programmes. He is a senior fellow of the U. of Georgia (CITS), doctoral student of the U. of Liege and author of many articles, especially on export control enforcement.

Ekaterina Chirkova is a PhD candidate at the Faculty of Law and Political Science, University of Liège (Belgium). She published several contributions on non-proliferation and export controls as well as undertook research internships in the EU, Russia and USA.

Sara Depauw is a researcher in the Flemish Peace Institute, a research institute that forms part of the Flemish parliament. Within the research programme on 'arms trade and arms production' she concentrates on the (sub)national, European and international juridical framework of external trade in strategic goods.

Pr. Shamsideen Babatunde Elegba obtained a first class M.Sc. Degree in Theoretical Nuclear Physics from Kharkov State University, in the former Soviet Union and a PhD in Theoretical Solid State Physics, at the University of Oregon, Eugene, USA. He has over 25 years of University research and teaching experience, having contributed as author and co-author to over 200 scientific publications and technical reports. In addition to nuclear safety and security, he has wide experience in energy planning and management.

Dr. Harald Hohmann is a "leading name in export control law", attorney of the law firm Hohmann Rechtsanwälte, near Frankfurt/Main (www.hohmann-rechtsanwaelte.com). He consults companies on EU & US export control law, EU & US customs trade law, criminal law (e.g. export and customs violations) and international contracts, notably. Dr. Hohmann is a senior lecturer at the University of Frankfurt and visiting professor at the Osaka City University, he has published 6 books on export control law and several articles and contributions to seminars worldwide.

Odette Jankowitsch (born Prevor), Austrian national; law doctorate, Vienna University; research fellow, NYU; former senior lawyer, IAEA. Independent expert on international nuclear law, associated with the University of Liège, EU Studies Unit; lecturer at Sorbonne University, Abu Dhabi, (PSUAD), Montpellier International School of Nuclear Law (ISNL); OECD/NEA Nuclear Law Essentials course (Paris); EU ESARDA course, Ispra (Italy).

John Kabange M. is a customs control officer of the Democratic Republic of Congo national bureau of liaison for intelligence. He is an expert of the chemical, biological, radiological and nuclear EU Centres of Excellence and participates to the missions organised by the World Customs Organisation in Africa and worldwide concerning intellectual property rights and the trafficking of drugs and other precursors.

Quentin Michel is Professor Ordinaire in European Studies at the University of Liège (Belgium). His Research Unit has developed a high level of expertise in the CBRN non-proliferation. He has worked in many projects related to sensitive trade control. He is a renowned expert in this field with more than 30 publications dedicated to this subject and is the initiator of the "Chaudfontaine Group" meetings.

Ivana Micic is a senior researcher in the European Studies Unit of the Department of Political Science at the University of Liège (Belgium). Prior of joining the Unit she worked as a Senior Researcher within the Dual-use and Arms Trade Control Programme at Stockholm International Peace Research Institute (SIPRI). In addition to research work on non-proliferation issues, she has designed and implemented a range of capacity-building activities to strengthen dual-use and arms trade control systems.

Sylvain Paile-Calvo is a senior researcher in the European Studies Unit of the Department of Political Science at the University of Liège

(Belgium). He published several contributions on nuclear law and the control of the trade of sensitive items, such as *Controlling the Dual-Use Goods – A Handbook* (Brussels, P.I.E. Peter Lang, 2013).

Martin Palmer is a partner in Supply Chain Compliance Ltd, a company specialising in the transport sector and has been involved with the distribution and logistics industry for over 35 years. During this period, he has held a number of senior roles within various areas of the transport sector, including Operations Director, Country Manager, Global Customs Director and was active in export control outreach programmes.

Crystal Pryor is a PhD Candidate in the Department of Political Science at the University of Washington (United States). Her dissertation is on multilateral export control regimes and domestic implementation of dual-use export controls in the United States, EU countries, and Japan. Her previous research was on U.S.-Japan outer space security policy.

Abdoul Rahimoune Massaoudou is Controller General at the "Patrimonial" Mining Company of Niger. He was previously Director Evaluation and Control of Mining Companies and General Manager of National Transport Company of Strategic Goods, giving him a broad view on the issue of export and transport of radioactive materials and the import of dangerous goods.

Anne-Valentine Rensonnet is graduated from the University of Liège. She studied Political Science with focus on European politics. She did her master thesis on the control of the trade of sensitive items and arms. Her main domains of interest encompass trade of sensitive items as well as European and International Law.

Rosa Rosanelli is International Trade Compliance Site Manager for Pratt and Whitney Belgium Engine Centre in Herstal (Belgium). She is specialised in export controls for the aeronautics and space sector and is author of several publications, including *US Export Control Regulations Explained to the European Exporter: A Handbook.*

Miguel Sousa Ferro is a graduate in law from the Lisbon University Law School, where he is a guest lecturer and is waiting to defend his doctorate in competition law. He holds an LLM in European Studies from the College of Europe. He has published widely in several fields, including nuclear law, having been awarded the INLA Prize in 2012.

Dr. Laszlo Stefan has worked many years for the trade licencing authority of Hungary in the area of export controls and is now the director of the Authority of Defence Industry and Export Control.

Dr. Andrea Viski joined the European Commission's Joint Research Centre in 2013 to contribute to the Nuclear Security Unit's work on export controls as well as the EU CBRN Centres of Excellence (CoE) initiative.

She previously worked in the Dual-Use and Arms Trade Control, as well as the Arms Control and Non-Proliferation, Programs at the Stockholm International Peace Research Institute (SIPRI). She received her PhD from the Law Department of the European University Institute, where she wrote her PhD on nuclear export control issues.

Velislava Zhivkova is a PhD scholar at the International Institute of Energy Policy and Diplomacy, Moscow State Institute of International Relations. Her area of specialisation covers energy policy, nuclear energy and international security issues.

Non-proliferation & security

The aim of this book series is to study the various aspects of risk linked to human activities.

Scientific and technological development is changing our society fundamentally and the concept of risk is crucial for the analysis of the ongoing social transformation process.

Progress in genetic engineering and the use of military technology by civilians, for instance, raise questions concerning ethical, political, environmental and public-health issues.

This series, therefore, opts for a multidisciplinary approach to the problem of risk, which involves the scientific community as much as the political world and civil society.

It publishes monographs and collected papers, mainly in French or English.

Series editors: Quentin MICHEL & Sébastien BRUNET,
Université de Liège (Belgium)

Published Books

N° 9 – Quentin MICHEL, Sylvain PAILE, Maryna TSUKANOVA, Andrea VISKI, *Controlling the Trade of the Dual-Use Items. A Handbook*, 2013.

N° 8 – Odette JANKOWITSCH-PREVOR, Quentin MICHEL (eds.), *European Dual-Use Trade Controls. Beyond Materiality and Borders*, 2013.

N° 7 – André DUMOULIN, Delphine DESCHAUX-BEAUME et Sylvain PAILE (dir.), *Politiques de communication, médias et défense. L'OTAN et la PSDC : visibilité en Belgique et chez ses voisins*, 2013.

N° 6 – Quentin MICHEL, *Concilier l'inconciliable. Les régimes internationaux et européens de contrôle du commerce nucléaire*, 2012

N° 5 – Quentin MICHEL (ed.), *Sensitive Trade. The Perspective of European States*, 2011

N° 4 – Quentin MICHEL (ed.), *Terrorisme. Regards croisés / Terrorism. Cross Analysis*, 2005

N° 3 – Sébastien BRUNET, Anne BERGMANS, Anne BERTRAND & Patrick BIREN (dir.), *L'expertise en questions. Domestiquer l'incertitude dans la société du risque*, 2002

N° 2 – Pierre HUPET (dir.), *Risque et systèmes complexes. Les enjeux de la communication*, 2001

N° 1 – CD-Rom, Quentin MICHEL, *Articles nucléaires et articles à double usage : régulation du commerce au sein de l'Union européenne. Doctrine, jurisprudence et législation*, 2001.

www.peterlang.com